THE ONE MINUTE BIBLE™

The Heart of the Bible Arranged into 366 One-Minute Readings

HOLMAN
**CHRISTIAN
STANDARD
BIBLE®**

242.5
DEVOTIONAL LITERATURE
BIBLE—STUDY

Printed in the United States of America
1 2 3 4 5 6 07 06 05 04 03

TABLE OF CONTENTS

Introduction to *The One-Minute Bible*™

Often the Bible is simply called "the Book." This description conveys the enormous influence it has wielded first on Western civilization and now on the whole world. Law, literature, architecture, painting, music, morals, and religion all have been shaped by the Bible. It continues to be the world's best-selling book with sales exceeding one hundred million annually. The Bible has been translated into more than 1,000 languages and dialects.

While the Bible is called "the Book," it is actually a library of 66 books written over a period of 1600 years by more than 40 authors as diverse as one could imagine. Yet from these very different times, places, cultures, and literary forms emerges a coherent theme of God's creation of the universe.

In the last letter Paul wrote, he reminded his young colleague Timothy that "all Scripture is inspired by God." God superintended that both the writing and the preservation of these writings have God as their author, salvation as their end, and inerrant truth for their content.

Because the Bible is God's word, it has evoked the same hostility as God's prophets and God's Son, Jesus Christ. The Roman Emperor Diocletian attempted to destroy the Scriptures. In A.D. 303 he issued an edict that both church buildings and the Scriptures be burned. Many manuscripts of the New Testament were lost during this persecution. But only 25 years after Diocletian's attack on the Bible, the new Emperor Constantine ordered 50 copies of the Scriptures to be produced at the expense of the Roman government.

Reading the Bible

We praise the Bible but often stop short of reading it. Perhaps our first attempts at reading it were far from satisfying. We are like someone who is inspired to take up golf after watching a professional sink a 30-foot putt. The novice golfer soon realizes there is a price to be paid to play golf with the skill of the men and women on the PGA tour. One must begin working on one-foot putts and then build on that.

The Bible is a difficult book for several reasons. In terms of sheer number of pages, it is a huge book. The Bible takes as many pages as four large novels. As we have already noted, the Bible was written in different times, places, cultures, and genres by writers of widely different personalities. We begin reading a passage, and soon feel like the Ethiopian official whom Philip addressed in Acts 8:30-31: "Do you understand what you're reading?"

"How can I," he said, "unless someone guides me?"

The One-Minute Bible gives guidance by providing a portion of Scripture that can be read in one minute. Now that's doable. A one-minute reading is given for each day of the year. These Scripture portions have been carefully chosen to provide the reader with

- Selections relating to every principal event in the Bible
- Readings on every primary Bible topic and theme
- Verses that deal with every major Christian doctrine
- All of the most-beloved passages of Scripture.

Taking just one minute a day, you can survey the heart of the Bible in one year. Each day of the year, from January 1 through December 31, is indicated at the top of each page. Using this daily approach, if you should miss a week, it will take you only seven minutes to get back on track. If you miss half a month, you can catch up in 15 minutes.

Although this calendar can guide you through a one-year reading plan, don't limit yourself to starting in January or reading one page a day. The related texts at the bottom of each page allow you to go deeper into a topic by directing you to nearly 1,800 passages of Scripture that will further your understanding of the topics covered in that day's reading. Many of these texts are in *The One-Minute Bible*, and you can find them by means of the Scripture Index found on pages 403-410. However, we recommend that you look up these verses in a full-text Bible so that you can read even more of the context surrounding the focal passage.

Topical Headings and Organization

The One-Minute Bible begins with the first verse of Genesis and ends with the last verse of Revelation. Readings follow the general flow of biblical history, interlaced with several topical series such as two weeks for Easter in April and a week for mothers in May. (A two-page Table of Contents precedes this introduction.) Some readings reproduce an entire passage of Scripture, such as Psalm 2 on December 22. Often, several passages are combined to show the whole spectrum of biblical teaching on a given topic.

For example, on January 1, Genesis 1:1-2 introduces you to the Bible itself and to creation in particular. John 1:1-5 introduces you to Jesus—the Word—through whom all things were created. Psalm 148:1-6 invites you to praise the Lord as the Creator. January 2 continues the creation account with five texts enlarging on the theme of light.

Blocks of text from different Bible passages are separated by a full space; Scripture references are listed at the end of each reading. The text follows the wording, paragraphing, and poetic formatting of the *Holman Christian Standard Bible®*. On occasions proper nouns have been substituted for pronouns to make the selection clearer. We want you to know when Jesus is speaking so we inserted [Jesus said,] into such readings as Matthew 11:28-30 on March 24.

The 700 selected scriptures and 1,800 related texts were chosen to represent the key themes of the Bible from each of its 66 books. Great care was taken to ensure that each text has the same meaning in *The One-Minute Bible* that it has in its larger context in the Holy Bible.

Each month is introduced by a selection of quotations on the importance of the Bible—34 quotations from international leaders in politics and religion, key figures in the arts, sciences, and humanities.

Indexes

The One-Minute Bible guides you through an overview of the Bible in daily one-minute readings. Immediately following the last reading are two daily reading plans that will guide you through the entire Bible in a year. The morning and evening schedule (Plan I) offers readings from both the Old and New Testaments for each day of the year. The chronological schedule (Plan II) takes the reader through the Bible in historical order.

More than 450 key topics and personalities are indexed in the Topical Index found on pages 411-416. With this index you can find every reference to *comfort*, *salvation*, or the *names of God* found in *The One-Minute Bible*. If you want to study any word more thoroughly, we recommend the *Holman Illustrated Bible Dictionary*. The Scripture Index, mentioned above, locates every text printed in *The One-Minute Bible*.

For more information on the geographical setting of the Bible, we recommend the *Holman Bible Atlas* or the *Holman QuickSource Guide: Atlas of Bible Lands*.

About the Translation

All Scriptures are from the *Holman Christian Standard Bible®* (HCSB®), a translation of the full Bible completed in 2003. Each translator of the HCSB® believes the Bible is God's inspired word, inerrant in the original manuscripts. The goals of this translation are

- To provide English-speaking people across the world with an accurate, readable Bible in contemporary English
- To equip serious Bible students with an accurate translation for personal study, private devotions, and memorization
- To give those who love God's word a text that is easy to read, visually attractive on the page, and appealing when heard
- To affirm the authority of the Scriptures as God's inerrant word and to champion its absolutes against cultural or social agendas that would compromise its accuracy

"'Blessed Lord,
who hast caused
all Holy Scriptures
to be written for
our learning;

Grant that we may...
hear them, read, mark,
learn and inwardly
digest them."
Book of Common Prayer

CREATION: *In the Beginning*

In the beginning God created the heavens and the earth.

Now the earth was formless and empty, darkness covered the surface of the watery depths, and the Spirit of God was hovering over the surface of the waters.

In the beginning was the Word; and the Word was with God, and the Word was God. He was with God in the beginning.

All things were created through Him, and apart from Him not one thing was created that has been created. In Him was life, and that life was the light of men. That light shines in the darkness, yet the darkness did not overcome it.

> Hallelujah!
> Praise the LORD from the heavens;
> praise Him in the heights.
> Praise Him, all His angels;
> praise Him, all His hosts.
> Praise Him, sun and moon;
> praise Him, all you shining stars.
> Praise Him, highest heavens,
> and you waters above the heavens.
> Let them praise the name of the LORD,
> for He commanded, and they were created.
> He set them in position forever and ever;
> He gave an order that will never pass away.

GENESIS 1:1-2; JOHN 1:1-5; PSALM 148:1-6

Related texts: PSALMS 102:25-28; 139:13-18; PROVERBS 8; ISAIAH 40:12-31; 45:18-25; HEBREWS 11:1-3

1

CREATION: *Let There Be Light*

Then God said, "Let there be light," and there was light. God saw that the light was good, and God separated the light from the darkness. God called the light "day," and He called the darkness "night." Evening came, and then morning: the first day.

LORD, You are my lamp;
the LORD illuminates my darkness.

The LORD is my light and my salvation—
whom should I fear?
The LORD is the stronghold of my life—
of whom should I be afraid?

Then Jesus spoke to them again: "I am the light of the world. Anyone who follows Me will never walk in the darkness, but will have the light of life."

There will no longer be any curse. The throne of God and of the Lamb will be in the city, and His servants will serve Him. They will see His face, and His name will be on their foreheads. Night will no longer exist, and people will not need lamplight or sunlight, because the Lord God will give them light. And they will reign forever and ever.

GENESIS 1:3-5; 2 SAMUEL 22:29; PSALM 27:1; JOHN 8:12; REVELATION 22:3-5

Related texts: LEVITICUS 24:1-4; JOB 24:13-17; 38:8-20; JOHN 3:19-21; 1 JOHN 1:5-8

CREATION: *The Sky Above*

Then God said, "Let there be an expanse between the waters, separating water from water." So God made the expanse and separated the water under the expanse from the water above the expanse. And it was so. God called the expanse "sky." Evening came, and then morning: the second day.

The heavens declare the glory of God,
and the sky proclaims the work of His hands.
Day after day they pour out speech;
night after night they communicate knowledge.
There is no speech; there are no words;
their voice is not heard.

I will praise You, Lord, among the peoples;
I will sing praises to You among the nations.
For Your faithful love is as high as the heavens;
Your faithfulness reaches to the clouds.
God, be exalted above the heavens;
let Your glory be over the whole earth.
He made the earth by His power,
established the world by His wisdom,
and spread out the heavens by His understanding.
When He thunders,
the waters in the heavens are in turmoil,
and He causes the clouds to rise
from the ends of the earth.
He makes lightning for the rain
and brings the wind from His storehouses.

GENESIS 1:6-8; PSALMS 19:1-3; 57:9-11; JEREMIAH 10:12-13

Related texts: 1 CHRONICLES 16:23-31; JOB 38:22-38;
PSALM 102:25-28; ACTS 1:1-12

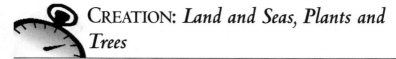

CREATION: *Land and Seas, Plants and Trees*

Then God said, "Let the water under the sky be gathered into one place, and let the dry land appear." And it was so. God called the dry land "earth," and He called the gathering of the water "seas." And God saw that it was good. Then God said, "Let the earth produce vegetation: seed-bearing plants, and fruit trees on the earth bearing fruit with seed in it, according to their kinds." And it was so. The earth brought forth vegetation: seed-bearing plants according to their kinds and trees bearing fruit with seed in it, according to their kinds. And God saw that it was good. Evening came, and then morning: the third day.

Do you not fear Me? This is the LORD's declaration.
Do you not tremble before Me,
the One who set the sand as the boundary of the
     sea,
an enduring barrier that it cannot cross?
The waves surge, but they cannot prevail.
They roar but cannot pass over it.

He causes grass to grow for the livestock
and provides crops for man to cultivate,
producing food from the earth,
wine that makes man's heart glad—
making his face shine with oil—
and bread that sustains man's heart.

GENESIS 1:9-13; JEREMIAH 5:22; PSALM 104:14-15

Related texts: JOB 12:7-12; 38:8:11; PSALM 104; REVELATION 20:11–21:4; 22:1-3

CREATION: *Sun, Moon, and Stars*

Then God said, "Let there be lights in the expanse of the sky to separate the day from the night. They will serve as signs for festivals and for days and years. They will be lights in the expanse of the sky to provide light on the earth." And it was so.

God made the two great lights—the greater light to have dominion over the day and the lesser light to have dominion over the night—as well as the stars. God placed them in the expanse of the sky to provide light on the earth, to dominate the day and the night, and to separate light from darkness. And God saw that it was good. Evening came, and then morning: the fourth day.

I did not see a sanctuary in it, because the Lord God the Almighty and the Lamb are its sanctuary. The city does not need the sun or the moon to shine on it, because God's glory illuminates it, and its lamp is the Lamb. The nations will walk in its light, and the kings of the earth will bring their glory into it.

Each day its gates will never close because it will never be night there. They will bring the glory and honor of the nations into it. Nothing profane will ever enter it: no one who does what is vile or false, but only those written in the Lamb's book of life.

GENESIS 1:14-19; REVELATION 21:22-27

Related texts: NEHEMIAH 9:5-6; JOB 9:1-9; PSALMS 19:1-6; 104:19-23; PROVERBS 4:18-19; EPHESIANS 5:8-16

CREATION: *All Creatures Great and Small*

Then God said, "Let the water swarm with living creatures, and let birds fly above the earth across the expanse of the sky." So God created the large sea creatures and every living creature that moves and swarms in the water, according to their kinds. He also created every winged bird according to its kind. And God saw that it was good. So God blessed them, "Be fruitful, multiply, and fill the waters of the seas, and let the birds multiply on the earth." Evening came, and then morning: the fifth day.

How countless are Your works, LORD!
In wisdom You have made them all;
the earth is full of Your creatures.
Here is the sea, vast and wide,
teeming with creatures beyond number—
living things both large and small.
There the ships move about,
and Leviathan, which You formed to play there.
All of them wait for You
to give them their food at the right time.
When You give it to them, they gather it;
when You open Your hand, they are satisfied with
      good things.

GENESIS 1:20-23; PSALM 104:24-28

Related texts: PSALMS 104:11-18; 148:7-12; MATTHEW 6:25-33; 10:29-31; REVELATION 5:11-13

CREATION: *The Cattle on a Thousand Hills*

Then God said, "Let the earth produce living creatures according to their kinds: livestock, creatures that crawl, and the wildlife of the earth according to their kinds." And it was so. So God made the wildlife of the earth according to their kinds, the livestock according to their kinds, and creatures that crawl on the ground according to their kinds. And God saw that it was good.

I do not rebuke you for your sacrifices
or for your burnt offerings, which are continually
    before Me.
I will not accept a bull from your household
or male goats from your pens,
for every animal of the forest is Mine,
the cattle on a thousand hills.
I know every bird of the mountains,
and the creatures of the field are Mine.
If I were hungry, I would not tell you,
for the world and everything in it is Mine.
Do I eat the flesh of bulls
or drink the blood of goats?
Sacrifice a thank offering to God,
and pay your vows to the Most High.
Call on Me in a day of trouble;
I will rescue you, and you will honor Me.

GENESIS 1:24-25; PSALM 50:8-15

Related texts: GENESIS 9:1-3; PSALM 8; PROVERBS 12:10; ISAIAH 11:1-10; 65:17-25

CREATION: *Mankind—The Image of God*

Then God said, "Let Us make man in Our image, according to Our likeness. They will rule the fish of the sea, the birds of the sky, the animals, all the earth, and the creatures that crawl on the earth."

So God created man in His own image;
He created him in the image of God;
He created them male and female.

God blessed them, and God said to them, "Be fruitful, multiply, fill the earth, and subdue it. Rule the fish of the sea, the birds of the sky, and every creature that crawls on the earth."

God also said, "Look, I have given you every seed-bearing plant on the surface of the entire earth, and every tree whose fruit contains seed. This food will be for you, for all the wildlife of the earth, for every bird of the sky, and for every creature that crawls on the earth—everything having the breath of life in it. I have given every green plant for food." And it was so.

God saw all that He had made, and it was very good. Evening came, and then morning: the sixth day.

GENESIS 1:26-31

Related texts: GENESIS 2:4-25; 9:6-7; PSALM 8;
1 CORINTHIANS 6:1-4; 2 CORINTHIANS 4:4-6; COLOSSIANS 1:9-20; 3:5-10

CREATION: *God Rests*

So the heavens and the earth and everything in them were completed. By the seventh day, God completed His work that He had done, and He rested on the seventh day from all His work that He had done. God blessed the seventh day and declared it holy, for on it He rested from His work of creation.

Remember to dedicate the Sabbath day. For the LORD made the heavens and the earth, the sea, and everything in them in six days; then He rested on the seventh day. Therefore the LORD blessed the Sabbath day and declared it holy.

On the Sabbath He was going through the grain-fields, and His disciples began to make their way picking some heads of grain. The Pharisees said to Him, "Look, why are they doing what is not lawful on the Sabbath?"

And He said to them, "Have you never read what David did when he was in need and hungry, he and his companions: how he entered the house of God in the time of Abiathar the high priest and ate the sacred bread—which is not lawful for anyone to eat except the priests—and also gave some to his companions?"

Then He told them, "The Sabbath was made for man, and not man for the Sabbath. Therefore the Son of Man is Lord even of the Sabbath."

GENESIS 2:1-3; EXODUS 20:8,11; MARK 2:23-28

Related texts: EXODUS 16:11-30; PSALM 62:1-5; MATTHEW 11:25-30; MARK 6:30-32; HEBREWS 4:1-4

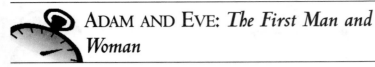

ADAM AND EVE: *The First Man and Woman*

Then the LORD God formed the man out of the dust from the ground and breathed the breath of life into his nostrils, and the man became a living being.

The LORD God took the man and placed him in the garden of Eden to work it and watch over it. And the LORD God commanded the man, "You are free to eat from any tree of the garden, but you must not eat from the tree of the knowledge of good and evil, for on the day you eat from it, you will certainly die."

Then the LORD God said, "It is not good for the man to be alone. I will make a helper who is like him."

But for the man no helper was found who was like him. So the LORD God caused a deep sleep to come over the man, and he slept. God took one of his ribs and closed the flesh at that place. Then the LORD God made the rib He had taken from the man into a woman and brought her to the man. And the man said:

This one, at last, is bone of my bone,
and flesh of my flesh;
this one will be called woman,
for she was taken from man.

This is why a man leaves his father and mother and bonds with his wife, and they become one flesh.

Both the man and his wife were naked, yet felt no shame.

GENESIS 2:7,15-18,20b-25

Related texts: GENESIS 1:26-29; MATTHEW 19:1-12; MARK 10:1-12; 1 CORINTHIANS 6:15–7:40

Rulers of God's Creation

Lord, our Lord,
how magnificent is Your name throughout the
    earth!
You have covered the heavens with Your majesty.
Because of Your adversaries, You have established a
    stronghold
from the mouths of children and nursing infants,
to silence the enemy and the avenger.
When I observe Your heavens, the work of Your
    fingers,
the moon and the stars, which You set in place,
what is man that You remember him,
the son of man that You look after him?
You made him little less than God
and crowned him with glory and honor.
You made him lord over the works of Your hands;
You put everything under his feet:
all the sheep and oxen,
as well as animals in the wild,
birds of the sky,
and fish of the sea
passing through the currents of the seas.
O Lord, our Lord,
how magnificent is Your name throughout the
    earth!

Psalm 8

The Fall of Mankind

Now the serpent was the most cunning of all the wild animals that the LORD God had made. He said to the woman, "Did God really say, 'You can't eat from any tree in the garden'?"

The woman said to the serpent, "We may eat the fruit from the trees in the garden. But about the fruit of the tree in the middle of the garden, God said, 'You must not eat it or touch it, or you will die.' "

"No! You will not die," the serpent said to the woman. "In fact, God knows that when you eat it your eyes will be opened and you will be like God, knowing good and evil." Then the woman saw that the tree was good for food and delightful to look at, and that it was desirable for obtaining wisdom. So she took some of its fruit and ate it; she also gave some to her husband, who was with her, and he ate it. Then the eyes of both of them were opened, and they knew they were naked; so they sewed fig leaves together and made loincloths for themselves.

Then the man and his wife heard the sound of the LORD God walking in the garden at the time of the evening breeze, and they hid themselves from the LORD God among the trees of the garden.

GENESIS 3:1-8

Related texts: EZEKIEL 28:13-19; ROMANS 5:12-19; 1 TIMOTHY 2:11-15; JAMES 1:12-15

God Judges the First Sin

So the LORD God called out to the man and said to him, "Where are you?"

And he said, "I heard You in the garden, and I was afraid because I was naked, so I hid."

Then He asked, "Who told you that you were naked? Did you eat from the tree that I had commanded you not to eat from?"

Then the man replied, "The woman You gave to be with me—she gave me some fruit from the tree, and I ate."

So the LORD God asked the woman, "What is this you have done?"

And the woman said, "It was the serpent. He deceived me, and I ate."

Then the LORD God said to the serpent:
Because you have done this,
you are cursed more than any livestock
and more than any wild animal.
You will move on your belly
and eat dust all the days of your life.
I will put hostility between you and the woman,
and between your seed and her seed.
He will strike your head,
and you will strike his heel.
He said to the woman:
I will intensify your labor pains;
you will bear children in anguish.
Your desire will be for your husband,
yet he will dominate you.

GENESIS 3:9-16; ROMANS 8:1

Related texts: DEUTERONOMY 32:1-6; ROMANS 3:9-18;
REVELATION 12:9; 20:1-3,7-15; 22:1-3

God Exiles Adam and Eve from the Garden

And He said to Adam, "Because you listened to your wife's voice and ate from the tree about which I commanded you, 'Do not eat from it':
The ground is cursed because of you.
You will eat from it by means of painful labor all the days of your life.
It will produce thorns and thistles for you, and you will eat the plants of the field.
You will eat bread by the sweat of your brow until you return to the ground, since you were taken from it.
For you are dust, and you will return to dust."
Adam named his wife Eve because she was the mother of all the living. The LORD God made clothing out of skins for Adam and his wife, and He clothed them.

The LORD God said, "Since man has become like one of Us, knowing good and evil, he must not reach out, and also take from the tree of life, and eat, and live forever." So the LORD God sent him away from the garden of Eden to work the ground from which he was taken. He drove man out, and east of the garden of Eden He stationed cherubim with a flaming, whirling sword to guard the way to the tree of life.

For just as in Adam all die, so also in Christ all will be made alive.

GENESIS 3:17-24; 1 CORINTHIANS 15:22

Related texts: GENESIS 18:16-33; PSALM 50; ROMANS 8:18-25; REVELATION 22

Death in Adam, Life in Christ

Therefore, just as sin entered the world through one man, and death through sin, in this way death spread to all men, because all sinned. In fact, sin was in the world before the law, but sin is not charged to one's account when there is no law.

Nevertheless, death reigned from Adam to Moses, even over those who did not sin in the likeness of Adam's transgression. He is a prototype of the Coming One.

But the gift is not like the trespass. For if by the one man's trespass the many died, how much more have the grace of God and the gift overflowed to the many by the grace of the one man, Jesus Christ. And the gift is not like the one man's sin, because from one sin came the judgment, resulting in condemnation, but from many trespasses came the gift, resulting in justification. Since by the one man's trespass, death reigned through that one man, how much more will those who receive the overflow of grace and the gift of righteousness reign in life through the one man, Jesus Christ.

For the wages of sin is death, but the gift of God is eternal life in Christ Jesus our Lord.

ROMANS 5:12-17; 6:23

Related texts: GENESIS 3; ROMANS 5:18–6:23; EPHESIANS 2:1-10; COLOSSIANS 3:1-17

CAIN AND ABEL: *The First Murder*

Adam knew his wife Eve intimately, and she conceived and gave birth to Cain. She said, "I have had a male child with the LORD's help." Then she also gave birth to his brother Abel.

Now Abel became a shepherd of a flock, but Cain cultivated the land. In the course of time Cain presented some of the land's produce as an offering to the LORD. And Abel also presented an offering—some of the firstborn of his flock and their fat portions. The LORD had regard for Abel and his offering, but He did not have regard for Cain and his offering. Cain was furious, and he was downcast.

Then the LORD said to Cain, "Why are you furious? And why are you downcast? If you do right, won't you be accepted? But if you do not do right, sin is crouching at the door. Its desire is for you, but you must master it."

Cain said to his brother Abel, "Let's go out to the field." And while they were in the field, Cain attacked his brother Abel and killed him.

Then the LORD said to Cain, "Where is your brother Abel?"

"I don't know," he replied. "Am I my brother's guardian?"

Then He said, "What have you done? Your brother's blood cries out to Me from the ground! So now you are cursed with alienation from the ground that opened its mouth to receive your brother's blood you have shed. If you work the land, it will never again give you its yield. You will be a restless wanderer on the earth."

GENESIS 4:1-12

Related texts: EXODUS 20:13; MATTHEW 5:21-26; HEBREWS 11:4; 1 JOHN 3:11-12

NOAH: *The Righteous Man*

These are the family records of Noah. Noah was a righteous man, blameless among his contemporaries; Noah walked with God. And Noah fathered three sons: Shem, Ham, and Japheth.

Now the earth was corrupt in God's sight, and the earth was filled with violence. God saw how corrupt the earth was, for all flesh had corrupted its way on the earth. Then God said to Noah, "I have decided to put an end to all flesh, for the earth is filled with violence because of them; therefore I am going to destroy them along with the earth.

"Make yourself an ark of gofer wood. Make rooms in the ark, and cover it with pitch inside and outside.

"Understand that I am bringing a deluge—floodwaters on the earth to destroy all flesh under heaven with the breath of life in it. Everything on earth will die. But I will establish My covenant with you, and you will enter the ark with your sons, your wife, and your sons' wives. You are also to bring into the ark two of every living thing of all flesh, male and female, to keep them alive with you. Take with you every kind of food that is eaten; gather it as food for you and for them." And Noah did this. He did everything that God had commanded him.

GENESIS 6:9-14,17-19,21-22

Related texts: PSALM 29:36; HEBREWS 11:1-7; 1 PETER 3:18-22

The Great Flood

Noah was 600 years old when the deluge came and water covered the earth. So Noah, his sons, his wife, and his sons' wives entered the ark because of the waters of the deluge. From the clean animals, unclean animals, birds, and every creature that crawls on the ground, two of each, male and female, entered the ark with Noah, just as God had commanded him. Seven days later the waters of the deluge came on the earth.

In the six hundredth year of Noah's life, in the second month, on the seventeenth day of the month, on that day all the sources of the watery depths burst open, the floodgates of the sky were opened.

The deluge continued 40 days on the earth; the waters increased and lifted up the ark so that it rose above the earth. The waters surged and increased greatly on the earth, and the ark floated on the surface of the water. Then the waters surged even higher on the earth, and all the high mountains under the whole sky were covered.

He wiped out every living thing that was on the surface of the ground, from mankind to livestock, to creatures that crawl, to the birds of the sky, and they were wiped off the earth. Only Noah was left, and those that were with him in the ark.

By faith Noah, after being warned about what was not yet seen, in reverence built an ark to deliver his family. By this he condemned the world and became an heir of the righteousness that comes by faith.

GENESIS 7:6-11,17-19,23; HEBREWS 11:7

Related texts: PSALM 93; NAHUM 1:1-8; MATTHEW 24:36-42; LUKE 17:26-36; 2 PETER 2:4-9

After the Flood

God remembered Noah, as well as all the wildlife and all the livestock that were with him in the ark. God caused a wind to pass over the earth, and the water began to subside.

After 40 days Noah opened the window of the ark that he had made, and he sent out a raven. It went back and forth until the waters had dried up from the earth. Then he sent out a dove to see whether the water on the earth's surface had gone down, but the dove found no resting place for her foot. She returned to him in the ark because water covered the surface of the whole earth. So Noah waited seven more days and sent out the dove from the ark again. When the dove came to him at evening, there was a plucked olive leaf in her beak. So Noah knew that the water on the earth's surface had gone down.

So Noah, along with his sons, his wife, and his sons' wives, came out.

Then Noah built an altar to the LORD. He took some of every kind of clean animal and every kind of clean bird and offered burnt offerings on the altar. When the LORD smelled the pleasing aroma, He said to Himself, "I will never again curse the ground because of man, even though man's inclination is evil from his youth. And I will never again strike down every living thing as I have done.

GENESIS 8:1,6-9a,10-11,18,20-21

Related texts: GENESIS 9; 2 PETER 3:1-14; REVELATION 21:1-4

God Calls Abram

The LORD said to Abram:
Go out from your land,
your relatives,
and your father's house
to the land that I will show you.
I will make you into a great nation,
I will bless you,
I will make your name great,
and you will be a blessing.
I will bless those who bless you,
I will curse those who treat you with contempt,
and all the peoples on earth
will be blessed through you.

So Abram went, as the LORD had told him, and Lot
went with him. Abram was 75 years old when he left
Haran. He took his wife Sarai, his nephew Lot, all the
possessions they had accumulated, and the people he
had acquired in Haran, and they set out for the land of
Canaan. When they came to the land of Canaan, Abram
passed through the land to the site of Shechem, at the
oak of Moreh. At that time the Canaanites were in the
land. But the LORD appeared to Abram and said, "I will
give this land to your offspring." So he built an altar
there to the LORD who had appeared to him.

GENESIS 12:1-7

Related texts: PSALM 67; ACTS 7:2-5; HEBREWS 6:13-16;
11:8-10

God Promises Abram a Son

After these events, the word of the Lord came to Abram in a vision:

Do not be afraid, Abram.

I am your shield;

your reward will be very great.

But Abram said, "Lord GOD, what can You give me, since I am childless and the heir of my house is Eliezer of Damascus?" Abram continued, "Look, You have given me no offspring, so a slave born in my house will be my heir."

Now the word of the LORD came to him: "This one will not be your heir; instead, one who comes from your own body will be your heir." He took him outside and said, "Look at the sky and count the stars, if you are able to count them." Then He said to him, "Your offspring will be that numerous."

Abram believed the LORD, and He credited it to him as righteousness.

Now it was credited to him was not written for Abraham alone, but also for us. It will be credited to us who believe in Him who raised Jesus our Lord from the dead. He was delivered up for our trespasses and raised for our justification.

GENESIS 15:1-6; ROMANS 4:23-25

Related texts: GENESIS 21:1-5; ROMANS 4; GALATIANS 3:1-9

ISHMAEL AND ISSAC: *Abram's Sons*

Abram's wife Sarai had not borne him children. She owned an Egyptian slave named Hagar. Sarai said to Abram, "Since the LORD has prevented me from bearing children, go to my slave; perhaps I can have children by her." And Abram agreed to what Sarai said. So Abram's wife Sarai took Hagar, her Egyptian slave, and gave her to her husband Abram as a wife for him. This happened after Abram had lived in the land of Canaan 10 years. He slept with Hagar, and she became pregnant.

So Hagar gave birth to Abram's son, and Abram gave the name Ishmael to the son Hagar had. Abram was 86 years old when Hagar bore Ishmael to him.

The LORD came to Sarah as He had said, and the LORD did for Sarah what He had promised. Sarah became pregnant and bore a son to Abraham in his old age, at the appointed time God had told him. Abraham named his son who was born to him—the one Sarah bore to him—Isaac. When his son Isaac was eight days old, Abraham circumcised him, as God had commanded him. Abraham was 100 years old when his son Isaac was born to him.

By faith even Sarah herself, when she was barren, received power to conceive offspring, even though she was past the age, since she considered that the One who had promised was faithful.

GENESIS 16:1-4a,15-16; 21:1-5; HEBREWS 11:11

Related texts: GENESIS 21:6-21; ACTS 7:1-8; ROMANS 4; GALATIANS 4:22-31

Abraham Offers Issac as a Sacrifice

After these things God tested Abraham and said to him, "Abraham!"

"Here I am," he answered.

"Take your son," He said, "your only son Isaac, whom you love, go to the land of Moriah, and offer him there as a burnt offering on one of the mountains I will tell you about."

When they arrived at the place that God had told him about, Abraham built the altar there and arranged the wood. He bound his son Isaac and placed him on the altar, on top of the wood. Then Abraham reached out and took the knife to slaughter his son.

But the Angel of the LORD called to him from heaven and said, "Abraham, Abraham!"

He replied, "Here I am."

Then He said, "Do not lay a hand on the boy or do anything to him. For now I know that you fear God, since you have not withheld your only son from Me." Abraham looked up and saw a ram caught by its horns in the thicket. So Abraham went and took the ram and offered it as a burnt offering in place of his son. And Abraham named that place The LORD Will Provide, so today it is said: "It will be provided on the LORD's mountain."

Love consists in this: not that we loved God, but that He loved us and sent His Son to be the propitiation for our sins.

GENESIS 22:1-2,9-14; 1 JOHN 4:10

Related texts: GENESIS 22:15-19; JOHN 3:16; ROMANS 8:31-39; HEBREWS 11:17-19

Esau and Jacob: *Issac's Sons*

These are the family records of Isaac son of Abraham. Abraham fathered Isaac. Isaac was 40 years old when he took as his wife Rebekah daughter of Bethuel the Aramean from Paddan-aram, and sister of Laban the Aramean. Isaac prayed to the LORD on behalf of his wife because she was barren. The LORD heard his prayer, and his wife Rebekah conceived. But the children inside her struggled with each other, and she said, "Why is this happening to me?" So she went to inquire of the LORD. And the LORD said to her:

Two nations are in your womb;
two people will come from you and be separated.
One people will be stronger than the other,
and the older will serve the younger.

When her time came to give birth, there were indeed twins in her womb. The first one came out reddish, covered with hair like a fur coat, and they named him Esau. After this, his brother came out grasping Esau's heel with his hand. So he was named Jacob. Isaac was 60 years old when they were born.

When the boys grew up, Esau became an expert hunter, an outdoorsman, but Jacob was a quiet man who stayed at home. Isaac loved Esau because he had a taste for wild game, but Rebekah loved Jacob.

GENESIS 25:19-28

Esau Sells His Inheritance to Jacob

Once when Jacob was cooking a stew, Esau came in from the field, exhausted. He said to Jacob, "Let me eat some of that red stuff, because I'm exhausted." That is why he was also named Edom.

Jacob replied, "First sell me your birthright."

"Look," said Esau, "I'm about to die, so what good is a birthright to me?"

Jacob said, "Swear to me first." So he swore to Jacob and sold his birthright to him. Then Jacob gave bread and lentil stew to Esau; he ate, drank, got up, and went away. So Esau despised his birthright.

"I have loved you," says the LORD.

"But you ask: How have You loved us?

"Wasn't Esau Jacob's brother?" This is the LORD's declaration. "Even so, I loved Jacob, but I hated Esau. I turned his mountains into a wasteland, and gave his inheritance to the desert jackals."

And see that there isn't any immoral or irreverent person like Esau, who sold his birthright in exchange for one meal. For you know that later, when he wanted to inherit the blessing, he was rejected because he didn't find any opportunity for repentance, though he sought it with tears.

GENESIS 25:29-34; MALACHI 1:2-3; HEBREWS 12:16-17

Related texts: GENESIS 27–36; PSALM 60; OBADIAH

JOSEPH THE DREAMER: *Jacob's Favorite Son*

At 17 years of age, Joseph tended sheep with his brothers. The young man was working with the sons of Bilhah and Zilpah, his father's wives, and he brought a bad report about them to their father.

Now Israel loved Joseph more than his other sons because Joseph was a son born to him in his old age, and he made a robe of many colors for him. When his brothers saw that their father loved him more than all his brothers, they hated him and could not bring themselves to speak peaceably to him.

Then Joseph had a dream. When he told it to his brothers, they hated him even more. He said to them, "Listen to this dream I had: There we were, binding sheaves of grain in the field. Suddenly my sheaf stood up, and your sheaves gathered around it and bowed down to my sheaf."

Then he had another dream and told it to his brothers. "Look," he said, "I had another dream, and this time the sun, moon, and 11 stars were bowing down to me."

He told his father and brothers, but his father rebuked him. "What kind of dream is this that you have had?" he said. "Are your mother and brothers and I going to bow down to the ground before you?" His brothers were jealous of him, but his father kept the matter in mind.

GENESIS 37:2b-7,9-11

Related texts: GENESIS 28:10-19; 41:1-45; JOEL 2:28-32; MATTHEW 1:18–2:22

Jacob Moves His Family to Egypt

Then He [God] gave him [Abraham] the covenant of circumcision. This being so, he fathered Isaac and circumcised him on the eighth day; Isaac did the same with Jacob, and Jacob with the 12 patriarchs.

The patriarchs became jealous of Joseph and sold him into Egypt, but God was with him and rescued him out of all his troubles. He gave him favor and wisdom in the sight of Pharaoh, king of Egypt, who appointed him governor over Egypt and over his whole household. Then a famine came over all of Egypt and Canaan, with great suffering, and our forefathers could find no food. When Jacob heard there was grain in Egypt, he sent our forefathers the first time. The second time, Joseph was revealed to his brothers, and Joseph's family became known to Pharaoh. Joseph then invited his father Jacob and all his relatives, 75 people in all, and Jacob went down to Egypt. He and our forefathers died there.

Now Jacob lived in the land of Egypt 17 years, and his life span was 147 years.

ACTS 7:8-15; GENESIS 47:28

JOSEPH: *God Intended It for Good*

When Joseph's brothers saw that their father was dead, they said to one another, "If Joseph is holding a grudge against us, he will certainly repay us for all the wrong we caused him."

So they sent this message to Joseph, "Before he died your father gave a command: 'Say this to Joseph: Please forgive your brothers' transgression and their sin—the wrong they caused you.' Therefore, please forgive the transgression of the servants of the God of your father." Joseph wept when their message came to him. Then his brothers also came to him, bowed down before him, and said, "We are your slaves!"

But Joseph said to them, "Don't be afraid. Am I in the place of God? You planned evil against me; God planned it for good to bring about the present result— the survival of many people. Therefore don't be afraid. I will take care of you and your little ones." And he comforted them and spoke kindly to them.

Joseph said to his brothers, "I am about to die, but God will certainly come to your aid and bring you up from this land to the land He promised Abraham, Isaac, and Jacob."

We know that all things work together for the good of those who love God: those who are called according to His purpose.

GENESIS 50:15-21,24; ROMANS 8:28

Related texts: GENESIS 37–50; EXODUS 1; 13:17-19; JOSHUA 24:32; PSALM 105:7-25; HEBREWS 11:21-22

JOB: *Blameless and Blessed*

There was a man in the country of Uz named Job. He was a man of perfect integrity, who feared God and turned away from evil. Job was the greatest man among all the people of the east.

One day the sons of God came to present themselves before the LORD, and Satan also came with them. The LORD asked Satan, "Where have you come from?"

"From roaming through the earth," Satan answered Him, "and walking around on it."

Then the LORD said to Satan, "Have you considered My servant Job? No one else on earth is like him, a man of perfect integrity, who fears God and turns away from evil."

Satan answered the LORD, "Does Job fear God for nothing? Haven't You placed a hedge around him, his household, and everything he owns? You have blessed the work of his hands, and his possessions are spread out in the land. But stretch out Your hand and strike everything he owns, and he will surely curse You to Your face."

"Very well," the LORD told Satan, "everything he owns is in your power. However, you must not lay a hand on Job himself." So Satan went out from the LORD'S presence.

JOB 1:1,3b,6-12

Job Loses His Wealth and His Children

One day when Job's sons and daughters were eating and drinking wine in their oldest brother's house, a messenger came to Job and reported: "While the oxen were plowing and the donkeys grazing nearby, the Sabeans swooped down and took them away. They struck down the servants with the sword, and I alone have escaped to tell you!"

He was still speaking when another messenger came and reported: "A lightning storm struck from heaven. It burned up the sheep and the servants, and devoured them, and I alone have escaped to tell you!"

That messenger was still speaking when yet another came and reported: "The Chaldeans formed three bands, made a raid on the camels, and took them away. They struck down the servants with the sword, and I alone have escaped to tell you!"

He was still speaking when another messenger came and reported: "Your sons and daughters were eating and drinking wine in their oldest brother's house. Suddenly a powerful wind swept in from the desert and struck the four corners of the house. It collapsed on the young people so that they died, and I alone have escaped to tell you!"

Then Job stood up, tore his robe and shaved his head. He fell to the ground and worshiped, saying:
Naked I came from my mother's womb,
and naked I will leave this life.
The LORD gives, and the LORD takes away.
Praise the name of the LORD.
Throughout all this Job did not sin or blame God for anything.

JOB 1:13-22

Related texts: HABAKKUK 3:17-19; 1 THESSALONIANS 5:16-18; REVELATION 7:13-17

Job Loses His Health

One day the sons of God came again to present themselves before the LORD, and Satan also came with them to present himself before the LORD. The LORD asked Satan, "Where have you come from?"

"From roaming through the earth," Satan answered Him, "and walking around on it."

Then the LORD said to Satan, "Have you considered My servant Job? No one else on earth is like him, a man of perfect integrity, who fears God and turns away from evil. He still retains his integrity, even though you incited Me against him, to destroy him without just cause."

"Skin for skin!" Satan answered the LORD. "A man will give up everything he owns in exchange for his life. But stretch out Your hand and strike his flesh and bones, and he will surely curse You to Your face."

"Very well," the LORD told Satan, "he is in your power; only spare his life." So Satan left the LORD's presence and infected Job with incurable boils from the sole of his foot to the top of his head. Then Job took a piece of broken pottery to scrape himself while he sat among the ashes.

His wife said to him, "Do you still retain your integrity? Curse God and die!"

"You speak as a foolish woman speaks," he told her. "Should we accept only good from God and not adversity?" Throughout all this Job did not sin in what he said.

JOB 2:1-10

Related texts: JOB 19:25-27; PROVERBS 11:2-6; PHILIPPIANS 3:7-11

A thorough knowledge of the Bible is worth more than a college education.

Theodore Roosevelt (1858–1919)
UNITED STATES PRESIDENT

I am a man of one book.

St. Thomas Aquinas (1227–1274)
ITALIAN THEOLOGIAN/PHILOSOPHER

The man of one book is always formidable; but when that book is the Bible he is irresistible.

William Mackergo Taylor (1829–1895)
SCOTTISH CLERGYMAN

Is Suffering Always Punishment?

Now when Job's three friends—Eliphaz the
Temanite, Bildad the Shuhite, and Zophar the
Naamathite—heard about all this adversity that had
happened to him, each of them came from his home.
They met together to go and offer sympathy and comfort to him. When they looked from a distance, they
could barely recognize him. They wept aloud, and each
man tore his robe and threw dust into the air and on
his head. Then they sat on the ground with him seven
days and nights, but no one spoke a word to him
because they saw that his suffering was very intense.

Then Eliphaz the Temanite replied:
Consider: who has perished when he was innocent?
Where have the honest been destroyed?
In my experience, those who plow injustice
and those who sow trouble reap the same.
They perish at a single blast from God
and come to an end by the breath of His nostrils.

However, if I were you, I would appeal to God
and would present my case to Him.
See how happy the man is God corrects;
so do not reject the discipline of the Almighty.
For He crushes but also binds up;
He strikes, but His hands also heal.
We have investigated this, and it is true!
Hear it and understand it for yourself.

JOB 2:11-13; 4:1,7-9; 5:8,17-18,27

Related texts: JOB 4–5; 8; 11; 15; 18; 20; 22; 25;
32–37; HEBREWS 12:5-11

Job Protests His Innocence

Then Job answered:
How long will you torment me
and crush me with words?
You have humiliated me ten times now,
and you mistreat me without shame.
Even if it is true that I have sinned,
my mistake concerns only me.
If you really want to appear superior to me
and would use my disgrace as evidence against me,
then understand that it is God who has wronged me
and caught me in His net.
I cry out: Violence! but get no response;
I call for help, but there is no justice.

Job continued his discourse, saying:
As God lives, who has deprived me of justice,
and the Almighty who has made me bitter,
as long as my breath is still in me
and the breath from God remains in my nostrils,
my lips will not speak unjustly,
and my tongue will not utter deceit.
I will never affirm that you are right.
I will maintain my integrity until I die.
I will cling to my righteousness and never let it go.
My conscience will not accuse me as long as I live!

JOB 19:1-7; 27:1-6

Related texts: JOB 3; 6–7; 9–10; 12–14; 16–17; 19; 21;
23–24; 26–31; PSALM 7; LUKE 18:1-8

God Answers Job

Then the LORD answered Job from the whirlwind.
    He said:
    Who is this who obscures My counsel
    with ignorant words?
    Get ready to answer Me like a man;
    when I question you, you will inform Me.
    Where were you when I established the earth?
    Tell Me, if you have understanding.
    Who fixed its dimensions? Certainly you know!
    Who stretched a measuring line across it?
    What supports its foundations?
    Or who laid its cornerstone
    while the morning stars sang together
    and all the sons of God shouted for joy?

The LORD answered Job:
    Will the one who contends with the Almighty
        correct Him?
    Let him who argues with God give an answer.
Then Job answered the LORD:
    I am so insignificant. How can I answer You?
    I place my hand over my mouth.
    I have spoken once, and I will not reply;
    twice, but now I can add nothing.
 Then the LORD answered Job from the whirlwind:
    Get ready to answer Me like a man;
    When I question you, you will inform Me.
    Would you really challenge My justice?
    Would you declare Me guilty to justify yourself?

JOB 38:1-7; 40:1-8

Related texts: PSALM 30; JOB 38–41; HABAKKUK 1:1–2:1;   *37*
ROMANS 9–10

God Vindicates and Restores Job

Then Job replied to the LORD:
> I know that You can do anything
> and no plan of Yours can be thwarted.
> You asked, "Who is this who conceals My counsel
> with ignorance?"
> Surely I spoke about things I did not understand,
> things too wonderful for me to know.
> You said, "Listen now, and I will speak.
> When I question you, you will inform Me."
> I had heard rumors about You,
> but now my eyes have seen You.
> Therefore I take back my words
> and repent in dust and ashes.

After the Lord had finished speaking to Job, He said to Eliphaz the Temanite: "I am angry with you and your two friends, for you have not spoken the truth about Me, as My servant Job has. Now take seven bulls and seven rams, go to My servant Job, and offer a burnt offering for yourselves. Then My servant Job will pray for you. I will surely accept his prayer and not deal with you as your folly deserves. For you have not spoken the truth about Me, as My servant Job has." Then Eliphaz the Temanite, Bildad the Shuhite, and Zophar the Naamathite went and did as the Lord had told them, and the Lord accepted Job's prayer.

After Job had prayed for his friends, the Lord restored his prosperity and doubled his previous possessions.

JOB 42:1-10

Related texts: PSALM 17:37; MATTHEW 5:1-6; JAMES 5:11

THE BEATITUDES: *Poor in Spirit*

When He saw the crowds, He went up on the mountain, and after He sat down, His disciples came to Him. Then He began to teach them, saying:
"Blessed are the poor in spirit,
because the kingdom of heaven is theirs."

The sacrifice pleasing to God is a broken spirit.
God, You will not despise a broken and humbled
   heart.

For the High and Exalted One
who lives forever, whose name is Holy says this:
"I live in a high and holy place,
and with the oppressed and lowly of spirit,
to revive the spirit of the lowly
and revive the heart of the oppressed."

My brothers, hold your faith in our glorious Lord Jesus Christ without showing favoritism. For suppose a man comes into your meeting wearing a gold ring, dressed in fine clothes, and a poor man dressed in dirty clothes also comes in. If you look with favor on the man wearing the fine clothes so that you say, "Sit here in a good place," and yet you say to the poor man, "Stand over there," or, "Sit here on the floor by my footstool," haven't you discriminated among yourselves and become judges with evil thoughts?

Listen, my dear brothers: Didn't God choose the poor in this world to be rich in faith and heirs of the kingdom that He has promised to those who love Him?

MATTHEW 5:1-3; PSALM 51:17; ISAIAH 57:15; JAMES 2:1-5

THE BEATITUDES: *Those Who Mourn*

Blessed are those who mourn,
because they will be comforted.

The Spirit of the Lord GOD is on Me,
because the LORD has anointed Me
to bring good news to the poor.
He has sent Me to heal the brokenhearted,
to proclaim liberty to the captives,
and freedom to the prisoners;
to proclaim the year of the LORD's favor,
and the day of our God's vengeance;
to comfort all who mourn,
to provide for those who mourn in Zion;
to give them a crown of beauty instead of ashes,
festive oil instead of mourning,
and splendid clothes instead of despair.
And they will be called righteous trees,
planted by the LORD,
to glorify Him.

Then I heard a loud voice from the throne:
Look! God's dwelling is with men,
and He will live with them.
They will be His people,
and God Himself will be with them and be their
God.
He will wipe away every tear from their eyes.
Death will exist no longer;
grief, crying, and pain will exist no longer,
because the previous things have passed away.

MATTHEW 5:4; ISAIAH 61:1-3; REVELATION 21:3-4

Related texts: NEHEMIAH 8:1-12; ECCLESIASTES 3:1-8; PSALM
119:49-50; LUKE 6:21; 2 CORINTHIANS 1:3-7; 7:8-11

THE BEATITUDES: *The Gentle*

Blessed are the gentle,
because they will inherit the earth.

Do not be agitated by evildoers;
do not envy those who do wrong.
For they wither quickly like grass
and wilt like tender green plants.
Trust in the LORD and do good;
dwell in the land and live securely.
Take delight in the LORD,
and He will give you your heart's desires.
Commit your way to the LORD;
trust in Him, and He will act,
making your righteousness shine like the dawn,
your justice like the noonday.
Be silent before the LORD and wait expectantly for
    Him;
do not be agitated by one who prospers in his way,
by the man who carries out evil plans.
Refrain from anger and give up your rage;
do not be agitated—it can only bring harm.
For evildoers will be destroyed,
but those who hope in the LORD will inherit the
    land.
A little while, and the wicked will be no more;
though you look for him, he will not be there.
But the humble will inherit the land
and will enjoy abundant prosperity.

MATTHEW 5:5; PSALM 37:1-11

Related texts: PSALM 25:12-13; 37:12-40; MATTHEW 11:25-30; GALATIANS 5:19-23; 2 CORINTHIANS 10:1-5

THE BEATITUDES: *Hungry for Righteousness*

Blessed are those who hunger and thirst for righteousness,
because they will be filled.

As a deer longs for streams of water,
so I long for You, God.
I thirst for God, the living God.
When can I come and appear before God?

Jesus said, "Everyone who drinks from this water
will get thirsty again. But whoever drinks from the
water that I will give him will never get thirsty again—
ever! In fact, the water I will give him will become a
well of water springing up within him for eternal life."

"I am the bread of life," Jesus told them. "No one
who comes to Me will ever be hungry, and no one who
believes in Me will ever be thirsty again."

On the last and most important day of the festival,
Jesus stood up and cried out, "If anyone is thirsty, he
should come to Me and drink! The one who believes in
Me, as the Scripture has said, will have streams of living
water flow from deep within him." He said this about
the Spirit, whom those who believed in Him were going
to receive, for the Spirit had not yet been received,
because Jesus had not yet been glorified.

MATTHEW 5:6; PSALM 42:1-2; JOHN 4:13-14; 6:35; 7:37-39

Related texts: PSALMS 107:1-9; 146; ISAIAH 55:1-2; LUKE
6:21; REVELATION 7:16-17; 22:17

THE BEATITUDES: *The Merciful*

Blessed are the merciful,
because they will be shown mercy.

He will not leave you, destroy you, or forget the covenant with your fathers that He swore to them by oath, because the LORD your God is a compassionate God.

I lift my eyes to You,
the One enthroned in heaven.
Like a servant's eyes on His master's hand,
like a servant girl's eyes on her mistress's hand,
so our eyes are on the LORD our God
until He shows us favor.
Show us favor, LORD, show us favor,
for we've had more than enough contempt.
We've had more than enough
scorn from the arrogant
and contempt from the proud.

He has told you men what is good
and what it is the LORD requires of you:
Only to act justly,
to love faithfulness,
and to walk humbly with your God.

Speak and act as those who will be judged by the law of freedom. For judgment is without mercy to the one who hasn't shown mercy. Mercy triumphs over judgment.

MATTHEW 5:7; DEUTERONOMY 4:31; PSALM 123; MICAH 6:8; JAMES 2:12-13

Related texts: PSALM 6; MICAH 7:18-19; HOSEA 6:6; ZECHARIAH 7:9-10; LUKE 6:27-38; 10:25-37; JUDE 20-23

THE BEATITUDES: *The Pure in Heart*

Blessed are the pure in heart,
because they will see God.

Who may ascend the mountain of the LORD?
Who may stand in His holy place?
The one who has clean hands and a pure heart,
who has not set his mind on what is false,
and who has not sworn deceitfully.
He will receive blessing from the LORD,
and righteousness from the God of his salvation.

God, create a clean heart for me
and renew a steadfast spirit within me.

Flee from youthful passions, and pursue righteousness, faith, love, and peace, along with those who call on the Lord from a pure heart.

Therefore, brothers, since we have boldness to enter the sanctuary through the blood of Jesus, by the new and living way that He has inaugurated for us, through the curtain (that is, His flesh); and since we have a great high priest over the house of God, let us draw near with a true heart in full assurance of faith, our hearts sprinkled clean from an evil conscience and our bodies washed in pure water.

MATTHEW 5:8; PSALMS 24:3-5; 51:10; 2 TIMOTHY 2:22;
HEBREWS 10:19-22

Related texts: 2 CHRONICLES 30:13-20; PROVERBS 20:5-11;
MARK 7:1-23; HEBREWS 3; 12:14-29

THE BEATITUDES: *The Peacemakers*

Blessed are the peacemakers,
because they will be called sons of God.

Come, children, listen to me;
I will teach you the fear of the LORD.
Who is the man who delights in life,
loving a long life to enjoy what is good?
Keep your tongue from evil
and your lips from deceitful speech.
Turn away from evil and do good;
seek peace and pursue it.

Watch the blameless and observe the upright,
for the man of peace will have a future.
But transgressors will all be eliminated;
the future of the wicked will be destroyed.

"There is no peace," says the LORD, "for the wicked."

If possible, on your part, live at peace with everyone.

But the wisdom from above is first pure, then peace-loving, gentle, compliant, full of mercy and good fruits, without favoritism and hypocrisy.

MATTHEW 5:9; PSALMS 34:11-14; 37:37-38; ISAIAH 48:22; ROMANS 12:18; JAMES 3:17

Related texts: ISAIAH 9:6-7; JOHN 1:1-13; ROMANS 8:9-23; GALATIANS 3:26–4:7; 1 JOHN 3:1-11

THE BEATITUDES: *The Persecuted Righteous*

Blessed are those who are persecuted for righteousness, because the kingdom of heaven is theirs.

Blessed are you when they insult you and persecute you, and say every kind of evil against you falsely because of Me. Be glad and rejoice, because your reward is great in heaven. For that is how they persecuted the prophets who were before you.

But the Lord is with me like a violent warrior.
Therefore, my persecutors will stumble and not prevail.
Since they have not succeeded, they will be utterly shamed,
an everlasting humiliation that will never be forgotten.

For it brings favor if, because of conscience toward God, someone endures grief from suffering unjustly. For what credit is there if you endure when you sin and are beaten? But when you do good and suffer, if you endure, it brings favor with God.

For you were called to this,
because Christ also suffered for you,
leaving you an example,
so that you should follow in His steps.

So because of Christ, I am pleased in weaknesses, in insults, in catastrophes, in persecutions, and in pressures. For when I am weak, then I am strong.

MATTHEW 5:10-12; JEREMIAH 20:11; 1 PETER 2:19-21; 2 CORINTHIANS 12:10

Related texts: JOB 36:15-17; ISAIAH 53; 1 PETER 1:3-9; 4:12-19

Unconditional Love

Who can separate us from the love of Christ?
Can affliction or anguish or persecution
or famine or nakedness or danger or sword?
As it is written:
Because of You we are being put to death all day
   long;
we are counted as sheep to be slaughtered.
No, in all these things we are more than victorious
through Him who loved us.
For I am persuaded that neither death nor life,
nor angels nor rulers,
nor things present, nor things to come, nor powers,
nor height, nor depth, nor any other created thing
will have the power to separate us
from the love of God that is in Christ Jesus our
   Lord!

And we have come to know and to believe the love
that God has for us. God is love, and the one who
remains in love remains in God, and God remains in
him.

In this, love is perfected with us so that we may
have confidence in the day of judgment; for we are as
He is in this world. There is no fear in love; instead,
perfect love drives out fear, because fear involves punishment. So the one who fears has not reached perfec-
tion in love. We love because He first loved us.

ROMANS 8:35-39; 1 JOHN 4:16-19

Related texts: DEUTERONOMY 7:7-11; 10:14-15; JOHN
3:16-19; ROMANS 5:8-11; EPHESIANS 2:4-10

The Greatest Is Love

If I speak the languages of men and of angels, but
    do not have love,
I am a sounding gong or a clanging cymbal.
If I have the gift of prophecy,
and understand all mysteries and all knowledge,
and if I have all faith, so that I can move mountains,
but do not have love, I am nothing.
And if I donate all my goods to feed the poor,
and if I give my body to be burned,
but do not have love, I gain nothing.
Love is patient; love is kind. Love does not envy;
is not boastful; is not conceited;
does not act improperly; is not selfish;
is not provoked; does not keep a record of wrongs;
finds no joy in unrighteousness, but rejoices in the
    truth;
bears all things, believes all things,
hopes all things, endures all things.
Love never ends.
Now these three remain: faith, hope, and love.
But the greatest of these is love.

Set me as a seal on your heart,
as a seal on your arm.
For love is as strong as death;
ardent love is as unrelenting as Sheol.
Love's flames are fiery flames —
the fiercest of all.

Husbands, love your wives, just as also Christ loved
the church and gave Himself for her.

1 CORINTHIANS 13:1-8a,13; SONG OF SONGS 8:6;
EPHESIANS 5:25

Related texts: DEUTERONOMY 6:1-5; PSALM 136; JOHN
15:9-17; 1 JOHN 3

Israelites Oppressed in Egypt

These are the names of the sons of Israel who came to Egypt with Jacob; each came with his family:
Reuben, Simeon, Levi, and Judah;
Issachar, Zebulun, and Benjamin;
Dan and Naphtali; Gad and Asher.
The total number of Jacob's descendants was 70; Joseph was already in Egypt.

Then Joseph and all his brothers and all that generation died. But the Israelites were fruitful, increased rapidly, multiplied, and became extremely numerous so that the land was filled with them.

A new king, who had not known Joseph, came to power in Egypt. He said to his people, "Look, the Israelite people are more numerous and powerful than we are. Let us deal shrewdly with them; otherwise they will multiply further, and if war breaks out, they may join our enemies, fight against us, and leave the country." So the Egyptians assigned taskmasters over the Israelites to oppress them with forced labor. They built Pithom and Rameses as supply cities for Pharaoh. But the more they oppressed them, the more they multiplied and spread so that the Egyptians came to dread the Israelites. They worked the Israelites ruthlessly.

Pharaoh then commanded all his people: "You must throw every son born to the Hebrews into the Nile, but let every daughter live."

EXODUS 1:1-13,22

Related texts: PSALM 105:23-25; ACTS 7:9-34;
1 CORINTHIANS 7:21-23; GALATIANS 3:26-28

The Birth of Moses

Now a man from the family of Levi married a Levite woman. The woman became pregnant and gave birth to a son; when she saw that he was beautiful, she hid him for three months. But when she could no longer hide him, she got a papyrus basket for him and coated it with asphalt and pitch. She placed the child in it and set it among the reeds by the bank of the Nile. Then his sister stood at a distance in order to see what would happen to him.

Pharaoh's daughter went down to bathe at the Nile while her servant girls walked along the riverbank. Seeing the basket among the reeds, she sent her slave girl to get it. When she opened it, she saw the child—a little boy, crying. She felt sorry for him and said, "This is one of the Hebrew boys."

Then his sister said to Pharaoh's daughter, "Should I go and call a woman from the Hebrews to nurse the boy for you?"

"Go." Pharaoh's daughter told her. So the girl went and called the boy's mother. Then Pharaoh's daughter said to her, "Take this child and nurse him for me, and I will pay your wages." So the woman took the boy and nursed him. When the child grew older, she brought him to Pharaoh's daughter, and he became her son. She named him Moses, "Because," she said, "I drew him out of the water."

EXODUS 2:1-10

Related texts: ISAIAH 49:13-19; ACTS 7:20-22; HEBREWS 11:23

Moses Flees from Egypt

Years later, after Moses had grown up, he went out to his own people and observed their forced labor. He saw an Egyptian beating a Hebrew, one of his people. Looking all around and seeing no one, he struck the Egyptian dead and hid him in the sand. The next day he went out and saw two Hebrews fighting. He asked the one in the wrong, "Why are you attacking your neighbor?"

"Who made you a leader and judge over us?" the man replied. "Are you planning to kill me as you killed the Egyptian?"

Then Moses became afraid and thought: What I did is certainly known. When Pharaoh heard about this, he tried to kill Moses. But Moses fled from Pharaoh and went to live in the land of Midian.

After a long time, the king of Egypt died. The Israelites groaned because of their difficult labor, and they cried out; and their cry for help ascended to God because of the difficult labor. So God heard their groaning, and He remembered His covenant with Abraham, Isaac, and Jacob. God saw the Israelites, and He took notice.

He has sent redemption to His people.
He has ordained His covenant forever.
His name is holy and awe-inspiring.

Exodus 2:11-15a,23-25; Psalm 111:9

Related texts: Numbers 32:23; Acts 7:23-29; Hebrews 11:24-27

The LORD Appears to Moses

Meanwhile Moses was shepherding the flock of his father-in-law Jethro, the priest of Midian. He led the flock to the far side of the wilderness and came to Horeb, the mountain of God. Then the Angel of the LORD appeared to him in a flame of fire within a bush. As Moses looked, he saw that the bush was on fire but was not consumed. So Moses thought: I must go over and look at this remarkable sight. Why isn't the bush burning up?

When the LORD saw that he had gone over to look, God called out to him from the bush, "Moses, Moses!"

"Here I am," he answered.

"Do not come closer," He said. "Take your sandals off your feet, for the place where you are standing is holy ground." Then He continued, "I am the God of your father, the God of Abraham, the God of Isaac, and the God of Jacob." Moses hid his face because he was afraid to look at God.

Then the LORD said, "I have observed the misery of My people in Egypt, and have heard them crying out because of their oppressors, and I know about their sufferings. I have come down to rescue them from the power of the Egyptians and to bring them from that land to a good and spacious land, a land flowing with milk and honey.

Therefore, go. I am sending you to Pharaoh so that you may lead My people, the Israelites, out of Egypt."

EXODUS 3:1-8a,10

Related texts: ISAIAH 6; ACTS 7:30-35; REVELATION 15:2-4

The LORD Reveals His Name to Moses

But Moses asked God, "Who am I that I should go to Pharaoh and that I should bring the Israelites out of Egypt?"

He answered, "I will certainly be with you, and this will be the sign to you that I have sent you: when you bring the people out of Egypt, you will all worship God at this mountain."

Then Moses asked God, "If I go to the Israelites and say to them: The God of your fathers has sent me to you, and they ask me, 'What is His name?' what should I tell them?"

God replied to Moses, "I AM WHO I AM. This is what you are to say to the Israelites: I AM has sent me to you."

God also said to Moses, "Say this to the Israelites: Yahweh, the God of your fathers, the God of Abraham, the God of Isaac, and the God of Jacob, has sent me to you. This is My name forever; this is how I am to be remembered in every generation.

Then God spoke to Moses, telling him, "I am Yahweh. I appeared to Abraham, Isaac, and Jacob as Almighty, but I did not make My name Yahweh known to them."

EXODUS 3:11-15; 6:2-3

Related texts: EXODUS 20:7; JOHN 6:35; 8:12,58; 10:7,11; 11:25; 14:6; 15:1; REVELATION 1:8

THE NAMES OF GOD: *The LORD*

The LORD is a refuge for the oppressed,
a refuge in times of trouble.
Those who know Your name trust in You
because You have not abandoned those who seek
You, LORD.

Do not misuse the name of the LORD your God,
because the LORD will punish anyone who misuses His
name.

For I will proclaim the LORD's name.
Declare the greatness of our God!
The Rock—His work is perfect;
all His ways are entirely just.
A faithful God, without prejudice,
He is righteous and true.

Give thanks to the LORD; call on His name;
proclaim His deeds among the peoples.
Sing to Him; sing praise to Him;
tell about all His wonderful works!
Honor His holy name;
let the hearts of those who seek the LORD rejoice.

The name of the LORD is a strong tower;
the righteous run to it and are protected.

LORD, there is no one like You.
You are great;
Your name is great in power.

PSALM 9:9-10; EXODUS 20:7; DEUTERONOMY 32:3-4; 1
CHRONICLES 16:8-10; PROVERBS 18:10; JEREMIAH 10:6

Related texts: EXODUS 15:1-3; ISAIAH 42:5-9; COLOSSIANS
3:16-17; HEBREWS 13:15

THE NAMES OF GOD: *The Sovereign* LORD

This is why You are great, Lord GOD. There is no one like You, and there is no God besides You, as all we have heard confirms. And who is like Your people Israel? God came to one nation on earth in order to redeem a people for Himself, to make a name for Himself, and to perform for them great and awesome acts, driving out nations and their gods before Your people You redeemed for Yourself from Egypt. You established Your people Israel Your own people forever, and You, LORD, have become their God.

> Our God is a God of salvation,
> and escape from death belongs to the Lord GOD.

> For You are my hope, Lord GOD,
> my confidence from my youth.

> Those far from You will certainly perish;
> You destroy all who are unfaithful to You.
> But as for me, God's presence is my good.
> I have made the Lord GOD my refuge,
> so I can tell about all You do.

2 SAMUEL 7:22-24; PSALMS 68:20; 71:5; 73:27-28

Related texts: ISAIAH 50:4-11; EZEKIEL 36; ACTS 4:23-35; EPHESIANS 5:19-20

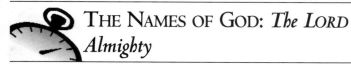

THE NAMES OF GOD: *The LORD Almighty*

Lift up your heads, you gates!
Rise up, ancient doors!
Then the King of glory will come in.
Who is this King of glory?
The LORD, strong and mighty,
the LORD, mighty in battle.
Lift up your heads, you gates!
Rise up, ancient doors!
Then the King of glory will come in.
Who is He, this King of glory?
The LORD of Hosts,
He is the King of glory.

I also saw something like a sea of glass mixed with
fire, and those who had won the victory from the beast,
his image, and the number of his name, were standing
on the sea of glass with harps from God. They sang the
song of God's servant Moses, and the song of the Lamb:
Great and awe-inspiring are Your works, Lord God,
the Almighty;
righteous and true are Your ways, King of the
Nations.
Lord, who will not fear and glorify Your name?
Because You alone are holy,
because all the nations will come and worship
before You,
because Your righteous acts have been revealed.

PSALM 24:7-10; REVELATION 15:2-4

Related texts: 1 SAMUEL 17:39-51; PSALM 46; ISAIAH 54:5

THE NAMES OF GOD: *The Almighty*

Therefore listen to me, you men of understanding.
It is impossible for God to do wrong,
And for the Almighty to act unjustly.
For He repays a person according to his deeds,
and He bring his ways on him.
Indeed, it is true that God does not act wickedly
and the Almighty does not pervert justice.

The Almighty—we cannot reach Him—
He is exalted in power!
In His justice and righteousness,
He will not oppress.
Therefore, men fear Him.
He does not look favorably on any who are wise in
    heart.

The one who lives under the protection of the Most
    High
dwells in the shadow of the Almighty.
I will say to the LORD, "My refuge and my fortress,
my God, in whom I trust."
He Himself will deliver you from the hunter's net,
from the destructive plague.
He will cover you with His feathers;
you will take refuge under His wings.
His faithfulness will be a protective shield.

"I am the Alpha and the Omega," says the Lord
God, "the One who is, who was, and who is coming,
the Almighty."

JOB 34:10-12; 37:23-24; PSALM 91:1-4; REVELATION 1:8

Related texts: GENESIS 17:1; 28:3; 35:11; 43:14; 48:3;
49:25; EXODUS 6:2-4; REVELATION 4:1-8; 15:2-4; 21:22-27

NAMES OF GOD: *The Lord*

For the LORD your God is the God of gods and Lord of lords, the great, mighty, and awesome God, showing no partiality and taking no bribe. He executes justice for the fatherless and the widow, and loves the foreign resident, giving him food and clothing.

O LORD, our Lord,
how magnificent is Your name throughout the earth!

Lord, You have been our refuge
in every generation.
Before the mountains were born,
before You gave birth to the earth and the world,
from eternity to eternity, You are God.

If you confess with your mouth, "Jesus is Lord," and believe in your heart that God raised Him from the dead, you will be saved. With the heart one believes, resulting in righteousness, and with the mouth one confesses, resulting in salvation. Now the Scripture says, No one who believes on Him will be put to shame, for there is no distinction between Jew and Greek, since the same Lord of all is rich to all who call on Him. For everyone who calls on the name of the Lord will be saved.

Therefore as you have received Christ Jesus the Lord, walk in Him, rooted and built up in Him and established in the faith, just as you were taught, and overflowing with thankfulness.

DEUTERONOMY 10:17-18; PSALMS 8:9; 90:1-2; ROMANS 10:9-13; COLOSSIANS 2:6-7

Related texts: JOB 28; PSALMS 8; 86; 110; DANIEL 9:1-19; PHILIPPIANS 2:5-11

NAMES OF GOD: *The Most High*

God is our refuge and strength,
a helper who is always found in times of trouble.
Therefore we will not be afraid, though the earth
    trembles
and the mountains topple into the depths of the seas,
though its waters roar and foam
and the mountains quake with its turmoil.
There is a river—its streams delight the city of God,
the holy dwelling place of the Most High.
God is within her; she will not be toppled.
God will help her when the morning dawns.
Nations rage, kingdoms topple;
the earth melts when He lifts His voice.
The LORD of Hosts is with us;
the God of Jacob is our stronghold.

Clap your hands, all you peoples;
shout to God with a jubilant cry.
For the LORD Most High is awe-inspiring,
a great King over all the earth.

It is good to praise the LORD,
to sing praise to Your name, Most High,
to declare Your faithful love in the morning
and Your faithfulness at night.
For You have made me rejoice, LORD, by what You
    have done;
I will shout for joy because of the works of Your
    hands.
How magnificent are Your works, LORD,
how profound Your thoughts!

PSALMS 46:1-7; 47:1-2; 92:1-2,4-5

Related texts: GENESIS 14:18-24; PSALMS 7; 9:1-2; 91;
LUKE 1:26-38

NAMES OF GOD: *The Creator*

So remember your Creator in the days of your youth:
Before the days of adversity come,
and the years approach when you will say,
"I have no delight in them";
before the sun and the light are darkened,
and the moon and the stars,
and the clouds return after the rain;
on the day when the guardians of the house tremble,
and the strong men stoop,
the women who grind cease because they are few,
and the ones who watch through the windows see
　　dimly,
and the doors at the street are shut
while the sound of the mill fades;
when one rises at the sound of a bird,
and all the daughters of song grow faint.
Also, they are afraid of heights and dangers on the
　　road;
the almond tree blossoms,
the grasshopper loses its spring,
and the caper berry has no effect;
for man is headed to his eternal home,
and mourners will walk around in the street;
before the silver cord is snapped,
and the golden bowl is broken,
and the jar is shattered at the spring,
and the wheel is broken into the well;
and the dust returns to the earth as it once was,
and the spirit returns to God who gave it.

ECCLESIASTES 12:1-7

Related texts: GENESIS 1; 14:18-24; ECCLESIASTES 12:9-14;
ISAIAH 40:27-31; REVELATION 4:11

NAMES OF GOD: *Everlasting God, King Eternal*

Jacob, why do you say,
and Israel, why do you assert:
"My way is hidden from the LORD,
and my claim is ignored by my God"?
Do you not know?
Have you not heard?
Yahweh is the everlasting God,
the Creator of the whole earth.
He never grows faint or weary;
there is no limit to His understanding.
He gives strength to the weary
and strengthens the powerless.
Youths may faint and grow weary,
and young men stumble and fall,
but those who trust in the LORD
will renew their strength;
they will soar on wings like eagles;
they will run and not grow weary;
they will walk and not faint.

This saying is trustworthy and deserving of full acceptance: "Christ Jesus came into the world to save sinners"—and I am the worst of them. But I received mercy because of this, so that in me, the worst of them, Christ Jesus might demonstrate the utmost patience as an example to those who would believe in Him for eternal life. Now to the King eternal, immortal, invisible, the only God, be honor and glory forever and ever. Amen.

ISAIAH 40:27-31; 1 TIMOTHY 1:15-17

Related texts: DEUTERONOMY 33:27; PSALM 90:1-2; ROMANS 16:25-27; HEBREWS 9:14

NAMES OF GOD: *The Holy One*

But You are holy,
enthroned on the praises of Israel.
Our fathers trusted in You;
they trusted, and You rescued them.
They cried to You and were set free;
they trusted in You and were not disgraced.

The fear of the LORD is the beginning of wisdom,
and the knowledge of the Holy One is understanding.
For by Wisdom your days will be many,
and years will be added to your life.
If you are wise, you are wise for your own benefit;
if you mock, you alone will bear the consequences.

The Holy One of Israel is our Redeemer;
the Lord of Hosts is His name.

In the synagogue there was a man with an unclean
demonic spirit who cried out with a loud voice, "Leave
us alone! What do You have to do with us, Jesus—
Nazarene? Have You come to destroy us? I know who
You are—the Holy One of God!"
But Jesus rebuked him and said, "Be quiet and
come out of him!"
And throwing him down before them, the demon
came out of him without hurting him at all. They were
all struck with amazement and kept saying to one
another, "What is this message? For with authority and
power He commands the unclean spirits, and they
come out!"

PSALM 22:3-5; PROVERBS 9:10-12; ISAIAH 47:4; LUKE 4:33-36

Related texts: PSALM 16; ISAIAH 40:25-31; 54:5; ACTS
2:22-39

NAMES OF GOD: *Judge*

But the LORD sits enthroned forever;
He has established His throne for judgment.
He judges the world with righteousness;
He executes judgment on the peoples with fairness.

LORD, God of vengeance—
God of vengeance, appear.
Rise up, Judge of the earth;
repay the proud what they deserve.

Then a shoot will grow from the stump of Jesse,
and a branch from his roots will bear fruit.
The Spirit of the LORD will rest on Him—
a Spirit of wisdom and understanding,
a Spirit of counsel and strength,
a Spirit of knowledge and of the fear of the LORD.
His delight will be in the fear of the LORD.
He will not judge
by what He sees with His eyes,
He will not execute justice
by what He hears with His ears,
but He will judge the poor righteously
and execute justice for the oppressed of the land.
He will strike the land
with discipline from His mouth,
and He will kill the wicked
with a command from His lips.
Righteousness and faithfulness
will be a belt around His waist.

For the LORD is our Judge.

PSALMS 9:7-8; 94:1-2; ISAIAH 11:1-5; 33:22

Related texts: JUDGES 11:27; PSALMS 7; 82; 96; JOHN 5:25-30;
ACTS 10:34-43; JAMES 4:11-12; REVELATION 19:11-16

*All human history as described in
the Bible, may be summarized in one phrase,
God in Search of Man. There are no words in
the world more knowing, more disclosing and
more indispensable, words both stern and
graceful, heart-rending and healing.*
Abraham Joshua Heschel (1907–1972)
AMERICAN THEOLOGIAN

*I was dazzled by the revelation of the truth
and obtained complete answers to the
questions: What is the meaning of my life?
And the meaning of other people's lives?*
Leo Tolstoy (1828–1910)
RUSSIAN NOVELIST
(On studying the Gospels)

*Prayer, in its turn, needs to be sustained
by reading the Holy Scripture.*
Francois Fenelon (1651–1715)
FRENCH ROMAN CATHOLIC BISHOP

NAMES OF GOD: *King*

The LORD sat enthroned at the flood;
the LORD sits enthroned, King forever.
The LORD gives His people strength;
the LORD blesses His people with peace.

I am the LORD, your Holy One,
the Creator of Israel, your King.

So Pilate asked Him, "Are You the King of the
    Jews?"
He answered him, "You have said it."

Then I saw heaven opened, and there was a white
horse! Its rider is called Faithful and True, and in righteousness He judges and makes war. His eyes were like a
fiery flame, and on His head were many crowns. He
had a name written that no one knows except Himself.
He wore a robe stained with blood, and His name is
called the Word of God. The armies that were in heav-
en followed Him on white horses, wearing pure white
linen. From His mouth came a sharp sword, so that
with it He might strike the nations. He will shepherd
them with an iron scepter. He will also trample the
winepress of the fierce anger of God, the Almighty. And
on His robe and on His thigh He has a name written:
KING OF KINGS AND LORD OF LORDS.

PSALM 29:10-11; ISAIAH 43:15; LUKE 23:3; REVELATION
19:11-16

Related texts: PSALMS 47; 95:1-7; ISAIAH 44:6-8; JEREMIAH
10:6-10; MATTHEW 21:1-5; 1 TIMOTHY 1:17; 6:15

NAMES OF GOD: *The Mighty One*

Instead of your being deserted and hated,
with no one passing through,
I will make you an object of eternal pride,
a joy from age to age.
You will nurse on the milk of nations,
and nurse at the breast of kings;
you will know that I, the Lord, am your Savior
and Redeemer, the Mighty One of Jacob.

And Mary said:
My soul proclaims the greatness of the Lord,
and my spirit has rejoiced in God my Savior,
because He has looked with favor
on the humble condition of His slave.
Surely, from now on all generations will call me blessed,
because the Mighty One has done great things for me,
and holy is His name.
His mercy is from generation to generation
on those who fear Him.
He has done a mighty deed with His arm;
He has scattered the proud because of the thoughts
of their hearts;
He has toppled the mighty from their thrones
and exalted the lowly.
He has satisfied the hungry with good things
and sent the rich away empty.
He has helped His servant Israel,
mindful of His mercy,
just as He spoke to our forefathers,
to Abraham and his descendants forever.

ISAIAH 60:15-16; LUKE 1:46-55

Related texts: JOSHUA 22:22; PSALMS 50; 132; ISAIAH
49:24-26; MARK 14:60-62

NAMES OF GOD: *Redeemer*

But I know my living Redeemer,
and He will stand on the dust at last.
Even after my skin has been destroyed,
yet I will see God in my flesh.
I will see Him myself;
my eyes will look at Him, and not as a stranger.
My heart longs within me.

Who perceives his unintentional sins?
Cleanse me from my hidden faults.
Moreover, keep Your servant from willful sins;
do not let them rule over me.
Then I will be innocent,
and cleansed from blatant rebellion.
May the words of my mouth and the meditation of
     my heart
be acceptable to You,
LORD, my rock and my Redeemer.

This is what the LORD, the King of Israel and its
     Redeemer, the LORD of Hosts, says:
I am the first and I am the last.
There is no God but Me.
Who, like Me, can announce the future?
Let him say so and make a case before Me,
     since I have established an ancient people.
Let these gods declare the coming things,
and what will take place.
Do not be startled or afraid.
Have I not told you and declared it long ago?
You are my witnesses!
Is there any God but Me?
There is no other Rock; I do not know any.

JOB 19:25-27; PSALM 19:12-14; ISAIAH 44:6-8

Related texts: ISAIAH 44:24-28; 54; LUKE 24:13-36;
GALATIANS 4:4-5; TITUS 2:11-14

NAMES OF GOD: *Refuge*

The LORD is a refuge for the oppressed,
a refuge in times of trouble.
Those who know Your name trust in You
because You have not abandoned those who seek
You, LORD.

God, hear my cry;
pay attention to my prayer.
I call to You from the ends of the earth when my
heart is without strength.
Lead me to a rock that is high above me,
for You have been a refuge for me,
a strong tower in the face of the enemy.
I will live in Your tent forever
and take refuge under the shelter of Your wings.

LORD, my strength and my stronghold,
my refuge in a time of distress,
the nations will come to You
from the ends of the earth, and they will say,
"Our fathers inherited only lies,
worthless idols of no benefit at all."
Can one make gods for himself?
But they are not gods.
"Therefore, I am about to inform them,
and this time I will make them know
My power and My might;
then they will know that My name is Yahweh."

PSALMS 9:9-10; 61:1-4; JEREMIAH 16:19-21

Related texts: 2 SAMUEL 22:3; 31; PSALMS 46; 59:16-17;
71; 91

NAMES OF GOD: *Rock*

Pay attention, heavens, and I will speak;
listen, earth, to the words of my mouth.
Let my teaching fall like rain
and my word settle like dew,
like gentle rain on new grass
and showers on tender plants.
For I will proclaim the LORD's name.
Declare the greatness of our God!
The Rock—His work is perfect;
all His ways are entirely just.
A faithful God, without prejudice,
He is righteous and true.

Hannah prayed:
My heart rejoices in the LORD;
my horn is lifted up by the LORD.
My mouth boasts over my enemies,
because I rejoice in Your salvation.
There is no one holy like the LORD.
There is no one besides You!
And there is no rock like our God.

The LORD is my rock, my fortress, and my deliverer,
my God, my mountain where I seek refuge,
my shield and the horn of my salvation, my
      stronghold.
I called to the LORD, who is worthy of praise,
and I was saved from my enemies.

DEUTERONOMY 32:1-4; 1 SAMUEL 2:1-2; PSALM 18:2-3

Related texts: DEUTERONOMY 32; 2 SAMUEL 22; PSALM 62;
ROMANS 9:30-33; 1 CORINTHIANS 10:1-4; 1 PETER 2:1-8

NAMES OF GOD: *Savior*

Why am I so depressed?
Why this turmoil within me?
Hope in God, for I will still praise Him,
my Savior and my God.

"You are My witnesses"—the LORD's declaration—
"and My servant whom I have chosen,
so that you may know and believe Me
and understand that I am He.
No god was formed before Me,
and there will be none after Me.
I, I am the LORD,
and there is no other Savior but Me.
I alone declared, saved, and proclaimed—
and not some foreign god among you.
So you are My witnesses"—the LORD's declaration—
"and I am God.
Also, from today on I am He alone,
and no one can take anything from My hand.
I act, and who can reverse it?"

For the grace of God has appeared, with salvation
for all people, instructing us to deny godlessness and
worldly lusts and to live in a sensible, righteous, and
godly way in the present age, while we wait for the
blessed hope and the appearing of the glory of our great
God and Savior, Jesus Christ. He gave Himself for us to
redeem us from all lawlessness and to cleanse for
Himself a special people, eager to do good works.

PSALM 42:11; ISAIAH 43:10-13; TITUS 2:11-14

Related texts: PSALM 68:19-20; MICAH 7:1-7; HABAKKUK
3:16-19; LUKE 1:47-55; 2:8-20; JOHN 4:40-42; ACTS 5:29-32

NAMES OF GOD: *Shepherd*

The LORD is my shepherd;
there is nothing I lack.

See, the Lord GOD comes with strength,
and His power establishes His rule.
His reward is with Him,
and His gifts accompany Him.
He protects His flock like a shepherd;
He gathers the lambs in His arms
and carries them in the fold of His garment.
He gently leads those that are nursing.

Now may the God of peace, who brought up from
the dead our Lord Jesus—the great Shepherd of the
sheep—with the blood of the everlasting covenant,
equip you with all that is good to do His will, working
in us what is pleasing in His sight, through Jesus Christ,
to whom be glory forever and ever. Amen.

For this reason they are before the throne of God,
and they serve Him day and night in His sanctuary.
The One seated on the throne will shelter them:
no longer will they hunger; no longer will they
thirst;
no longer will the sun strike them, or any heat.
Because the Lamb who is at the center of the
throne will shepherd them;
He will guide them to springs of living waters,
and God will wipe away every tear from their eyes.

PSALM 23:1; ISAIAH 40:10-11; HEBREWS 13:20-21;
REVELATION 7:15-17

Related texts: PSALMS 23; 80:1-7; EZEKIEL 34; MICAH 5:2-5;
JOHN 10:11-15; 1 PETER 2:21-25; 5:1-4

The Fruit of the Spirit

Now the works of the flesh are obvious: sexual immorality, moral impurity, promiscuity, idolatry, sorcery, hatreds, strife, jealousy, outbursts of anger, selfish ambitions, dissensions, factions, envy, drunkenness, carousing, and anything similar, about which I tell you in advance—as I told you before—that those who practice such things will not inherit the kingdom of God.

But the fruit of the Spirit is love, joy, peace, patience, kindness, goodness, faith, gentleness, self-control. Against such things there is no law.

For you were once darkness, but now you are light in the Lord. Walk as children of light—for the fruit of the light results in all goodness, righteousness, and truth—discerning what is pleasing to the Lord. Don't participate in the fruitless works of darkness, but instead, expose them.

A good tree doesn't produce bad fruit, nor again does a bad tree produce good fruit. For each tree is known by its own fruit. Figs aren't gathered from thornbushes, or grapes picked from a bramble bush. A good man produces good out of the good storeroom of his heart, and an evil man produces evil out of the evil storeroom. For his mouth speaks from the overflow of the heart.

GALATIANS 5:19-23; EPHESIANS 5:8-11; LUKE 6:43-45

Related texts: PSALMS 1; 112; ISAIAH 27:2-3; JOHN 15:1-16; ROMANS 7:1-6

THE FRUIT OF THE SPIRIT: *Love*

I love You, LORD, my strength.

"This is the most important [commandment]," Jesus answered:
"Hear, O Israel! The Lord our God is one Lord. And you shall love the Lord your God with all your heart, with all your soul, with all your mind, and with all your strength.
"The second is: You shall love your neighbor as yourself. There is no other commandment greater than these."

"I give you a new commandment: that you love one another. Just as I have loved you, you should also love one another. By this all people will know that you are My disciples, if you have love for one another."

"You have heard that it was said, You shall love your neighbor and hate your enemy. But I tell you, love your enemies, and pray for those who persecute you, so that you may be sons of your Father in heaven. For He causes His sun to rise on the evil and the good, and sends rain on the righteous and the unrighteous. For if you love those who love you, what reward will you have? Don't even the tax collectors do the same?"

Therefore, God's chosen ones, holy and loved, put on heartfelt compassion, kindness, humility, gentleness, and patience, accepting one another and forgiving one another if anyone has a complaint against another. Just as the Lord has forgiven you, so also you must forgive. Above all, put on love—the perfect bond of unity.

PSALM 18:1; MARK 12:29-31; JOHN 13:34-35; MATTHEW 5:43-46; COLOSSIANS 3:12-14

Related texts: DEUTERONOMY 6:4-6; JOHN 14–15; 21:15-17; 1 CORINTHIANS 13; 1 JOHN 4:7-21; 1 PETER 4:7-8

God Is Love

The LORD came down in a cloud, stood with him there, and proclaimed His name Yahweh. Then the LORD passed in front of him and proclaimed:

Yahweh—Yahweh is a compassionate and gracious God, slow to anger and rich in faithful love and truth, maintaining faithful love to a thousand generations, forgiving wrongdoing, rebellion, and sin. But He will not leave the guilty unpunished, bringing the consequences of the fathers' wrongdoing on the children and grandchildren to the third and fourth generation.

He loves righteousness and justice;
the earth is full of the LORD's unfailing love.

"For God loved the world in this way: He gave His One and Only Son, so that everyone who believes in Him will not perish but have eternal life."

But God proves His own love for us in that while we were still sinners Christ died for us!
For I am persuaded that neither death nor life,
nor angels nor rulers,
nor things present, nor things to come, nor powers,
nor height, nor depth, nor any other created thing
will have the power to separate us
from the love of God that is in Christ Jesus our
Lord!

God is love, and the one who remains in love remains in God, and God remains in him.

EXODUS 34:5-7; PSALM 33:5; JOHN 3:16; ROMANS 5:8; 8:38-39; 1 JOHN 4:16b

Related texts: PSALM 136; ISAIAH 63:7; JEREMIAH 9:23-24; ZEPHANIAH 3:16-17; TITUS 3:3-5a; 1 JOHN 4:7-21

THE FRUIT OF THE SPIRIT: *Joy*

Rejoice in the LORD, you righteous ones;
praise from the upright is beautiful.
Praise the LORD with the lyre;
make music to Him with a ten-stringed harp.
Sing a new song to Him;
play skillfully on the strings, with a joyful shout.
For the word of the LORD is right,
and all His work is trustworthy.

Though the fig tree does not bud
and there is no fruit on the vines,
though the olive crop fails
and the fields produce no food,
though there are no sheep in the pen
and no cattle in the stalls,
yet I will rejoice in the LORD;
I will rejoice in the God of my salvation!

Now may the God of hope fill you with all joy and
peace in believing, so that you may overflow with hope
by the power of the Holy Spirit.

Rejoice in the Lord always. I will say it again:
Rejoice!

Dear friends, when the fiery ordeal arises among
you to test you, don't be surprised by it, as if something
unusual were happening to you. Instead, as you share
in the sufferings of the Messiah rejoice, so that you may
also rejoice with great joy at the revelation of His glory.

PSALM 33:1-4; HABAKKUK 3:17-18; ROMANS 15:13;
PHILIPPIANS 4:4; 1 PETER 4:12-13

Related texts: NEHEMIAH 8:1-12; PSALMS 28:6-9; 30:4-5;
PROVERBS 11:10; ISAIAH 61

God Is Joyful

May the glory of the LORD endure forever;
may the LORD rejoice in His works.
He looks at the earth, and it trembles;
He touches the mountains, and they pour out
    smoke.
I will sing to the LORD all my life;
I will sing praise to my God while I live.
May my meditation be pleasing to Him;
I will rejoice in the LORD.

On that day it will be said to Jerusalem:
"Do not fear;
Zion, do not let your hands grow weak.
The LORD your God is among you,
a warrior who saves.
He will rejoice over you with gladness.
He will bring you quietness with His love.
He will delight in you with shouts of joy."

Keeping our eyes on Jesus, the source and perfecter
of our faith, who for the joy that lay before Him endured
a cross and despised the shame, and has sat down at
the right hand of God's throne.

PSALM 104:31-34; ZEPHANIAH 3:16-17; HEBREWS 12:2-3

Related texts: 1 CHRONICLES 16:23-33; NEHEMIAH 8:1-12;
PSALM 21:1-7; ISAIAH 62:4-7

THE FRUIT OF THE SPIRIT: *Peace*

The LORD bless you and protect you;
the LORD make His face shine on you,
and be gracious to you;
the LORD look with favor on you
and give you peace.

Abundant peace belongs to those who love Your
instruction;
nothing makes them stumble.

You will keep in perfect peace
the mind that is dependent on You,
for it is trusting in You.
Trust in the LORD forever,
because in Yah, the LORD, is an everlasting rock!

"Peace I leave with you. My peace I give to you. I do not give to you as the world gives. Your heart must not be troubled or fearful."

Don't worry about anything, but in everything, through prayer and petition with thanksgiving, let your requests be made known to God. And the peace of God, which surpasses every thought, will guard your hearts and your minds in Christ Jesus.

And let the peace of the Messiah, to which you were also called in one body, control your hearts. Be thankful.

NUMBERS 6:24-26; PSALM 119:165; ISAIAH 26:3-4; JOHN 14:27; PHILIPPIANS 4:6-7; COLOSSIANS 3:15

Related texts: PROVERBS 12:20; ISAIAH 32:17; 57:21;
MICAH 4:1-5; LUKE 2:13-14; ROMANS 8:1-6

God Is Peaceful

The LORD gives His people strength;
the LORD blesses His people with peace.

For a child will be born for us,
a son will be given to us,
and the government will be on His shoulders.
He will be named
Wonderful Counselor, Mighty God,
Eternal Father, Prince of Peace.
The dominion will be vast,
and its prosperity will never end.
He will reign on the throne of David
and over his kingdom,
to establish and sustain it
with justice and righteousness from now on and
forever.
The zeal of the LORD of Hosts will accomplish this.

Therefore, since we have been declared righteous by faith, we have peace with God through our Lord Jesus Christ. Also through Him, we have obtained access by faith into this grace in which we stand, and we rejoice in the hope of the glory of God.

Now may the God of peace Himself sanctify you completely. And may your spirit, soul, and body be kept sound and blameless for the coming of our Lord Jesus Christ.

May the Lord of peace Himself give you peace always in every way. The Lord be with all of you.

PSALM 29:11; ISAIAH 9:6-7; ROMANS 5:1-2;
1 THESSALONIANS 5:23; 2 THESSALONIANS 3:16

Related texts: ECCLESIASTES 3:1-8; ROMANS 15:33; 16:20;
2 CORINTHIANS 13:11; PHILIPPIANS 4:6-9

THE FRUIT OF THE SPIRIT: *Patience*

Be silent before the LORD and wait expectantly for Him;
do not be agitated by one who prospers in his way,
by the man who carries out evil plans.
Refrain from anger and give up your rage;
do not be agitated—it can only bring harm.
For evildoers will be destroyed,
but those who hope in the LORD will inherit the land.

I waited patiently for the LORD,
and He turned to me and heard my cry for help.
He brought me up from a desolate pit,
out of the muddy clay,
and set my feet on a rock,
making my steps secure.
He put a new song in my mouth,
a hymn of praise to our God.
Many will see and fear,
and put their trust in the LORD.

A patient person shows great understanding,
but a quick-tempered one promotes foolishness.

Love is patient; love is kind. Love does not envy; is not boastful; is not conceited.

Therefore, brothers, be patient until the Lord's coming. See how the farmer waits for the precious fruit of the earth and is patient with it until it receives the early and the late rains. You also must be patient. Strengthen your hearts, because the Lord's coming is near.

PSALMS 37:7-9; 40:1-3; PROVERBS 14:29; 1 CORINTHIANS 13:4; JAMES 5:7-8

Related texts: PROVERBS 15:18; 16:32; 19:11; 25:15; ECCLESIASTES 7:8; ROMANS 12:9-12

God Is Patient

This saying is trustworthy and deserving of full acceptance: "Christ Jesus came into the world to save sinners"—and I am the worst of them. But I received mercy because of this, so that in me, the worst of them, Christ Jesus might demonstrate the utmost patience as an example to those who would believe in Him for eternal life.

The Lord does not delay His promise, as some understand delay, but is patient with you, not wanting any to perish, but all to come to repentance.

But the Day of the Lord will come like a thief; on that day the heavens will pass away with a loud noise, the elements will burn and be dissolved, and the earth and the works on it will be disclosed. Since all these things are to be destroyed in this way, it is clear what sort of people you should be in holy conduct and godliness as you wait for and earnestly desire the coming of the day of God, because of which the heavens will be on fire and be dissolved, and the elements will melt with the heat. But based on His promise, we wait for new heavens and a new earth, where righteousness will dwell.

Therefore, dear friends, while you wait for these things, make every effort to be found in peace without spot or blemish before Him. Also, regard the patience of our Lord as an opportunity for salvation, just as our dear brother Paul, according to the wisdom given to him, has written to you.

1 TIMOTHY 1:15-16; 2 PETER 3:9-15

Related texts: ISAIAH 7:13; 65:17-25; ROMANS 2:1-4; 3:21-28; 1 PETER 3:18-20; REVELATION 21:1-8

THE FRUIT OF THE SPIRIT: *Kindness*

A gracious woman gains honor,
but violent men gain only riches.
A kind man benefits himself,
but a cruel man brings disaster on himself.

The one who despises his neighbor sins,
but whoever shows kindness to the poor will be
happy.

The one who oppresses the poor insults their Maker,
but one who is kind to the needy honors Him.

Kindness to the poor is a loan to the LORD,
and He will give a reward to the lender.

And be kind and compassionate to one another, forgiving one another, just as God also forgave you in Christ.

Therefore, God's chosen ones, holy and loved, put on heartfelt compassion, kindness, humility, gentleness, and patience, accepting one another and forgiving one another if anyone has a complaint against another. Just as the Lord has forgiven you, so also you must forgive. Above all, put on love—the perfect bond of unity.

PROVERBS 11:16-17; 14:21,31; 19:17; EPHESIANS 4:32;
COLOSSIANS 3:12-14

God Is Kind

I will make known the LORD's faithful love
and the LORD's praiseworthy acts,
because of all the LORD has done for us—
even the many good things
He has done for the house of Israel
and has done for them based on His compassions
and the abundance of His faithful love.

This is what the LORD says:
The wise must not boast in his wisdom;
the mighty must not boast in his might;
the rich must not boast in his riches.
But the one who boasts should boast in this,
that he understands and knows Me—
that I am the LORD, showing faithful love,
justice, and righteousness on the earth,
for I delight in these things.

This is the LORD's declaration.
For we too were once foolish, disobedient,
deceived, captives of various passions and pleasures,
living in malice and envy, hateful, detesting one
another.
But when the goodness and love for man
appeared from God our Savior,
He saved us—
not by works of righteousness that we had done,
but according to His mercy.

ISAIAH 63:7; JEREMIAH 9:23-24; TITUS 3:3-5a

Related texts: PSALM 18:30-36; ISAIAH 53:1-9;
2 CORINTHIANS 10:1

THE FRUIT OF THE SPIRIT: *Goodness*

The good obtain favor from the LORD,
but He condemns a man who schemes.

I know that there is nothing better for them than to rejoice and enjoy the good life. It is also the gift of God whenever anyone eats, drinks, and enjoys all his efforts.

A good tree doesn't produce bad fruit, nor again does a bad tree produce good fruit. For each tree is known by its own fruit. Figs aren't gathered from thornbushes, or grapes picked from a bramble bush. A good man produces good out of the good storeroom of his heart, and an evil man produces evil out of the evil storeroom. For his mouth speaks from the overflow of the heart.

So we must not get tired of doing good, for we will reap at the proper time if we don't give up. Therefore, as we have opportunity, we must work for the good of all, especially for those who belong to the household of faith.

For we are His creation—created in Christ Jesus for good works, which God prepared ahead of time so that we should walk in them.

Dear friend, do not imitate what is evil, but what is good. The one who does good is of God; the one who does evil has not seen God.

PROVERBS 12:2; ECCLESIASTES 3:12-13; LUKE 6:43-45; GALATIANS 6:9-10; EPHESIANS 2:10; 3 JOHN 11

Related texts: PSALM 34:8-14; PROVERBS 3:27; 11:27; 1 PETER 2:12-15

God Is Good

Taste and see that the LORD is good.
How happy is the man who takes refuge in Him!

I will praise You forever for what You have done.
In the presence of Your faithful people,
I will place my hope in Your name, for it is good.

God is indeed good to Israel,
to the pure in heart.
For the LORD is good, and His love is eternal;
His faithfulness endures through all generations.

Give thanks to the LORD, for He is good;
His faithful love endures forever.

You are good, and You do what is good;
teach me Your statutes.

Praise the LORD, for the LORD is good;
sing praise to His name, for it is delightful.

The LORD is good to everyone;
His compassion rests on all He has made.

PSALMS 34:8; 52:9; 73:1; 100:5; 118:29; 119:68;
135:3; 145:9

Related texts: 2 CHRONICLES 6:41: PSALM 84:9-12; MARK
10:17-18; ROMANS 8:18-28; 3 JOHN 11

THE FRUIT OF THE SPIRIT: *Faithfulness*

Above all, fear the LORD and worship Him faithfully with all your heart, considering the great things He has done for you.

With the faithful
You prove Yourself faithful;
with the blameless man
You prove Yourself blameless;
with the pure
You prove Yourself pure,
but with the crooked
You prove Yourself shrewd.
You rescue an afflicted people,
but Your eyes are set against the proud—
You humble them.

Love the LORD, all His faithful ones.
The LORD protects the loyal,
but fully repays the arrogant.
Be strong and courageous,
all you who hope in the LORD.

This saying is trustworthy:
For if we have died with Him, we will also live with
    Him;
if we endure, we will also reign with Him;
if we deny Him, He will also deny us;
if we are faithless, He remains faithful,
for He cannot deny Himself.

1 SAMUEL 12:24; 2 SAMUEL 22:26-28; PSALM 31:23-24; 2 TIMOTHY 2:11-13

Related texts: PSALM 101; PROVERBS 3:1-4; MATTHEW 24:45-51; 25:14-30

God Is Faithful

Know that Yahweh your God is God, the faithful God who keeps His gracious covenant loyalty for a thousand generations with those who love Him and keep His commands. But He directly pays back and destroys those who hate Him. He will not hesitate to directly pay back the one who hates Him.

> I will sing about the LORD's faithful love forever;
> with my mouth I will proclaim Your faithfulness to
>   all generations.
> For I will declare, "Faithful love is built up forever;
> You establish Your faithfulness in the heavens."

> This I bring to mind;
> therefore, I will have hope.
> The Lord's faithful love does not cease,
> His compassions have no end.
> They are new every morning;
> great is Your faithfulness.

Therefore, whoever thinks he stands must be careful not to fall! No temptation has overtaken you except what is common to humanity. God is faithful and He will not allow you to be tempted beyond what you are able, but with the temptation He will also provide a way of escape, so that you are able to bear it.

If we confess our sins, He is faithful and righteous to forgive us our sins and to cleanse us from all unrighteousness.

DEUTERONOMY 7:9-10; PSALM 89:1-2; LAMENTATIONS 3:21-23; 1 CORINTHIANS 10:12-13; 1 JOHN 1:9

Related texts: DEUTERONOMY 31:30–32:4; 2 THESSALONIANS 3:3; 2 TIMOTHY 2:11-13; REVELATION 19:11-16

THE FRUIT OF THE SPIRIT: *Gentleness*

A gentle answer turns away anger,
but a harsh word stirs up wrath.

A ruler can be persuaded through patience,
and a gentle tongue can break a bone.

With all humility and gentleness, with patience,
accepting one another in love, diligently keeping the
unity of the Spirit with the peace that binds us.

Rejoice in the Lord always. I will say it again:
Rejoice! Let your graciousness be known to everyone.
The Lord is near. Don't worry about anything, but in
everything, through prayer and petition with thanksgiving,
let your requests be made known to God. And the
peace of God, which surpasses every thought, will
guard your hearts and your minds in Christ Jesus.

And who will harm you if you are passionate for
what is good? But even if you should suffer for righteousness, you are blessed. Do not fear what they fear or
be disturbed, but set apart the Messiah as Lord in your
hearts, and always be ready to give a defense to anyone
who asks you for a reason for the hope that is in you.
However, do this with gentleness and respect, keeping
your conscience clear, so that when you are accused,
those who denounce your Christian life will be put to
shame.

PROVERBS 15:1; 25:15; EPHESIANS 4:2-3; PHILIPPIANS 4:4-7;
1 PETER 3:13-16

Related texts: ISAIAH 8:12-15; 1 TIMOTHY 6:3-11;
2 TIMOTHY 2:24-25; 1 PETER 3:1-6

God Is Gentle

See, the Lord GOD comes with strength,
and His power establishes His rule.
His reward is with Him,
and His gifts accompany Him.
He protects His flock like a shepherd;
He gathers the lambs in His arms
and carries them in the fold of His garment.
He gently leads those that are nursing.

Rejoice greatly, Daughter Zion!
Shout in triumph, Daughter Jerusalem!
See, your King is coming to you;
He is righteous and victorious,
humble and riding on a donkey,
on a colt, the foal of a donkey.

[Jesus said] "Come to Me, all you who are weary and
burdened, and I will give you rest. Take My yoke upon
you and learn from Me, because I am gentle and humble in heart, and you will find rest for your souls. For
My yoke is easy and My burden is light."

ISAIAH 40:10-11; ZECHARIAH 9:9; MATTHEW 11:28-30

Related texts: 1 KINGS 19:9-12; 2 CORINTHIANS 10:1;
MATTHEW 21:1-12

THE FRUIT OF THE SPIRIT:
Self-Control

A man who does not control his temper
is like a city whose wall is broken down.

But you must speak what is consistent with sound teaching. Older men are to be self-controlled, worthy of respect, sensible, and sound in faith, love, and endurance. In the same way, older women are to be reverent in behavior, not slanderers, not addicted to much wine. They are to teach what is good, so that they may encourage the young women to love their husbands and children, to be sensible, pure, good home-makers, and submissive to their husbands, so that God's message will not be slandered.

Likewise, encourage the young men to be sensible.

For this very reason, make every effort to supplement your faith with goodness, goodness with knowledge, knowledge with self-control, self-control with endurance, endurance with godliness, godliness with brotherly affection, and brotherly affection with love. For if these qualities are yours and are increasing, they will keep you from being useless or unfruitful in the knowledge of our Lord Jesus Christ.

PROVERBS 25:28; TITUS 2:1-6; 2 PETER 1:5-8

God Is Slow to Anger

The LORD is compassionate and gracious,
slow to anger and full of faithful love.
He will not always accuse us
or be angry forever.
He has not dealt with us as our sins deserve
or repaid us according to our offenses.
For as high as the heavens are above the earth,
so great is His faithful love toward those who fear
Him.
As far as the east is from the west,
so far has He removed our transgressions from us.

The LORD is gracious and compassionate,
slow to anger and great in faithful love.
The LORD is good to everyone;
His compassion rests on all He has made.

The LORD is a jealous and avenging God;
the LORD takes vengeance
and is fierce in wrath.
The LORD takes vengeance against His foes;
He is furious with His enemies.
The LORD is slow to anger but great in power;
the LORD will never leave the guilty unpunished.
His path is in the whirlwind and storm,
and clouds are the dust beneath His feet.

PSALMS 103:8-12; 145:8-9; NAHUM 1:2-3

Related texts: EXODUS 34:5-7; PSALM 86:15-17; JOEL
2:12-14; JONAH 3–4; 2 PETER 3:8-15

God Sends Moses to Egypt

God also said to Moses, "Say this to the Israelites: Yahweh, the God of your fathers, the God of Abraham, the God of Isaac, and the God of Jacob, has sent me to you. This is My name forever; this is how I am to be remembered in every generation.

"Go and assemble the elders of Israel and say to them: Yahweh, the God of your fathers, the God of Abraham, Isaac, and Jacob, has appeared to me and said: I have paid close attention to you and to what has been done to you in Egypt. And I have promised you that I will bring you up from the misery of Egypt to the land of the Canaanites, Hittites, Amorites, Perizzites, Hivites, and Jebusites—a land flowing with milk and honey. They will listen to what you say. Then you, along with the elders of Israel, must go to the king of Egypt and say to him: The LORD, the God of the Hebrews, has met with us. Now please let us go on a three-day trip into the wilderness so that we may sacrifice to the LORD our God.

"However, I know that the king of Egypt will not allow you to go, unless he is forced by a strong hand. I will stretch out My hand and strike Egypt with all My miracles that I will perform in it. After that, he will let you go. And I will give this people such favor in the sight of the Egyptians that when you go, you will not go empty-handed. Each woman will ask her neighbor and any woman staying in her house for silver and gold jewelry, and clothing, and you will put them on your sons and daughters. So you will plunder the Egyptians."

EXODUS 3:15-22

Related texts: GENESIS 13:12-17; 15:12-16; HAGGAI 2:4-8; ACTS 7:30-36

Moses Confronts Pharaoh

The LORD instructed Moses, "When you go back to Egypt, make sure you do in front of Pharaoh all the wonders I have put within your power. But I will harden his heart so that he won't let the people go. Then you will say to Pharaoh: This is what the LORD says: Israel is My firstborn son. I told you: Let My son go so that he may worship Me, but you refused to let him go. Now I will kill your firstborn son!"

Now the LORD had said to Aaron, "Go and meet Moses in the wilderness." So he went and met him at the mountain of God and kissed him. Moses told Aaron everything the LORD had sent him to say, and about all the signs He had commanded him to do. Then Moses and Aaron went and assembled all the elders of the Israelites. Aaron repeated everything the LORD had said to Moses and performed the signs before the people. The people believed, and when they heard that the LORD had paid attention to them and that He had seen their misery, they bowed down and worshiped.

Later, Moses and Aaron went in and said to Pharaoh, "This is what the LORD, the God of Israel, says: Let My people go, so that they may hold a festival for Me in the wilderness."

But Pharaoh responded, "Who is the LORD that I should obey Him by letting Israel go? I do not know the LORD, and what's more, I will not let Israel go."

EXODUS 4:21-23,27-31; 5:1-2

Related texts: EXODUS 1:8-13; 9:13-16; PROVERBS 29:1-2; JOHN 10:33-38

God Hardens Pharaoh's Heart

The LORD answered Moses, "See, I have made you like God to Pharaoh, and Aaron your brother will be your prophet. You must say whatever I command you; then Aaron your brother must declare it to Pharaoh so that he will let the Israelites go from his land. But I will harden Pharaoh's heart and multiply My signs and wonders in the land of Egypt. Pharaoh will not listen to you, but I will put My hand on Egypt and bring out the ranks of My people the Israelites, out of the land of Egypt by great acts of judgment. The Egyptians will know that I am the LORD when I stretch out My hand against Egypt, and bring out the Israelites from among them."

The LORD said to Moses and Aaron, "When Pharaoh tells you: Perform a miracle, tell Aaron: Take your staff and throw it down before Pharaoh. It will become a serpent." So Moses and Aaron went in to Pharaoh and did just as the LORD had commanded. Aaron threw down his staff before Pharaoh and his officials, and it became a serpent. But then Pharaoh called the wise men and sorcerers—the magicians of Egypt, and they also did the same thing by their occult practices. Each one threw down his staff, and it became a serpent. But Aaron's staff swallowed their staffs. However, Pharaoh's heart hardened, and he did not listen to them, as the LORD had said.

EXODUS 7:1-5,8-13

Related texts: EXODUS 8:7,18-19; ROMANS 9:14-21; 2 TIMOTHY 3:8-9

The Plagues Against Egypt

My people, hear my instruction;
listen to what I say.
I will declare wise sayings;
I will speak mysteries from the past—
things we have heard and known
and that our fathers have passed down to us.
We must not hide them from their children,
but must tell a future generation the praises of the LORD,
His might, and the wonderful works He has performed.

He performed His miraculous signs in Egypt
and His marvels in the region of Zoan.
He turned their rivers into blood,
and they could not drink from their streams.
He sent among them swarms of flies, which fed on them,
and frogs, which devastated them.
He gave their crops to the caterpillar
and the fruit of their labor to the locust.
He killed their vines with hail
and their sycamore-fig trees with a flood.
He handed over their livestock to hail
and their cattle to lightning bolts.
He sent His burning anger against them:
fury, indignation, and calamity—
a band of deadly messengers.
He cleared a path for His anger.
He did not spare them from death,
but delivered their lives to the plague.
He struck all the firstborn in Egypt,
the first progeny of the tents of Ham.

PSALM 78:1-4,43-51

Related texts: EXODUS 7:15–10:29; DEUTERONOMY 4:32-38;
1 SAMUEL 4:2-8; ACTS 7:30-36

God Kills the Firstborn in Egypt

The LORD said to Moses, "I will bring one more plague on Pharaoh and on Egypt. After that, he will let you go from here. When he lets you go, he will drive you out of here. Now announce to the people that both men and women should ask their neighbors for gold and silver jewelry." The LORD gave the people favor in the sight of the Egyptians. And the man Moses was feared in the land of Egypt, by Pharaoh's officials and the people.

So Moses said, "This is what the LORD says: 'About midnight I will go throughout Egypt and every firstborn male in the land of Egypt will die, from the firstborn of Pharaoh who sits on his throne to the firstborn of the servant girl who is behind the millstones, as well as every firstborn of the livestock. Then there will be a great cry of anguish through all the land of Egypt such as never was before, or ever will be again. But against all the Israelites, whether man or beast, not even a dog will snarl, so that you may know that the LORD makes a distinction between Egypt and Israel. All these officials of yours will come down to me and bow before me, saying: Leave, you and all the people who follow you. After that, I will leave.' " And he left Pharaoh's presence in fierce anger.

The LORD said to Moses, "Pharaoh will not listen to you, so that My wonders may be multiplied in the land of Egypt." Moses and Aaron did all these wonders before Pharaoh, but the LORD hardened Pharaoh's heart, and he would not let the Israelites go out of his land.

EXODUS 11:1-10

Related texts: EXODUS 4:22-23; PSALMS 105:23-38;
135:8-9; 136:10-12; ROMANS 9:14-21; HEBREWS 11:28

*So great is my veneration for the
Bible that the earlier my children
begin to read it, the more confident
will be my hope that they will prove
useful citizens to their country and
respectable members of society.*

John Quincy Adams (1767–1848)
UNITED STATES PRESIDENT

*It ain't those parts of the Bible
that I can't understand
that bother me, it is the parts
that I do understand.*

Mark Twain (1835–1910)
AMERICAN AUTHOR

*No sciences are better attested
than the religion of the Bible.*

Sir Issac Newton (1642–1727)
ENGLISH SCIENTIST

The First Passover

Then Moses summoned all the elders of Israel and said to them, "Go, select an animal from the flock according to your families, and slaughter the Passover lamb. Take a cluster of hyssop, dip it in the blood that is in the basin, and brush the lintel and the two doorposts with some of the blood in the basin. None of you may go out the door of his house until morning. When the Lord passes through to strike Egypt and sees the blood on the lintel and the two doorposts, He will pass over the door and not let the destroyer enter your houses to strike you.

"Keep this command permanently as a statute for you and your descendants. When you enter the land that the Lord will give you as He promised, you are to observe this ritual. When your children ask you, 'What does this ritual mean to you?' you are to reply, 'It is the Passover sacrifice to the Lord, for He passed over the houses of the Israelites in Egypt when He struck the Egyptians and spared our homes.' " So the people bowed down and worshiped. Then the Israelites went and did this, they did just as the Lord had commanded Moses and Aaron.

Exodus 12:21-28

The Prophecy of the Suffering Servant

See, My servant will act wisely;
He will be raised and lifted up and greatly exalted.

He was despised and rejected by men,
a man of suffering who knew what sickness was.
He was like one people turned away from;
He was despised, and we didn't value Him.
Yet He Himself bore our sicknesses,
and He carried our pains;
but we in turn regarded Him stricken,
struck down by God, and afflicted.
But He was pierced because of our transgressions,
crushed because of our iniquities;
punishment for our peace was on Him,
and we are healed by His wounds.
We all went astray like sheep;
we all have turned to our own way;
and the LORD has punished Him
for the iniquity of us all.
He was oppressed and afflicted,
yet He did not open His mouth.
Like a lamb led to the slaughter
and like a sheep silent before her shearers,
He did not open His mouth.

Yet the LORD was pleased to crush Him,
and He made Him sick.
When You make Him a restitution offering,
He will see His seed, He will prolong His days,
and the will of the LORD will succeed by His hand.

ISAIAH 52:13; 53:3-7,10

Related texts: Psalm 22; Mark 10:45; Acts 8:26-39;
1 Peter 2:21-25

JESUS: *The Lamb of God*

The next day John saw Jesus coming toward him and said, "Here is the Lamb of God, who takes away the sin of the world! This is the One I told you about: 'After me comes a man who has surpassed me, because He existed before me.' I didn't know Him, but I came baptizing with water so He might be revealed to Israel."

And John testified, "I watched the Spirit descending from heaven like a dove, and He rested upon Him. I didn't know Him, but He who sent me to baptize with water told me, 'The One on whom you see the Spirit descending and resting—He is the One baptizing with the Holy Spirit.' I have seen and testified that He is the Son of God!"

Then I looked, and heard the voice of many angels around the throne, and also of the living creatures, and of the elders. Their number was countless thousands, plus thousands of thousands. They said with a loud voice:

> The Lamb who was slaughtered is worthy
>
> to receive power and riches
>
> and wisdom and strength
>
> and honor and glory and blessing!

JOHN 1:29-34; REVELATION 5:11-12

Related texts: GENESIS 22:1-19; HEBREWS 9:11-28; 1 PETER 1:18-20; REVELATION 5–7; 21:9–22:4

Jesus Predicts His Resurrection

And Jesus called them over and said to them, "You know that those who are regarded as rulers of the Gentiles dominate them, and their men of high positions exercise power over them. But it must not be like that among you. On the contrary, whoever wants to become great among you must be your servant, and whoever wants to be first among you must be a slave to all. For even the Son of Man did not come to be served, but to serve, and to give His life—a ransom for many."

Once when He was praying in private, and His disciples were with Him, He asked them, "Who do the crowds say that I am?"

And they answered, "John the Baptist; others, Elijah; still others, that one of the ancient prophets has come back."

"But you," He asked them, "who do you say that I am?"

Peter answered, "God's Messiah!"

But He strictly warned and instructed them to tell this to no one, saying, "The Son of Man must suffer many things and be rejected by the elders, chief priests, and scribes, be killed, and be raised the third day."

MARK 10:42-45; LUKE 9:18-22

Related texts: PSALM 16; ISAIAH 53; MATTHEW 12:38-41; MARK 10:32-34; LUKE 24:13-32; ACTS 2:14-40

Jesus' Triumphal Entry

When they approached Jerusalem and came to Bethphage at the Mount of Olives, Jesus then sent two disciples, telling them, "Go into the village ahead of you. At once you will find a donkey tied there, and a colt with her. Untie them and bring them to Me. If anyone says anything to you, you should say that the Lord needs them, and immediately he will send them."

This took place so that what was spoken through the prophet might be fulfilled:

Tell Daughter Zion,

"See, your King is coming to you,

gentle, and mounted on a donkey,

even on a colt, the foal of a beast of burden."

The disciples went and did just as Jesus directed them. They brought the donkey and the colt, laid their robes on them, and He sat on them. A very large crowd spread their robes on the road; others were cutting branches from the trees and spreading them on the road. Then the crowds who went before Him and those who followed kept shouting:

Hosanna to the Son of David!

Blessed is He who comes in the name of the Lord!

Hosanna in the highest heaven!

When He entered Jerusalem, the whole city was shaken, saying, "Who is this?" And the crowds kept saying, "This is the prophet Jesus from Nazareth in Galilee!"

Matthew 21:1-11

Related texts: Psalm 118; Zechariah 9:9; Mark 11:1-11; Luke 19:28-40; John 12:12-16

Jesus Cleanses the Temple

As He approached and saw the city, He wept over it, saying, "If you knew this day what leads to peace—but now it is hidden from your eyes. For the days will come upon you when your enemies will build an embankment against you, surround you, and hem you in on every side. They will crush you and your children within you to the ground, and they will not leave one stone on another in you, because you did not recognize the time of your visitation."

Jesus went into the temple complex and drove out all those buying and selling in the temple. He overturned the money changers' tables and the chairs of those selling doves. And He said to them, "It is written, My house will be called a house of prayer. But you are making it a den of thieves!"

The blind and the lame came to Him in the temple complex, and He healed them. When the chief priests and the scribes saw the wonders that He did, and the children in the temple complex cheering, "*Hosanna* to the Son of David!" they were indignant and said to Him, "Do You hear what these children are saying?"

"Yes," Jesus told them. "Have you never read:

From the mouths of children and nursing infants
You have prepared praise?"

LUKE 19:41-44; MATTHEW 21:12-16

Related texts: PSALM 8; ISAIAH 56; JEREMIAH 7:9-11; MARK 11:15-18; JOHN 2:13-17

Whose Son Is the Messiah?

While the Pharisees were together, Jesus questioned them, "What do you think about the Messiah? Whose Son is He?"

"David's," they told Him.

He asked them, "How is it then that David, inspired by the Spirit, calls Him 'Lord':

**The Lord said to my Lord,
'Sit at My right hand
until I put Your enemies under Your feet'?**

"If, then, David calls Him 'Lord,' how is He his Son?" No one was able to answer Him at all, and from that day no one dared to question Him any more.

After six days Jesus took Peter, James, and John, and led them up on a high mountain by themselves to be alone. He was transformed in front of them.

A cloud appeared, overshadowing them, and a voice came from the cloud:

**This is My beloved Son
listen to Him!**

For we did not follow cleverly contrived myths when we made known to you the power and coming of our Lord Jesus Christ; instead, we were eyewitnesses of His majesty. For when He received honor and glory from God the Father, a voice came to Him from the Majestic Glory:

This is My beloved Son.
I take delight in Him!

MATTHEW 22:41-46; MARK 9:2,7; 2 PETER 1:16-17

Related texts: PSALM 110; MATTHEW 27:45-54; MARK 1:9-11;
LUKE 9:28-36; ACTS 2

The Last Supper

Then the Day of Unleavened Bread came, on which the Passover lamb had to be sacrificed. Jesus sent Peter and John, saying, "Go and prepare the Passover meal for us, so we may eat it."

When the hour came, He reclined at the table, and the apostles with Him. Then He said to them, "I have fervently desired to eat this Passover with you before I suffer. For I tell you, I will not eat it again until it is fulfilled in the kingdom of God." Then He took a cup, and after giving thanks, He said, "Take this and share it among yourselves. For I tell you, from now on I will not drink of the fruit of the vine until the kingdom of God comes."

And He took bread, gave thanks, broke it, gave it to them, and said, "This is My body, which is given for you. Do this in remembrance of Me."

In the same way He also took the cup after supper and said, "This cup is the new covenant in My blood, which is shed for you. But look, the hand of the one betraying Me is at the table with Me! For the Son of Man will go away as it has been determined, but woe to that man by whom He is betrayed!"

Luke 22:7-8,14-22

Related texts: Jeremiah 31:31-36; Matthew 26:17-30; Mark 14:12-26; Revelation 19:4-9

Jesus Is Betrayed

After Jesus had said these things, He went out with His disciples across the Kidron ravine, where there was a garden into which He and His disciples entered. Judas, who betrayed Him, also knew the place, because Jesus often met there with His disciples. So Judas took a company of soldiers and some temple police from the chief priests and the Pharisees and came there with lanterns, torches, and weapons.

Then Jesus, knowing everything that was about to happen to Him, went out and said to them, "Who is it you're looking for?"

"Jesus the Nazarene," they answered.

"I am He," Jesus told them.

Judas, who betrayed Him, was also standing with them. When He told them, "I am He," they stepped back and fell to the ground.

Then He asked them again, "Who is it you're looking for?"

"Jesus the Nazarene," they said.

"I told you I am He," Jesus replied. "So if you're looking for Me, let these men go." This was to fulfill the words He had said: "I have not lost one of those You have given Me."

JOHN 18:1-9

Related texts: GENESIS 37; MATTHEW 26:47-56; MARK 14:43-50; LUKE 22:47-54; JOHN 6:35-40; 17:1-12

Jesus Is Condemned to Death

The chief priests and the whole Sanhedrin were looking for false testimony against Jesus so they could put Him to death. But they could not find any, even though many false witnesses came forward. Finally, two who came forward stated, "This man said, 'I can demolish God's sanctuary and rebuild it in three days.' "

The high priest then stood up and said to Him, "Don't You have an answer to what these men are testifying against You?" But Jesus kept silent. Then the high priest said to Him, "By the living God I place You under oath: tell us if You are the Messiah, the Son of God!"

"You have said it," Jesus told him. "But I tell you, in the future you will see the Son of Man seated at the right hand of the Power, and coming on the clouds of heaven."

Then the high priest tore his robes and said, "He has blasphemed! Why do we still need witnesses? Look, now you've heard the blasphemy! What is your decision?"

They answered, "He deserves death!" Then they spit in His face and beat Him; and others slapped Him and said, "Prophesy to us, Messiah! Who hit You?"

MATTHEW 26:59-68

Related texts: LEVITICUS 24:13-16; DANIEL 7:13-14; MARK 14:55-65; LUKE 23:63-71

Jesus Is Crucified

And they brought Him to the place called Golgotha (which means Skull Place). They tried to give Him wine mixed with myrrh, but He did not take it. Then they crucified Him and divided His clothes, casting lots for them to decide what each would get. Now it was nine in the morning when they crucified Him. The inscription of the charge written against Him was:

> THE KING OF THE JEWS

They crucified two criminals with Him, one on His right and one on His left. [So the Scripture was fulfilled that says: And He was counted among outlaws.] Those who passed by were yelling insults at Him, shaking their heads, and saying, "Ha! The One who would demolish the sanctuary and build it in three days, save Yourself by coming down from the cross!" In the same way, the chief priests with the scribes were mocking Him to one another and saying, "He saved others; He cannot save Himself! Let the Messiah, the King of Israel, come down now from the cross, so that we may see and believe." Even those who were crucified with Him were taunting Him.

But Jesus let out a loud cry and breathed His last. Then the curtain of the sanctuary was split in two from top to bottom. When the centurion, who was standing opposite Him, saw the way He breathed His last, he said, "This man really was God's Son!"

MARK 15:22-32,37-39

Related texts: PSALM 22; ISAIAH 53; MATTHEW 27:33-56; LUKE 23:26-48; JOHN 3:13-16; 19:16-37

Alive Again!

After the Sabbath, as the first day of the week was dawning, Mary Magdalene and the other Mary went to view the tomb. Suddenly there was a violent earthquake, because an angel of the Lord descended from heaven and approached the tomb. He rolled back the stone and was sitting on it. His appearance was like lightning, and his robe was as white as snow. The guards were so shaken from fear of him that they became like dead men.

But the angel told the women, "Don't be afraid, because I know you are looking for Jesus who was crucified. He is not here! For He has been resurrected, just as He said. Come and see the place where He lay. Then go quickly and tell His disciples, 'He has been raised from the dead. In fact, He is going ahead of you to Galilee; you will see Him there.' Listen, I have told you."

So, departing quickly from the tomb with fear and great joy, they ran to tell His disciples the news. Just then Jesus met them and said, "Rejoice!" They came up, took hold of His feet, and worshiped Him. Then Jesus told them, "Do not be afraid. Go and tell My brothers to leave for Galilee, and they will see Me there."

MATTHEW 28:1-10

Related texts: PSALM 16:8-11; MARK 16:1-8; LUKE 24:1-10; JOHN 20:1-18; 1 CORINTHIANS 15

The All-Importance of the Resurrection

Now if Christ is preached as raised from the dead, how can some of you say, "There is no resurrection of the dead"? But if there is no resurrection of the dead, then Christ has not been raised; and if Christ has not been raised, then our preaching is without foundation, and so is your faith. In addition, we are found to be false witnesses about God, because we have testified about God that He raised up Christ—whom He did not raise up if in fact the dead are not raised. For if the dead are not raised, Christ has not been raised. And if Christ has not been raised, your faith is worthless; you are still in your sins. Therefore those who have fallen asleep in Christ have also perished. If we have placed our hope in Christ for this life only, we should be pitied more than anyone.

But now Christ has been raised from the dead, the firstfruits of those who have fallen asleep. For since death came through a man, the resurrection of the dead also comes through a man. For just as in Adam all die, so also in Christ all will be made alive.

1 Corinthians 15:12-22

JESUS CHRIST: *Our Passover*

Your boasting is not good. Don't you know that a little yeast permeates the whole batch of dough? Clean out the old yeast so that you may be a new batch, since you are unleavened. For Christ our Passover has been sacrificed. Therefore, let us observe the feast, not with old yeast, or with the yeast of malice and evil, but with the unleavened bread of sincerity and truth.

And if you address as Father the One who judges impartially based on each one's work, you are to conduct yourselves in reverence during this time of temporary residence. For you know that you were redeemed from your empty way of life inherited from the fathers, not with perishable things, like silver or gold, but with the precious blood of Christ, like that of a lamb without defect or blemish. He was destined before the foundation of the world, but was revealed at the end of the times for you who through Him are believers in God, who raised Him from the dead and gave Him glory, so that your faith and hope are in God.

By obedience to the truth, having purified yourselves for sincere love of the brothers, love one another earnestly from a pure heart.

1 CORINTHIANS 5:6-8; 1 PETER 1:17-22

Related texts: EXODUS 12–13; JOHN 1:19-36; HEBREWS 2:11-18; REVELATION 13:8

The Israelites Leave Egypt

Now at midnight the LORD struck every firstborn male in the land of Egypt, from the firstborn of Pharaoh who sat on his throne to the firstborn of the prisoner who was in the dungeon, and every firstborn of the livestock. During the night Pharaoh got up, he along with all his officials and all the Egyptians, and there was a loud wailing throughout Egypt because there wasn't a house without someone dead. He summoned Moses and Aaron during the night and said, "Get up, leave my people, both you and the Israelites, and go, worship the LORD as you have asked. Take even your flocks and your herds as you asked, and leave, and this will also be a blessing to me."

Now the Egyptians pressured the people in order to send them quickly out of the country, for they said, "We're all going to die!" So the people took their dough before it was leavened, with their kneading bowls wrapped up in their clothes on their shoulders.

The Israelites acted on Moses' word and asked the Egyptians for silver and gold jewelry and for clothing. And the LORD gave the people such favor in the Egyptians' sight that they gave them what they requested. In this way they plundered the Egyptians.

The LORD went ahead of them in a pillar of cloud to lead them on their way during the day and in a pillar of fire to give them light at night, so that they could travel day or night. The pillar of cloud by day and the pillar of fire by night never left its place in front of the people.

EXODUS 12:29-36; 13:21-22

Related texts: DEUTERONOMY 16:1-8; PSALMS 78:41-52;
105:26-38; 2 THESSALONIANS 1:5-10

Pharaoh Pursues the Israelites

The Egyptians—all Pharaoh's horses and chariots, his horsemen, and his army—chased after them and caught up with them as they camped by the sea beside Pi-hahiroth, in front of Baal-zephon.

As Pharaoh approached, the Israelites looked up and saw the Egyptians coming after them. Then the Israelites were terrified and cried out to the LORD for help. They said to Moses: "Is it because there are no graves in Egypt that you took us to die in the wilderness? What have you done to us by bringing us out of Egypt? Isn't this what we told you in Egypt: Leave us alone so that we may serve the Egyptians? It would have been better for us to serve the Egyptians than to die in the wilderness."

But Moses said to the people, "Don't be afraid. Stand firm and see the LORD's salvation He will provide for you today; for the Egyptians you see today, you will never see again. The LORD will fight for you; you must be quiet."

The LORD said to Moses, "Why are you crying out to Me? Tell the Israelites to break camp. As for you, lift up your staff, stretch out your hand over the sea, and divide it so that the Israelites can go through the sea on dry ground. I am going to harden the hearts of the Egyptians so that they will go in after them, and I will receive glory by means of Pharaoh, all his army, and his chariots and horsemen. The Egyptians will know that I am the LORD when I receive glory through Pharaoh, his chariots, and his horsemen."

EXODUS 14:9-18

Related texts: PSALM 37:7; 46:10; ISAIAH 59:1; ROMANS 9:14-24; HEBREWS 11:1-2

Crossing the Red Sea

Then Moses stretched out his hand over the sea. The LORD drove the sea back with a powerful east wind all that night and turned the sea into dry land. So the waters were divided, and the Israelites went through the sea on dry ground, with the waters like a wall to them on their right and their left.

The Egyptians set out in pursuit—all Pharaoh's horses, his chariots, and his horsemen—and went into the sea after them. Then during the morning watch, the LORD looked down on the Egyptian forces from the pillar of fire and cloud, and threw them into confusion. He caused their chariot wheels to swerve and made them drive with difficulty. "Let's get away from Israel," the Egyptians said, "because the LORD is fighting for them against Egypt!"

Then the LORD said to Moses, "Stretch out your hand over the sea so that the waters may come back on the Egyptians, on their chariots and horsemen." So Moses stretched out his hand over the sea, and at daybreak the sea returned to its normal depth. While the Egyptians were trying to escape from it, the LORD overthrew them in the sea. The waters came back and covered the chariots and horsemen, the entire army of Pharaoh, that had gone after them into the sea. None of them survived.

EXODUS 14:21-28

Related texts: PSALMS 114; 136:13-15; DEUTERONOMY 11:1-4; JOSHUA 24:5-7; HEBREWS 11:23-29

The LORD Is a Warrior

That day the Lord saved Israel from the power of the Egyptians, and Israel saw the Egyptians dead on the seashore. When Israel saw the great power that the Lord used against the Egyptians, the people feared the Lord and believed in Him and in His servant Moses.

Then Moses and the Israelites sang this song to the Lord. They said:
I will sing to the Lord,
for He is highly exalted;
He has thrown the horse
and its rider into the sea.
The LORD is my strength and my song;
He has become my salvation.
This is my God, and I will praise Him,
my father's God, and I will exalt Him.
The LORD is a warrior;
 Yahweh is His name.

He threw Pharaoh's chariots
and his army into the sea;
the elite of his officers
were drowned in the Red Sea.

LORD, who is like You among the gods?
Who is like You, glorious in holiness,
revered with praises, performing wonders?
You will lead the people
You have redeemed
with Your faithful love.
You will guide them to Your holy dwelling
with Your strength.
The LORD will reign forever and ever!

EXODUS 14:30-31; 15:1-4,11,13,18

Related texts: PSALM 136; EPHESIANS 5:19-20; REVELATION 15:2-4

God's Care in the Desert

Give thanks to the Lord, call on His name;
proclaim His deeds among the peoples.
Sing to Him, sing praise to Him;
tell about all His wonderful works!
Honor His holy name;
let the hearts of those who seek the LORD rejoice.
Search for the LORD and for His strength;
seek His face always.
Remember the wonderful works He has done,
His wonders, and the judgments He has pronounced,
You offspring of Abraham His servant,
Jacob's descendants—His chosen ones.

Then He brought Israel out with silver and gold,
and no one among His tribes stumbled.
Egypt was glad when they left,
for dread of Israel had fallen on them.
He spread a cloud as a covering
and gave a fire to light up the night.
They asked, and He brought quail
and satisfied them with bread from heaven.
He opened a rock, and water gushed out;
it flowed like a stream in the desert.
For He remembered His holy promise
to Abraham His servant.
He brought His people out with rejoicing,
His chosen ones with shouts of joy.
He gave them the lands of the nations,
and they inherited what other peoples had worked for.
All this happened so that they might keep His statutes
and obey His laws.
  Hallelujah!

PSALM 105:1-6,37-45

Related texts: GENESIS 15; EXODUS 15:19–18:27; JOHN 6;   *119*
ACTS 7:36-38; 1 CORINTHIANS 10:1-4

God Makes a Covenant with Israel

In the third month, on the same day of the month that the Israelites had left the land of Egypt, they entered the Wilderness of Sinai. After they departed from Rephidim, they entered the Wilderness of Sinai and camped in the wilderness, and Israel camped there in front of the mountain.

Moses went up the mountain to God, and the LORD called to him from the mountain: "This is what you must say to the house of Jacob, and explain to the Israelites: You have seen what I did to the Egyptians and how I carried you on eagles' wings and brought you to Me. Now if you will listen to Me and carefully keep My covenant, you will be My own possession out of all the peoples, although all the earth is Mine, and you will be My kingdom of priests and My holy nation. These are the words that you are to say to the Israelites."

After Moses came back, He summoned the elders of the people, and put before them all these words that the LORD had commanded him. Then all the people responded together, "We will do all that the LORD has spoken." So Moses brought the people's words back to the LORD.

The LORD said to Moses, "I am going to come to you in a dense cloud, so that the people will hear when I speak with you and will always believe you." Then Moses reported the people's words to the LORD.

EXODUS 19:1-9

Related texts: DEUTERONOMY 4:1-20; JEREMIAH 31:31-34; HEBREWS 8

THE TEN COMMANDMENTS:
No Other Gods

I am the Lord your God, who brought you out of
the land of Egypt, out of the place of slavery.
Do not have other gods besides Me.

Sing to the LORD, all the earth.
Proclaim His salvation from day to day.
Declare His glory among the nations,
His wonderful works among all peoples.
For the LORD is great and is highly praised;
He is feared above all gods.
For all the gods of the peoples are idols,
but the LORD made the heavens.
Splendor and majesty are before Him;
strength and joy are in His place.
Ascribe to the LORD, families of the peoples,
ascribe to the LORD glory and strength.
Ascribe to the LORD the glory of His name;
bring an offering and come before Him.
Worship the LORD in His holy majesty;
tremble before Him, all the earth.
The world is firmly established;
it cannot be shaken.
Let the heavens be glad and the earth rejoice,
and let them say among the nations, "The LORD is
    King!"

EXODUS 20:2-3; 1 CHRONICLES 16:23-31

Related texts: EXODUS 18:8-10; DEUTERONOMY 4:32-39;
5:1-21; 13:1-16; ISAIAH 37:15-20; EPHESIANS 4:4-6

THE TEN COMMANDMENTS:
No Idols

Do not make an idol for yourself, whether in the shape of anything in the heavens above or on the earth below or in the waters under the earth. You must not bow down to them or worship them; for I, the LORD your God, am a jealous God, punishing the children for the fathers' sin, to the third and fourth generations of those who hate Me, but showing faithful love to a thousand generations of those who love Me and keep My commands.

Not to us, LORD, not to us,
but to Your name give glory
because of Your faithful love, because of Your truth.
Why should the nations say,
"Where is their God?"
Our God is in heaven
and does whatever He pleases.
Their idols are silver and gold,
made by human hands.
They have mouths, but cannot speak,
eyes, but cannot see.
They have ears, but cannot hear,
noses, but cannot smell.
They have hands, but cannot feel,
feet, but cannot walk.
They cannot make a sound with their throats.
Those who make them are just like them,
as are all who trust in them.

EXODUS 20:4-6; PSALM 115:1-8

Related texts: DEUTERONOMY 7; ISAIAH 44:6-19; JEREMIAH 10:1-16; 16:19-21; MATTHEW 6:19-24; 1 JOHN 5:21

THE TEN COMMANDMENTS:
God's Name

> Do not misuse the name of the LORD your God,
>> because the LORD will punish anyone who misuses
>> His name.

Now the son of an Israelite mother and an Egyptian father was among the Israelites. A fight broke out in the camp between the Israelite woman's son and an Israelite man. Her son cursed and blasphemed the Name, and they brought him to Moses. (His mother's name was Shelomith, a daughter of Dibri of the tribe of Dan.) They put him in custody until the Lord's decision could be made clear to them.

  Then the LORD spoke to Moses: "Bring the one who has cursed to the outside of the camp and have all who heard him lay their hands on his head; then have the whole community stone him. And tell the Israelites: If anyone curses his God, he will bear the consequences of his sin. Whoever blasphemes the name of the LORD is to be put to death; the whole community must stone him. If he blasphemes the Name, he is to be put to death, whether the foreign resident or the native."

> The name of the Lord is a strong tower;
> the righteous run to it and are protected.

EXODUS 20:7; LEVITICUS 24:10-16; PROVERBS 18:10

THE TEN COMMANDMENTS:
The Sabbath

Remember to dedicate the Sabbath day. For the Lord made the heavens and the earth, the sea, and everything in them in six days; then He rested on the seventh day. Therefore the Lord blessed the Sabbath day and declared it holy.

Moving on from there, He entered their synagogue. There He saw a man who had a paralyzed hand. And in order to accuse Him they asked Him, "Is it lawful to heal on the Sabbath?"

But He said to them, "What man among you, if he had a sheep that fell into a pit on the Sabbath, wouldn't take hold of it and lift it out? A man is worth far more than a sheep, so it is lawful to do good on the Sabbath."

Then He told the man, "Stretch out your hand." So he stretched it out, and it was restored, as good as the other.

EXODUS 20:8-11; MATTHEW 12:9-13

Related texts: GENESIS 2:1-3; EXODUS 16:11-30; PSALM 62:1-5; MARK 2:23-28; HEBREWS 4:1-4

THE TEN COMMANDMENTS: *Parents*

Honor your father and your mother so that you may
have a long life in the land that the Lord your
God is giving you.

"Whoever strikes his father or his mother must be
put to death."

"If anyone curses his father or mother, he must be
put to death. He has cursed his father or
mother; his blood is on his own hands."

Solomon's proverbs:
A wise son brings joy to his father,
but a foolish son, heartache to his mother.

Listen to your father who gave you life,
and don't despise your mother when she is old.
Buy—and do not sell—truth,
wisdom, instruction, and understanding.
The father of a righteous son will rejoice greatly,
and one who fathers a wise son will delight in him.
Let your father and mother have joy,
and let her who gave birth to you rejoice.

Children, obey your parents in the Lord, because
this is right. Honor your father and mother—which is
the first commandment with a promise— that it may go
well with you and that you may have a long life in the
land.

EXODUS 20:12; 21:15; LEVITICUS 20:9; PROVERBS 10:1;
23:22-25; EPHESIANS 6:1-3

Related texts: MALACHI 4:5-6; COLOSSIANS 3:20-21;
2 TIMOTHY 3:1-5; TITUS 1:6-9

THE TEN COMMANDMENTS: *Murder*

Do not murder.

Whoever sheds man's blood,
his blood will be shed by man,
for God made man
in His image.

"You have heard that it was said to our ancestors, **You shall not murder,** and whoever murders will be subject to judgment. But I tell you, everyone who is angry with his brother will be subject to judgment. And whoever says to his brother, 'Fool!' will be subject to the Sanhedrin. But whoever says, 'You moron!' will be subject to hellfire."

For this is the message you have heard from the beginning: we should love one another, unlike Cain, who was of the evil one and murdered his brother. And why did he murder him? Because his works were evil, and his brother's were righteous. Do not be surprised, brothers, if the world hates you. We know that we have passed from death to life because we love our brothers. The one who does not love remains in death. Everyone who hates his brother is a murderer, and you know that no murderer has eternal life residing in him.

This is how we have come to know love: He laid down His life for us. We should also lay down our lives for our brothers.

EXODUS 20:13; GENESIS 9:6; MATTHEW 5:21-22; 1 JOHN 3:11-16

Related texts: GENESIS 4:1-16; NUMBERS 35:9-34; MATTHEW 15:10-20; JOHN 8:42-44; ROMANS 1:28-32

THE TEN COMMANDMENTS: *Adultery*

Do not commit adultery.

Why, my son, would you be infatuated with a for-
    bidden woman
or embrace the breast of a stranger?
For a man's ways are before the Lord's eyes,
and He considers all his paths.
A wicked man's iniquities entrap him;
he is entangled in the ropes of his own sin.
He will die because there is no instruction,
and be lost because of his great stupidity.

"You have heard that it was said, You shall not commit adultery. But I tell you, everyone who looks at a
woman to lust for her has already committed adultery
with her in his heart. If your right eye causes you to sin,
gouge it out and throw it away. For it is better that you
lose one of your members than for your whole body to
be thrown into hell. And if your right hand causes you
to sin, cut it off and throw it away. For it is better that
you lose one of your members than for your whole body
to go into hell!
    "It was also said, Whoever divorces his wife must
give her a written notice of divorce. But I tell you,
everyone who divorces his wife, except in a case of sexual immorality, causes her to commit adultery. And
whoever marries a divorced woman commits adultery."

Marriage must be respected by all, and the marriage
bed kept undefiled, because God will judge immoral
people and adulterers.

Exodus 20:14; Proverbs 5:20-23; Matthew 5:27-28;
Hebrews 13:4

Related texts: PROVERBS 5:1-19; 6:20-35; ROMANS 1:18-27;
EPHESIANS 4:17-24; COLOSSIANS 3:1-7; 1 THESSALONIANS 4:3-8

THE TEN COMMANDMENTS: *Stealing*

Do not steal.

Place no trust in oppression,
or false hope in robbery.
If wealth increases,
pay no attention to it.
God has spoken once;
I have heard this twice:
strength belongs to God,
and faithful love belongs to You, LORD.
For You repay each according to his works.

Instruct those who are rich in the present age not to
be arrogant or to set their hope on the uncertainty of
wealth, but on God, who richly provides us with all
things to enjoy. Instruct them to do good, to be rich in
good works, to be generous, willing to share, storing up
for themselves a good foundation for the age to come,
so that they may take hold of life that is real.

The thief must no longer steal. Instead, he must do
honest work with his own hands, so that he has something to share with anyone in need.

EXODUS 20:15: PSALM 62:10-12; 1 TIMOTHY 6:17-19;
EPHESIANS 4:28

Related texts: PROVERBS 1:10-19; 10:2; ISAIAH 10:1-4;
MALACHI 3:6-12; TITUS 2:9-10

THE TEN COMMANDMENTS:
False Witness

Do not give false testimony against your neighbor.

"If a malicious witness testifies against someone accusing him of a crime, the two people in the dispute must stand in the presence of the Lord before the priests and judges in authority at the time. The judges are to make a careful investigation, and if the witness turns out to be a liar who has falsely accused his brother, you must do to him as he intended to do to his brother. You must purge the evil from you. Then everyone else will hear and be afraid, and they will never again do anything evil like this among you."

LORD, who can dwell in Your tent?
Who can live on Your holy mountain?
The one who lives honestly, practices righteousness,
and acknowledges the truth in his heart —
who does not slander with his tongue,
who does not harm his friend
or discredit his neighbor,
who despises the one rejected by the LORD,
but honors those who fear the LORD,
who keeps his word whatever the cost,
who does not lend his money at interest
or take a bribe against the innocent—
the one who does these things will never be moved.

EXODUS 20:16; DEUTERONOMY 19:16-20; PSALM 15

Related texts: PROVERBS 12:17-18; 25:18; ISAIAH 29:19-21;
MATTHEW 15:10-20; MARK 14:53-64

THE TEN COMMANDMENTS: *Coveting*

Do not covet your neighbor's house. Do not covet your neighbor's wife, his male or female slave, his ox or donkey, or anything that belongs to your neighbor.

Do not owe anyone anything, except to love one another, for the one who loves another has fulfilled the law. The commandments:

You shall not commit adultery,
you shall not murder,
you shall not steal,
you shall not covet,

and if there is any other commandment—all are summed up by this: You shall love your neighbor as yourself.

But godliness with contentment is a great gain.

For we brought nothing into the world,
and we can take nothing out.

But if we have food and clothing, we will be content with these.

Your life should be free from the love of money. Be satisfied with what you have, for He Himself has said, I will never leave you or forsake you.

EXODUS 20:17; ROMANS 13:8-10; 1 TIMOTHY 6:6-8; HEBREWS 13:5

Related texts: DEUTERONOMY 31:6; PROVERBS 1:10-19; PHILIPPIANS 4:11-12; 1 TIMOTHY 6:9-11; JAMES 4:1-3; 1 JOHN 2:15-17

*When I read... the Holy Scriptures...
all seems luminous, a single
word opens up infinite horizons
to my soul.*

St. Terese of Lisieux (1873–1897)
FRENCH NUN

*The highest earthly enjoyments
are but a shadow of the joy I
find in reading God's word.*

Lady Jane Grey (1537–1554)
QUEEN OF ENGLAND FOR NINE DAYS

*The most stupendous book, the most
sublime literature, even apart from
its sacred character, in the history
of the world.*

Blanche Mary Kelly (1881–1966)
AMERICAN AUTHOR

The Greatest Commandment

"Listen, Israel: The LORD our God, the LORD is One. Love the LORD your God with all your heart, with all your soul, and with all your strength. These words that I am giving you today are to be in your heart. Repeat them to your children. Talk about them when you sit in your house and when you walk along the road, when you lie down and when you get up. Bind them as a sign on your hand and let them be a symbol on your forehead. Write them on the doorposts of your house and on your gates."

"You must not take revenge or bear a grudge against members of your community, but you must love your neighbor as yourself, I am the LORD.

"When a foreigner lives with you in your land, you must not oppress him. You must regard the foreigner who lives with you as the native-born among you. You are to love him as yourself, for you were foreigners in the land of Egypt; I am the LORD your God."

"Teacher, which commandment in the law is the greatest?"

He said to him, "**You shall love the Lord your God with all your heart, with all your soul, and with all your mind.** This is the greatest and most important commandment. The second is like it: **You shall love your neighbor as yourself.** All the Law and the Prophets depend on these two commandments."

DEUTERONOMY 6:4-9; LEVITICUS 19:18,33-34; MATTHEW 22:36-40

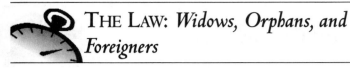

THE LAW: *Widows, Orphans, and Foreigners*

"You must not mistreat any widow or fatherless child. If you do mistreat them, they will no doubt cry to Me, and I will certainly hear their cry. My anger will burn, and I will kill you with the sword; then your wives will be widows and your children fatherless."

"Do not deny justice to a foreign resident or fatherless child, and do not take a widow's garment as security. Remember that you were a slave in Egypt, and the LORD your God redeemed you from there. Therefore I am commanding you to do this.

"When you reap the harvest in your field, and you forget a sheaf in the field, do not go back to get it. It is to be left for the foreign resident, the fatherless, and the widow, so that the LORD your God may bless you in all the work of your hands. When you knock down the fruit from your olive tree, you must not go over the branches again. What remains will be for the foreign resident, the fatherless, and the widow. When you gather the grapes of your vineyard, you must not glean what is left. What remains will be for the foreign resident, the fatherless, and the widow. Remember that you were a slave in the land of Egypt. Therefore I am commanding you to do this."

Pure and undefiled religion before our God and Father is this: to look after orphans and widows in their distress and to keep oneself unstained by the world.

EXODUS 22:22-24; DEUTERONOMY 24:17-22; JAMES 1:27

Related texts: DEUTERONOMY 10:17-20; PSALMS 68:5; 146:9; 1 TIMOTHY 5:3-16

THE LAW: *Restitution*

"When a man steals an ox or a sheep and butchers it or sells it, he must repay five cattle for the ox or four sheep for the sheep. If a thief is caught in the act of breaking in, and he is beaten to death, no one is guilty of bloodshed. But if this happens after sunrise, there is guilt of bloodshed. A thief must make full restitution. If he is unable, he is to be sold because of his theft. If what was stolen—whether ox, donkey, or sheep—is actually found alive in his possession, he must repay double.

"When a man lets a field or vineyard be grazed in, and then allows his animals to go and graze in someone else's field, he must repay with the best of his own field or vineyard.

"When a fire gets out of control, spreads to thorn-bushes, and consumes stacks of cut grain, standing grain, or a field, the one who started the fire must make full restitution for what was burned.

"When a man gives his neighbor money or goods to keep, but they are stolen from that person's house, the thief, if caught, must repay double. If the thief is not caught, the owner of the house must present himself to the judges to determine whether or not he has taken his neighbor's property. In any case of wrongdoing involving an ox, a donkey, a sheep, a garment, or anything else lost, and someone claims: That's mine, the case between the two parties is to come before the judges. The one the judges condemn must repay double to his neighbor."

EXODUS 22:1-9

THE LAW: *Eye for Eye*

"When men get in a fight, and hit a pregnant woman so that her children are born prematurely, but there is no injury, the one who hit her must be fined as the woman's husband demands from him, and he must pay according to judicial assessment. If there is an injury, then you must give life for life, eye for eye, tooth for tooth, hand for hand, foot for foot, burn for burn, bruise for bruise, wound for wound."

"If a man kills anyone, he must be put to death. Whoever kills an animal is to make restitution for it, life for life. If any man inflicts a permanent injury on his neighbor, whatever he has done is to be done to him: fracture for fracture, eye for eye, tooth for tooth. Whatever injury he inflicted on the person, the same is to be inflicted on him. Whoever kills an animal is to make restitution for it, but whoever kills a person is to be put to death. You are to have the same law for the foreign resident and the native, because I am the LORD your God."

"You have heard that it was said, **An eye for an eye and a tooth for a tooth.** But I tell you, don't resist an evildoer. On the contrary, if anyone slaps you on your right cheek, turn the other to him also."

EXODUS 21:22-25; LEVITICUS 24:17-22; MATTHEW 5:38-39

Related texts: DEUTERONOMY 19:16-21; PSALM 103:8-12; MATTHEW 5:40-42

THE LAW: *Capital Punishment*

"Whoever strikes a person so that he dies must be put to death."

"Whoever strikes his father or his mother must be put to death."

"Whoever kidnaps a person must be put to death, whether he sells him or the person is found in his possession."

"Whoever sacrifices to any gods, except the LORD alone, is to be set apart for destruction."

"Observe the Sabbath, for it is holy to you. Whoever profanes it must be put to death. If anyone does work on it, that person must be cut off from his people."

"If anyone curses his father or mother, he must be put to death. He has cursed his father or mother; his blood is on his own hands. If a man commits adultery with a married woman—if he commits adultery with his neighbor's wife—both the adulterer and the adulteress must be put to death. If a man sleeps with his father's wife, he has shamed his father. Both of them must be put to death; their blood is on their own hands. If a man sleeps with his daughter-in-law, both of them must be put to death. They have acted perversely; their blood is on their own hands. If a man sleeps with a man as with a woman, they have both committed an abomination. They must be put to death; their blood is on their own hands."

EXODUS 21:12,15-16; 22:20; 31:14; LEVITICUS 20:9-13

Related texts: GENESIS 9:6; LEVITICUS 24:17-22; DEUTERONOMY 24:16; MATTHEW 21:33-44

THE LAW: *Clean and Unclean*

The LORD spoke to Moses and Aaron: "Tell the Israelites: You may eat all these kinds of land animals. You may eat any animal with divided hooves and that chews the cud.

"This is what you may eat from all that is in the water: You may eat everything in the water that has fins and scales, whether in the seas or streams. But these are to be detestable to you: everything that does not have fins and scales in the seas or streams, among all the swarming things and other living creatures in the water. They are to remain detestable to you; you must not eat any of their meat, and you must detest their carcasses.

"All winged insects that walk on all fours are to be detestable to you. But you may eat these kinds of all the winged insects that walk on all fours: those that have jointed legs above their feet for hopping on the ground.

"All the creatures that swarm on the earth are detestable; they must not be eaten. Do not eat any of the creatures that swarm on the earth, anything that moves on its belly or walks on all fours or on many feet, for they are detestable. Do not become contaminated by any creature that swarms; do not become unclean or defiled by them. For I am the LORD your God, so you must consecrate yourselves and be holy because I am holy. You must not defile yourselves by any swarming creature that crawls on the ground. For I am the LORD, who brought you up from the land of Egypt to be your God, so you must be holy because I am holy."

LEVITICUS 11:1-3,9-11,20-21,44-45

Related texts: GENESIS 7:1-4; MATTHEW 15:1-20; MARK 7:1-23; ACTS 10; ROMANS 14

THE LAW: *The Festivals*

"Observe the month of Abib and celebrate the Passover to the LORD your God, because the LORD your God brought you out of Egypt by night in the month of Abib. Sacrifice to the LORD your God a Passover animal from the herd or flock in the place where the LORD chooses to have His name dwell.

"You must eat unleavened bread for six days. On the seventh day there is to be a solemn assembly to the LORD your God, and you must not do any work.

"You are to count seven weeks, counting the weeks from the time the sickle is first put to the standing grain. You are to celebrate the Festival of Weeks to the LORD your God with a freewill offering that you give in proportion to how the LORD your God has blessed you.

"You are to celebrate the Festival of Booths for seven days when you have gathered in everything from your threshing floor and winepress.

"You are to hold a seven-day festival for the LORD your God in the place He chooses, because the LORD your God will bless you in all your produce and in all the work of your hands, and you will have abundant joy.

"All your males are to appear three times a year before the LORD your God in the place He chooses: at the Festival of Unleavened Bread, the Festival of Weeks, and the Festival of Booths. No one is to appear before the LORD empty-handed. Everyone must appear with a gift suited to his means, according to the blessing the LORD your God has given you."

DEUTERONOMY 16:1-2,8-10,13,15-17

Related texts: EXODUS 12; 23:14-17; LEVITICUS 23; COLOSSIANS 2:16-23

Honor Your Mother

Honor your father and your mother, as the Lord your God has commanded you, so that you may live long and so that you may prosper in the land the Lord your God is giving you.

Then Pharisees and scribes came from Jerusalem to Jesus and asked, "Why do Your disciples break the tradition of the elders? For they don't wash their hands when they eat!"

He answered them, "And why do you break God's commandment because of your tradition? For God said:

Honor your father and your mother; and,
The one who speaks evil of father or mother
must be put to death.

But you say, 'Whoever tells his father or mother, "Whatever benefit you might have received from me is a gift committed to the temple"—he does not have to honor his father.' In this way, you have revoked God's word because of your tradition. Hypocrites! Isaiah prophesied correctly about you when he said:

This people honors Me with their lips,
but their heart is far from Me.
They worship Me in vain,
teaching as doctrines the commands of men."

DEUTERONOMY 5:16; MATTHEW 15:1-9

Related texts: EXODUS 20:12; 21:15; LEVITICUS 20:9; EPHESIANS 6:1-2

The Lord Has a Mother's Compassion

Shout for joy, you heavens!
Earth, rejoice!
Mountains break into joyful shouts!
For the LORD has comforted His people,
and will have compassion on His afflicted ones.
Zion says, "The LORD has abandoned me;
The Lord has forgotten me!"
"Can a woman forget her nursing child,
or lack compassion for the child of her womb?
Even if these forget,
yet I will not forget you.
Look, I have inscribed you on the palms of My
    hands;
your walls are continually before Me.
Your builders hurry;
those who destroy and devastate you will leave you.
Look up, and look around.
They all gather together; they come to you.
As I live"—the LORD's declaration—
"you will wear all your children as jewelry,
and put them on as a bride does.
For your waste and desolate places
and your land marked by ruins—
will now be indeed too small for the inhabitants,
and those who swallowed you up will be far away."

ISAIAH 49:13-19

A Happy Mother

Hallelujah!
Give praise, servants of the LORD;
praise the name of the LORD.
Let the name of the LORD be praised
both now and forever.
From the rising of the sun to its setting,
let the name of the LORD be praised.
The LORD is exalted above all the nations,
His glory above the heavens.
Who is like the LORD our God—
the One enthroned on high,
who stoops down to look
on the heavens and the earth?
He raises the poor from the dust
and lifts the needy from the garbage pile
in order to seat them with nobles—
with the nobles of His people.
He gives the childless woman a household,
making her the joyful mother of children.
Hallelujah!

PSALM 113

Related texts: 1 SAMUEL 2:1-10; JOB 42:12-16; PSALM
127:3-5; PROVERBS 17:6; ISAIAH 54:1-8; LUKE 1

A Mother's Teaching

Listen, my son, to your father's instruction,
and don't reject your mother's teaching,
for they will be a garland of grace on your head
and a gold chain around your neck.

The words of King Lemuel,
an oracle that his mother taught him:
What should I say, my son?
What, son of my womb?
What, son of my vows?
Don't spend your energy on women
or your efforts on those who destroy kings.
It is not for kings, Lemuel,
it is not for kings to drink wine
or for rulers to desire beer.
Otherwise, they will drink, forget what is decreed,
and pervert justice for all the oppressed.
Give beer to one who is dying,
and wine to one whose life is bitter.
Let him drink so that he can forget his poverty
and remember his trouble no more.
Speak up for those who have no voice,
for the justice of all who are dispossessed.
Speak up, judge righteously,
and defend the cause of the oppressed and needy.

PROVERBS 1:8-9; 31:1-9

Related texts: EXODUS 2:1-9; PROVERBS 6:20-24; 2 TIMOTHY 1:5; 3:14-17

THE CAPABLE WIFE: *Part 1*

A capable wife is her husband's crown,
but a wife who causes shame is like rottenness in
his bones.

Who can find a capable wife?
She is far more precious than jewels.
The heart of her husband trusts in her,
and he will not lack anything good.
She rewards him with good, not evil,
all the days of her life.
She selects wool and flax
and works with willing hands.
She is like the merchant ships,
bringing her food from far away.
She rises while it is still night
and provides food for her household
and portions for her servants.
She evaluates a field and buys it;
she plants a vineyard with her earnings.
She draws on her strength
and reveals that her arms are strong.
She sees that her profits are good,
and her lamp never goes out at night.
She extends her hands to the spinning staff,
and her hands hold the spindle.
Her hands reach out to the poor,
and she extends her hands to the needy.

PROVERBS 12:4; 31:10-20

THE CAPABLE WIFE: *Part 2*

Who can find a capable wife?
She is far more precious than jewels.

She is not afraid for her household when it snows,
for all in her household are doubly clothed.
She makes her own bed coverings;
her clothing is fine linen and purple.
Her husband is known at the city gates,
where he sits among the elders of the land.
She makes and sells linen garments;
she delivers belts to the merchants.
Strength and honor are her clothing,
and she can laugh at the time to come.
She opens her mouth with wisdom,
and loving instruction is on her tongue.
She watches over the activities of her household
and is never idle.
Her sons rise up and call her blessed.
Her husband also praises her:
"Many women are capable,
but you surpass them all!"
Charm is deceptive and beauty is fleeting,
but a woman who fears the LORD will be praised.
Give her the reward of her labor,
and let her works praise her at the city gates.

A man who finds a wife finds a good thing
and obtains favor from the LORD.

PROVERBS 31:10,21-31; 18:22

Your Maker Is Your Husband

"Rejoice, barren one, who did not give birth;
burst into song and shout,
you who have not been in labor!
For the children of the forsaken one will be more
than the children of the married woman,"
says the LORD.
"Enlarge the site of your tent,
and let your tent curtains be stretched out;
do not hold back;
lengthen your ropes,
and drive your pegs deep.

"Do not be afraid, for you will not be put to shame;
don't be humiliated, for you will not be disgraced.
For you will forget the shame of your youth,
and you will no longer remember
the disgrace of your widowhood.
For your husband is your Maker—
His name is Yahweh of Hosts—
and the Holy One of Israel is your Redeemer;
He is called the God of all the earth.
For the LORD has called you,
like a wife deserted and wounded in spirit,
a wife of one's youth when she is rejected,"
says your God.
"I deserted you for a brief moment,
but I will take you back with great compassion.
In a surge of anger
I hid My face from you for a moment,
but I will have compassion on you
with everlasting love,"
says the LORD your Redeemer.

ISAIAH 54:1-2,4-8

Related texts: PSALM 45; SONG OF SONGS 4; ISAIAH 62:1-7;
REVELATION 19:5-9; 21:1-4

THE LAW: *Women's Rights*

"When a man sells his daughter as a slave, she is not to leave as the male slaves do. If she is displeasing to her master, who chose her for himself, then he must let her be redeemed. He has no right to sell her to foreigners because he has acted treacherously toward her. Or if he chooses her for his son, he must deal with her according to the customary treatment of daughters. If he takes an additional wife, he must not reduce the food, clothing, or marital rights of the first wife. And if he does not do these three things for her, she may leave free of charge, without any exchange of money."

"Do not debase your daughter by making her a prostitute, or the land will be prostituted and filled with depravity."

"When brothers live on the same property and one of them dies without a son, the wife of the dead man may not marry a stranger outside the family. Her brother-in-law is to take her as his wife, have sexual relations with her, and perform the duty of a brother-in-law for her. The first son she bears will carry on the name of the dead brother, so his name will not be blotted out from Israel."

EXODUS 21:7-11; LEVITICUS 19:29; DEUTERONOMY 25:5-6

THE LAW: *The Tabernacle*

Now the first covenant also had regulations for ministry and an earthly sanctuary. For a tabernacle was set up; and in the first room, which is called "the holy place," were the lampstand, the table, and the presentation loaves. Behind the second curtain, the tabernacle was called "the holy of holies." It contained the gold altar of incense and the ark of the covenant, covered with gold on all sides, in which there was a gold jar containing the manna, Aaron's rod that budded, and the tablets of the covenant. The cherubim of glory were above it overshadowing the mercy seat. It is not possible to speak about these things in detail right now.

These things having been set up this way, the priests enter the first room repeatedly, performing their ministry. But the high priest alone enters the second room, and that only once a year, and never without blood, which he offers for himself and for the sins of the people committed in ignorance.

Now the Messiah has appeared, high priest of the good things that have come. In the greater and more perfect tabernacle not made with hands (that is, not of this creation), He entered the holy of holies once for all, not by the blood of goats and calves, but by His own blood, having obtained eternal redemption.

HEBREWS 9:1-7,11-12

Related texts: EXODUS 25–27; 35–40; MARK 15:37-38; HEBREWS 9:13-28; 10:9-23

THE LAW: *The Priesthood*

The Lord said to Aaron, "You, your sons, and your ancestral house will be responsible for sin against the sanctuary. You and your sons will be responsible for sin involving your priesthood. But also bring your brothers with you from the tribe of Levi, your ancestral tribe, so they may join you and serve with you and your sons in front of the tent of the testimony.

"You are to guard the sanctuary and the altar so that wrath may not fall on the Israelites again. Look, I have selected your fellow Levites from the Israelites as a gift for you, assigned by the LORD to work at the tent of meeting. But you and your sons will carry out your priestly responsibilities for everything concerning the altar and for what is inside the veil, and you will do that work. I am giving you the work of the priesthood as a gift, but an unauthorized person who comes near the sanctuary will be put to death."

"I give to you and to your sons and daughters all the holy contributions that the Israelites present to the LORD as a perpetual statute. It is a perpetual covenant of salt before the LORD for you as well as your offspring."

The LORD told Aaron, "You will not have an inheritance in their land; there will be no portion among them for you. I am your portion and your inheritance among the Israelites."

NUMBERS 18:1-2,5-7,19-20

Related texts: LEVITICUS 1–7; 21–22; NUMBERS 3; HEBREWS 7–9; 1 PETER 2:4-10

THE LAW: *Driving Out the Nations*

"When the Lord your God brings you into the land you are entering to possess, and He drives out many nations before you—the Hittites, Girgashites, Amorites, Canaanites, Perizzites, Hivites and Jebusites, seven nations more numerous and powerful than you—and when the Lord your God delivers them over to you and you defeat them, you must completely destroy them. Make no treaty with them and show them no mercy. Do not intermarry with them. Do not give your daughters to their sons or take their daughters for your sons, because they will turn your sons away from Me to worship other gods. Then the Lord's anger will burn against you, and He will swiftly destroy you. Instead, this is what you are to do to them: tear down their altars, smash their standing pillars, cut down their Asherah poles, and burn up their carved images. For you are a holy people belonging to the Lord your God. The Lord your God has chosen you to be His own possession out of all the peoples on the face of the earth.

"The LORD was devoted to you and chose you, not because you were more numerous than all peoples, for you were the fewest of all peoples. But because the LORD loved you and kept the oath He swore to your fathers, He brought you out with a strong hand and redeemed you from the place of slavery, from the power of Pharaoh king of Egypt."

DEUTERONOMY 7:1-8

Related texts: DEUTERONOMY 8:18–9:5; JUDGES 2:10-23; 2 CORINTHIANS 6:14–7:1; COLOSSIANS 4:4-6; 1 PETER 2:1-12

THE LAW: *Not Too Difficult*

"This command that I give you today is certainly not too difficult or beyond your reach. It is not in heaven, so that you have to ask, 'Who will go up to heaven, get it for us, and proclaim it to us so that we may follow it?' And it is not across the sea, so that you have to ask, 'Who will cross the sea, get it for us, and proclaim it to us so that we may follow it?' But the message is very near you, in your mouth and in your heart, so that you may follow it. See, today I have set before you life and prosperity, death and adversity. For I am commanding you today to love the Lord your God, to walk in His ways, and to keep His commands, statutes, and ordinances, so that you may live and multiply, and the Lord your God may bless you in the land you are entering to possess. But if your heart turns away and you do not listen and you are led astray to bow down to other gods and worship them, I tell you today that you will certainly perish and will not live long in the land you are entering to possess across the Jordan. I call heaven and earth as witnesses against you today that I have set before you life and death, blessing and curse. Choose life so that you and your descendants may live, love the Lord your God, obey Him, and remain faithful to Him. For He is your life, and He will prolong your life in the land the Lord swore to give to your fathers Abraham, Isaac, and Jacob."

DEUTERONOMY 30:11-20

Related texts: DEUTERONOMY 7:9-15; 10:12-13; MICAH 6:6-8; JOHN 14:15; ROMANS 10:5-13; 1 JOHN 5:3

SERMON ON THE MOUNT:
The Beatitudes

When He saw the crowds, He went up on the mountain, and after He sat down, His disciples came to Him. Then He began to teach them, saying:

"Blessed are the poor in spirit,
because the kingdom of heaven is theirs.
Blessed are those who mourn,
because they will be comforted.
Blessed are the gentle,
because they will inherit the earth.
Blessed are those who hunger and thirst for
righteousness,
because they will be filled.
Blessed are the merciful,
because they will be shown mercy.
Blessed are the pure in heart,
because they will see God.
Blessed are the peacemakers,
because they will be called sons of God.
Blessed are those who are persecuted for righteousness,
because the kingdom of heaven is theirs."

MATTHEW 5:1-10

Related texts: GENESIS 12:1-3; PSALM 1; LUKE 6:17-26; 11:27-28; JOHN 20:24-29

SERMON ON THE MOUNT:
Salt and Light

"Blessed are you when they insult you and persecute you, and say every kind of evil against you falsely because of Me. Be glad and rejoice, because your reward is great in heaven. For that is how they persecuted the prophets who were before you.

"You are the salt of the earth. But if the salt should lose its taste, how can it be made salty? It's no longer good for anything but to be thrown out and trampled on by men.

"You are the light of the world. A city situated on a hill cannot be hidden. No one lights a lamp and puts it under a basket, but rather on a lampstand, and it gives light for all who are in the house. In the same way, let your light shine before men, so that they may see your good works and give glory to your Father in heaven."

For you were once darkness, but now you are light in the Lord. Walk as children of light—for the fruit of the light results in all goodness, righteousness, and truth—discerning what is pleasing to the Lord.

MATTHEW 5:11-16; EPHESIANS 5:8-10

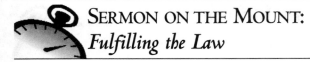

SERMON ON THE MOUNT:
Fulfilling the Law

"Don't assume that I came to destroy the Law or the Prophets. I did not come to destroy but to fulfill. For I assure you: Until heaven and earth pass away, not the smallest letter or one stroke of a letter will pass from the law until all things are accomplished. Therefore, whoever breaks one of the least of these commandments and teaches people to do so will be called least in the kingdom of heaven. But whoever practices and teaches these commandments will be called great in the kingdom of heaven. For I tell you, unless your righteousness surpasses that of the scribes and Pharisees, you will never enter the kingdom of heaven."

Therefore, no condemnation now exists for those in Christ Jesus, because the Spirit's law of life in Christ Jesus has set you free from the law of sin and of death. What the law could not do since it was limited by the flesh, God did. He condemned sin in the flesh by sending His own Son in flesh like ours under sin's domain, and as a sin offering, in order that the law's requirement would be accomplished in us who do not walk according to the flesh but according to the Spirit.

MATTHEW 5:17-20; ROMANS 8:1-4

Related texts: PSALM 119:161-176: MATTHEW 22:34-40; ROMANS 3:21-31; 7–8

Sermon on the Mount: *Murder and Hate*

"You have heard that it was said to our ancestors, You shall not murder, and whoever murders will be subject to judgment. But I tell you, everyone who is angry with his brother will be subject to judgment. And whoever says to his brother, 'Fool!' will be subject to the Sanhedrin. But whoever says, 'You moron!' will be subject to hellfire. So if you are offering your gift on the altar, and there you remember that your brother has something against you, leave your gift there in front of the altar. First go and be reconciled with your brother, and then come and offer your gift. Reach a settlement quickly with your adversary while you're on the way with him, or your adversary will hand you over to the judge, the judge to the officer, and you will be thrown into prison. I assure you: You will never get out of there until you have paid the last penny!"

The one who says he is in the light but hates his brother is in the darkness until now. The one who loves his brother remains in the light, and there is no cause for stumbling in him. But the one who hates his brother is in the darkness, walks in the darkness, and doesn't know where he's going, because the darkness has blinded his eyes.

Matthew 5:21-26; 1 John 2:9-11

SERMON ON THE MOUNT: *Adultery*

"You have heard that it was said, You shall not commit adultery. But I tell you, everyone who looks at a woman to lust for her has already committed adultery with her in his heart. If your right eye causes you to sin, gouge it out and throw it away. For it is better that you lose one of your members than for your whole body to be thrown into hell. And if your right hand causes you to sin, cut it off and throw it away. For it is better that you lose one of your members than for your whole body to go into hell!

"It was also said, Whoever divorces his wife must give her a written notice of divorce. But I tell you, everyone who divorces his wife, except in a case of sexual immorality, causes her to commit adultery. And whoever marries a divorced woman commits adultery."

For this is God's will, your sancification: that you abstain from sexual immorality, so that each of you knows how to possess his own vessel in sanctification and honor, not with lustful desires, like the Gentiles who don't know God. This means one must not transgress against and defraud his brother in this matter, because the Lord is an avenger of all these offenses, as we also previously told and warned you. For God has not called us to impurity, but to sanctification. therefore, the person who rejects this does not reject man, but God, who also gives you His Holy Spirit.

MATTHEW 5:27-32; 1 THESSALONIANS 4:3-8

Related texts: DEUTERONOMY 24:1-4; PROVERBS 5; MALACHI 2:10-16; MATTHEW 19:3-12; 1 CORINTHIANS 7

SERMON ON THE MOUNT: *Love, Not Revenge*

"You have heard that it was said, An eye for an eye and a tooth for a tooth. But I tell you, don't resist an evildoer. On the contrary, if anyone slaps you on your right cheek, turn the other to him also. As for the one who wants to sue you and take away your shirt, let him have your coat as well. And if anyone forces you to go one mile, go with him two. Give to the one who asks you, and don't turn away from the one who wants to borrow from you.

"You have heard that it was said, You shall love your neighbor and hate your enemy. But I tell you, love your enemies, and pray for those who persecute you, so that you may be sons of your Father in heaven. For He causes His sun to rise on the evil and the good, and sends rain on the righteous and the unrighteous. For if you love those who love you, what reward will you have? Don't even the tax collectors do the same? And if you greet only your brothers, what are you doing out of the ordinary? Don't even the Gentiles do the same? Be perfect, therefore, as your heavenly Father is perfect."

Dear friends, let us love one another, because love is from God, and everyone who loves has been born of God and knows God. The one who does not love does not know God, because God is love.

MATTHEW 5:38-48; 1 JOHN 4:7-8

Related texts: GENESIS 12:1-3; LEVITICUS 24:17-20; LUKE 6:27-37; ROMANS 12:14-18

SERMON ON THE MOUNT: *Treasure in Heaven*

"Be careful not to practice your righteousness in front of people, to be seen by them. Otherwise, you will have no reward from your Father in heaven. So whenever you give to the poor, don't sound a trumpet before you, as the hypocrites do in the synagogues and on the streets, to be applauded by people. I assure you: They've got their reward! But when you give to the poor, don't let your left hand know what your right hand is doing, so that your giving may be in secret. And your Father who sees in secret will reward you.

"Don't collect for yourselves treasures on earth, where moth and rust destroy and where thieves break in and steal. But collect for yourselves treasures in heaven, where neither moth nor rust destroys, and where thieves don't break in and steal. For where your treasure is, there your heart will be also.

"The eye is the lamp of the body. If your eye is generous, your whole body will be full of light. But if your eye is stingy, your whole body will be full of darkness. So if the light within you is darkness—how deep is that darkness!

"No one can be a slave of two masters, since either he will hate one and love the other, or be devoted to one and despise the other. You cannot be slaves of God and of money."

MATTHEW 6:1-4,19-24

Related texts: PROVERBS 11:24-25; MARK 10:17-31; LUKE 6:38; 12:32-34; ACTS 20:32-35; 2 CORINTHIANS 9:6-15

Sermon on the Mount: *Prayer*

"Whenever you pray, you must not be like the hypocrites, because they love to pray standing in the synagogues and on the street corners to be seen by people. I assure you: They've got their reward! But when you pray, go into your private room, shut your door, and pray to your Father who is in secret. And your Father who sees in secret will reward you. When you pray, don't babble like the idolaters, since they imagine they'll be heard for their many words. Don't be like them, because your Father knows the things you need before you ask Him.

"Therefore, you should pray like this:

> Our Father in heaven,
> Your name be honored as holy.
> Your kingdom come.
> Your will be done
> on earth as it is in heaven.
> Give us today our daily bread.
> And forgive us our debts,
> as we also have forgiven our debtors.
> And do not bring us into temptation,
> but deliver us from the evil one.
> [For Yours is the kingdom and the power
> and the glory forever. Amen.]

"For if you forgive people their wrongdoing, your heavenly Father will forgive you as well. But if you don't forgive people, your Father will not forgive your wrongdoing."

MATTHEW 6:5-15

SERMON ON THE MOUNT: *Fasting*

"Whenever you fast, don't be sad-faced like the hypocrites. For they make their faces unattractive so they may show their fasting to people. I assure you: They've got their reward! But when you fast, brush your hair and wash your face, so that you don't show your fasting to people, but to your Father who is in secret. And your Father who sees in secret will reward you."

Now John's disciples and the Pharisees were fasting. People came and asked Him, "Why do John's disciples and the Pharisees' disciples fast, but Your disciples do not fast?"

Jesus said to them, "The wedding guests cannot fast while the groom is with them, can they? As long as they have the groom with them, they cannot fast. But the time will come when the groom is taken away from them, and then they will fast in that day. No one sews a patch of unshrunk cloth on an old garment. Otherwise, the new patch pulls away from the old cloth, and a worse tear is made. And no one puts new wine into old wineskins. Otherwise, the wine will burst the skins, and the wine is lost as well as the skins. But new wine is for fresh wineskins."

MATTHEW 6:16-18; MARK 2:18-22

Related texts: ESTHER 3–4; ISAIAH 58; JONAH 3; ZECHARIAH 7–8; ACTS 14:21-23

SERMON ON THE MOUNT:
Why Worry?

"This is why I tell you: Don't worry about your life, what you will eat or what you will drink; or about your body, what you will wear. Isn't life more than food and the body more than clothing? Look at the birds of the sky: they don't sow or reap or gather into barns, yet your heavenly Father feeds them. Aren't you worth more than they? Can any of you add a single cubit to his height by worrying? And why do you worry about clothes? Learn how the wildflowers of the field grow: they don't labor or spin thread. Yet I tell you that not even Solomon in all his splendor was adorned like one of these! If that's how God clothes the grass of the field, which is here today and thrown into the furnace tomorrow, won't He do much more for you—you of little faith? So don't worry, saying, 'What will we eat?' or 'What will we drink?' or 'What will we wear?' For the Gentiles eagerly seek all these things, and your heavenly Father knows that you need them. But seek first the kingdom of God and His righteousness, and all these things will be provided for you. Therefore don't worry about tomorrow, because tomorrow will worry about itself. Each day has enough trouble of its own."

MATTHEW 6:25-34

SERMON ON THE MOUNT:
Judging and Asking

"Do not judge, so that you won't be judged. For with the judgment you use, you will be judged, and with the measure you use, it will be measured to you. Why do you look at the speck in your brother's eye, but don't notice the log in your own eye? Or how can you say to your brother, 'Let me take the speck out of your eye,' and look, there's a log in your eye? Hypocrite! First take the log out of your eye, and then you will see clearly to take the speck out of your brother's eye. Don't give what is holy to dogs or toss your pearls before pigs, or they will trample them with their feet, turn, and tear you to pieces.

"Keep asking, and it will be given to you. Keep searching, and you will find. Keep knocking, and the door will be opened to you. For everyone who asks receives, and the one who searches finds, and to the one who knocks, the door will be opened. What man among you, if his son asks him for bread, will give him a stone? Or if he asks for a fish, will give him a snake? If you then, who are evil, know how to give good gifts to your children, how much more will your Father in heaven give good things to those who ask Him! Therefore, whatever you want others to do for you, do also the same for them—this is the Law and the Prophets."

MATTHEW 7:1-12

Related texts: ROMANS 14:1-13; JOHN 16:24;
1 CORINTHIANS 5; JAMES 4:1-3; 1 JOHN 3:21-22

SERMON ON THE MOUNT:
The Two Ways

"Enter through the narrow gate; because the gate is wide and the road is broad that leads to destruction, and there are many who go through it. How narrow is the gate and difficult the road that leads to life; and few find it.

"Not everyone who says to Me, 'Lord, Lord!' will enter the kingdom of heaven, but the one who does the will of My Father in heaven. On that day many will say to Me, 'Lord, Lord, didn't we prophesy in Your name, drive out demons in Your name, and do many miracles in Your name?' Then I will announce to them, 'I never knew you! Depart from Me, you lawbreakers!'

"Therefore, everyone who hears these words of Mine and acts on them will be like a sensible man who built his house on the rock. The rain fell, the rivers rose, and the winds blew and pounded that house. Yet it didn't collapse, because its foundation was on the rock. But everyone who hears these words of Mine and doesn't act on them will be like a foolish man who built his house on the sand. The rain fell, the rivers rose, the winds blew and pounded that house, and it collapsed. And its collapse was great!"

When Jesus had finished this sermon, the crowds were astonished at His teaching. For He was teaching them like one who had authority, and not like their scribes.

MATTHEW 7:13-14,21-29

Related texts: PROVERBS 14:11-12; LUKE 13:22-30; JOHN 10:1-10; EPHESIANS 2:13-22

By the reading of Scripture I am so renewed that all nature seems renewed around me and with me. The whole world is charged with the glory of God and I feel fire and music under my feet.

Thomas Merton (1915–1968)
AMERICAN MONK

The Scripture…dispels the darkness and gives us a clear view of the true God.

John Calvin (1509–1564)
FRENCH THEOLOGIAN AND REFORMER

Give me a used Bible and I will, I think, be able to tell you about a man by the places that are edged with the dirt of seeking fingers.

John Steinbeck (1902–1968)
AMERICAN NOVELIST

The Golden Calf

When the people saw that Moses delayed in coming down from the mountain, they gathered around Aaron and said to him, "Come, make us a god who will go before us because this Moses, the man who brought us up from the land of Egypt—we don't know what has happened to him!"

Then Aaron replied to them, "Take off the gold rings that are on the ears of your wives, your sons, and your daughters and bring them to me." So all the people took off the gold rings that were on their ears and brought them to Aaron. He took the gold from their hands, fashioned it with an engraving tool, and made it into an image of a calf.

Then they said, "Israel, this is your God, who brought you up from the land of Egypt!"

When Aaron saw this, he built an altar before it; then he made an announcement: "There will be a festival to the LORD tomorrow." Early the next morning they arose, offered burnt offerings, and presented fellowship offerings. The people sat down to eat and drink, then got up to revel.

The LORD spoke to Moses: "Go down at once! For your people you brought up from the land of Egypt have acted corruptly. They have quickly turned from the way I commanded them; they have made for themselves an image of a calf. They have bowed down to it, sacrificed to it, and said, 'Israel, this is your God, who brought you up from the land of Egypt.' " The LORD also said to Moses: "I have seen this people, and they are indeed a stiff-necked people. Now leave Me alone, so that My anger can burn against them and I can destroy them. Then I will make you into a great nation."

EXODUS 32:1-2,4-10

Related texts: DEUTERONOMY 9:7-15; NEHEMIAH 9:16-19; PSALM 106:19-22; ACTS 7:37-41

Moses Pleads for the Israelites

But Moses interceded with the LORD his God: "LORD, why does Your anger burn against Your people You brought out of the land of Egypt with great power and a strong hand? Why should the Egyptians say, 'He brought them out with an evil intent to kill them in the mountains and wipe them off the face of the earth'? Turn from Your great anger and change Your mind about this disaster planned for Your people. Remember that You swore to Your servants Abraham, Isaac, and Israel by Yourself and declared to them, 'I will make your offspring as numerous as the stars of the sky and will give your offspring all this land that I have promised, and they will inherit it forever.' " So the LORD changed His mind about the disaster He said He would bring on His people.

Then Moses turned and went down the mountain with the two tablets of the testimony in his hands. They were inscribed on both sides—inscribed front and back. The tablets were the work of God, and the writing was God's writing, engraved on the tablets.

As he approached the camp and saw the calf and the dancing, Moses became enraged and threw the tablets out of his hands, smashing them at the base of the mountain. Then he took the calf they had made, burned it up, and ground it to powder. He scattered the powder over the surface of the water and forced the Israelites to drink the water.

EXODUS 32:11-16,19-20

Related texts: GENESIS 15:1-5; 22:15-18; 26:2-4; DEUTERONOMY 9:16-21; PSALM 106:23; JONAH 3; ACTS 7:40-42

Israel's History Is Our Warning

Now I want you to know, brothers, that our fathers were all under the cloud, all passed through the sea, and all were baptized into Moses in the cloud and in the sea. They all ate the same spiritual food, and all drank the same spiritual drink. For they drank from a spiritual rock that followed them, and that rock was Christ. But God was not pleased with most of them, for they were struck down in the desert.

Now these things became examples for us, so that we will not desire evil as they did. Don't become idolaters as some of them were; as it is written, The people sat down to eat and drink, and got up to play. Let us not commit sexual immorality as some of them did, and in a single day 23,000 people fell dead.

Now these things happened to them as examples, and they were written as a warning to us, on whom the ends of the ages have come. Therefore, whoever thinks he stands must be careful not to fall! No temptation has overtaken you except what is common to humanity. God is faithful and He will not allow you to be tempted beyond what you are able, but with the temptation He will also provide a way of escape, so that you are able to bear it.

1 CORINTHIANS 10:1-8,11-13

Related texts: EXODUS 14; 17:1-7; JOHN 6; HEBREWS 2:9-18; JAMES 1:12-15

God Forgives Those Who Repent

The LORD said to Moses, "Cut two stone tablets like the first ones, and I will write on them the words that were on the first tablets, which you broke."

Moses cut two stone tablets like the first ones. He got up early in the morning, and taking the two stone tablets in his hand, he climbed Mount Sinai, just as the LORD had commanded him.

The Lord came down in a cloud, stood with him there, and proclaimed His name Yahweh. Then the Lord passed in front of him and proclaimed:

> Yahweh—Yahweh is a compassionate and gracious God, slow to anger and rich in faithful love and truth, maintaining faithful love to a thousand generations, forgiving wrongdoing, rebellion, and sin. But He will not leave the guilty unpunished, bringing the consequences of the fathers' wrongdoing on the children and grandchildren to the third and fourth generation.

Moses immediately bowed down to the ground and worshiped. Then he said, "My Lord, if I have indeed found favor in Your sight, my Lord, please go with us. Even though this is a stiff-necked people, forgive our wrongdoing and sin, and accept us as Your own possession."

And the LORD responded: "Look, I am making a covenant. I will perform wonders in the presence of all your people that have never been done in all the earth or in any nation. All the people you live among will see the LORD's work, for what I am doing with you is awe-inspiring.

EXODUS 34:1,4-10

Related texts: PSALMS 86:15; 103:8; 145:8; JOHN 3:16-21; 1 JOHN 1:9

God Is Compassionate

"Don't be like your fathers and your brothers who were unfaithful to the LORD God of their ancestors so that He made them an object of horror as you yourselves see. Don't become obstinate now like your fathers did. Give your allegiance to the LORD, and come to His sanctuary that He has consecrated forever. Serve the LORD your God so that He may turn His fierce wrath away from you, for when you return to the LORD, your brothers and your sons will receive mercy in the presence of their captors and will return to this land. For the LORD your God is gracious and merciful; He will not turn His face away from you if you return to Him."

The LORD is gracious and compassionate,
slow to anger and great in faithful love.
The LORD is good to everyone;
His compassion rests on all He has made.

Blessed be the God and Father of our Lord Jesus Christ, the Father of mercies and the God of all comfort. He comforts us in all our affliction, so that we may be able to comfort those who are in any kind of affliction, through the comfort we ourselves receive from God. For as the sufferings of Christ overflow to us, so our comfort overflows through Christ.

2 CHRONICLES 30:7-9; PSALM 145:8-9; 2 CORINTHIANS 1:3-5

Related texts: EXODUS 33:19; 2 CHRONICLES 30:7-9; NEHEMIAH 9:16-19; PSALM 103; LAMENTATIONS 3:19-23

God Is Forgiving

Who is a God like You,
removing iniquity and passing over rebellion
for the remnant of His inheritance?
He does not hold on to His anger forever,
because He delights in faithful love.
He will again have compassion on us;
He will vanquish our iniquities.
You will cast all our sins
into the depths of the sea.
You will show loyalty to Jacob
and faithful love to Abraham,
as You swore to our fathers
from days long ago.

Now this is the message we have heard from Him
and declare to you: God is light, and there is absolutely
no darkness in Him. If we say, "We have fellowship
with Him," and walk in darkness, we are lying and are
not practicing the truth. But if we walk in the light as
He Himself is in the light, we have fellowship with one
another, and the blood of Jesus His Son cleanses us from
all sin. If we say, "We have no sin," we are deceiving
ourselves, and the truth is not in us. If we confess our
sins, He is faithful and righteous to forgive us our sins
and to cleanse us from all unrighteousness. If we say,
"We have not sinned," we make Him a liar, and His
word is not in us.

Micah 7:18-20; 1 John 1:5-10

Related texts: Numbers 14:1-35; 1 Kings 8:27-53; Psalm
32:1-5; Daniel 9:1-9; Matthew 6:14-15; 18:21-35

God Is Gracious

The LORD is gracious and righteous;
our God is compassionate.
The LORD guards the inexperienced;
I was helpless, and He saved me.
Return to your rest, my soul,
for the LORD has been good to you.

> The Word became flesh
> and took up residence among us.
> We observed His glory,
> the glory as the One and Only Son from the
> Father,
> full of grace and truth.
> For we have all received grace after grace
> from His fullness.
> For the law was given through Moses;
> grace and truth came through Jesus Christ.

But God, who is abundant in mercy, because of His great love that He had for us, made us alive with the Messiah even though we were dead in trespasses. By grace you are saved! He also raised us up with Him and seated us with Him in the heavens, in Christ Jesus, so that in the coming ages He might display the immeasurable riches of His grace in His kindness to us in Christ Jesus. For by grace you are saved through faith, and this is not from yourselves; it is God's gift—not from works, so that no one can boast.

PSALM 116:5-7; JOHN 1:14,16-17; EPHESIANS 2:4-9

Related texts: NUMBERS 6:24-26; PROVERBS 3:33-35; ROMANS 5:12-21

God Is Holy

"For I am the LORD, who brought you up from the land of Egypt to be your God, so you must be holy because I am holy."

In the year that King Uzziah died, I saw the Lord seated on a high and lofty throne, and His robe filled the temple. Seraphim were standing above Him; each one had six wings: with two he covered his face, with two he covered his feet, and with two he flew. And one called to another:
Holy, holy, holy is the LORD of Hosts;
His glory fills the whole earth.

For the High and Exalted One
who lives forever, whose name is Holy says this:
"I live in a high and holy place,
and with the oppressed and lowly of spirit,
to revive the spirit of the lowly
and revive the heart of the oppressed.
For I will not accuse you forever,
and I will not always be angry;
for then the spirit would grow weak before Me,
even the breath of man, which I have made."

As obedient children, do not be conformed to the desires of your former ignorance but, as the One who called you is holy, you also are to be holy in all your conduct; for it is written, Be holy, because I am holy.

LEVITICUS 11:45; ISAIAH 6:1-3; 57:15-16; 1 PETER 1:14-16

Related texts: EXODUS 15:11; LEVITICUS 22:31-33; PSALM 99; REVELATION 4; 15:2-4

God Is Merciful

Listen, LORD, and answer me,
for I am poor and needy.
Protect my life, for I am faithful.
You are my God; save Your servant who trusts in You.
Be gracious to me, Lord,
for I call to You all day long.
Bring joy to Your servant's life,
since I set my hope on You, Lord.
You rescue an afflicted people,
For You, Lord, are kind and ready to forgive,
abundant in faithful love to all who call on You.
LORD, hear my prayer;
listen to my plea for mercy.
I call on You in the day of my distress,
for You will answer me.

And you were dead in your trespasses and sins in which you previously walked according to this worldly age, according to the ruler of the atmospheric domain, the spirit now working in the disobedient. We too all previously lived among them in our fleshly desires, carrying out the inclinations of our flesh and thoughts, and by nature we were children under wrath, as the others were also. But God, who is abundant in mercy, because of His great love that He had for us, made us alive with the Messiah even though we were dead in trespasses. By grace you are saved!

PSALM 86:1-7; EPHESIANS 2:1-5

Related texts: EXODUS 33:19; DEUTERONOMY 4:31; NEHEMIAH 9:29-31; MICAH 7:18-20; ROMANS 9:11-18

God Is All-Powerful

Then Job replied to the Lord:
"I know that You can do anything
and no plan of Yours can be thwarted."

Ascribe power to God.
His majesty is over Israel,
His power among the clouds.
God, You are awe-inspiring in Your sanctuaries.
The God of Israel gives power and strength to His
    people.
May God be praised!

Ah, Lord GOD! You Yourself made the heavens and
earth by Your great power and with Your outstretched
arm. Nothing is too difficult for You! 18 You show faithful love to thousands but lay the fathers' sins on their
sons' laps after them, great and mighty God whose
name is the LORD of Hosts, 19 the One great in counsel
and mighty in deed, whose eyes are on all the ways of
the sons of men in order to give to each person according to his ways and the result of his deeds.

Our Lord and God,
You are worthy to receive
glory and honor and power,
because You have created all things,
and because of Your will
they exist and were created.

JOB 42:1-2; PSALM 68:34-35; JEREMIAH 32:17-19;
REVELATION 4:11

Related texts: GENESIS 18:14; EXODUS 15:1-18; PSALM 29;
MARK 4:35-41

God Is Everywhere

Where can I go to escape Your Spirit?
Where can I flee from Your presence?
If I go up to heaven, You are there;
if I make my bed in Sheol, You are there.
If I live at the eastern horizon
or settle at the western limits,
even there Your hand will lead me;
Your right hand will hold on to me.
If I say, "Surely the darkness will hide me,
and the light around me will become night"—
even the darkness is not dark to You.
The night shines like the day;
darkness and light are alike to You.

"Am I a God who is only near"—this is the LORD's declaration—"and not a God who is far away? Can a man hide himself in secret places where I cannot see him?"—the LORD's declaration. "Do I not fill the heavens and the earth?"—the LORD's declaration.

Then Jesus came near and said to them, "All authority has been given to Me in heaven and on earth. Go, therefore, and make disciples of all nations, baptizing them in the name of the Father and of the Son and of the Holy Spirit, teaching them to observe everything I have commanded you. And remember, I am with you always, to the end of the age."

PSALM 139:7-12; JEREMIAH 23:23-24; MATTHEW 28:18-20

Related texts: DEUTERONOMY 4:7; 1 KINGS 8:27; JOHN 1:45-49; 14:16-17

God Knows Everything

LORD, You have searched me and known me.
You know when I sit down and when I stand up;
You understand my thoughts from far away.
You observe my travels and my rest;
You are aware of all my ways.
Before a word is on my tongue,
You know all about it, LORD.
You have encircled me;
You have placed Your hand on me.
This extraordinary knowledge is beyond me.
It is lofty; I am unable to reach it.

> Oh, the depth of the riches
> both of the wisdom and the knowledge of God!
> How unsearchable His judgments
> and untraceable His ways!
> For who has known the mind of the Lord?
> Or who has been His counselor?
> Or who has ever first given to Him,
> and has to be repaid?
> For from Him and through Him and to Him are
>   all things.
> To Him be the glory forever. Amen.

For the word of God is living and effective and sharper than any two-edged sword, penetrating as far as to divide soul, spirit, joints, and marrow; it is a judge of the ideas and thoughts of the heart. No creature is hidden from Him, but all things are naked and exposed to the eyes of Him to whom we must give an account.

PSALM 139:1-6; ROMANS 11:33-36; HEBREWS 4:12-13

Related texts: 2 CHRONICLES 16:9; PSALM 94:1-11;
PROVERBS 5:21; JOHN 3:19-20; 1 CORINTHIANS 1:18-25

God Is One

"Listen, Israel: The LORD our God, the LORD is One. Love the LORD your God with all your heart, with all your soul, and with all your strength."

On that day Yahweh will become king over all the earth—Yahweh alone, and His name alone.

Or is God for Jews only? Is He not also for Gentiles? Yes, for Gentiles too, since there is one God who will justify the circumcised by faith and the uncircumcised through faith.

For even if there are so-called gods, whether in heaven or on earth—as there are many "gods" and many "lords"—

> yet for us there is one God, the Father,
> from whom are all things, and we for Him;
> and one Lord, Jesus Christ,
> through whom are all things, and we through
>   Him.

There is one body and one Spirit, just as you were called to one hope at your calling; one Lord, one faith, one baptism, one God and Father of all, who is above all and through all and in all.

DEUTERONOMY 6:4-5; ZECHARIAH 14:9; ROMANS 3:29-30; 1 CORINTHIANS 8:5-6; EPHESIANS 4:4-6

Related texts: ISAIAH 44:6-8; MALACHI 2:10; MATTHEW 19:16-17; 23:1-10; MARK 12:28-34

God Is Righteous

Rise up, LORD, in Your anger;
lift Yourself up against the fury of my adversaries;
awake for me; You have ordained a judgment.
Let the assembly of peoples gather around You;
take Your seat on high over it.
The LORD judges the peoples;
vindicate me, LORD,
according to my righteousness and my integrity.
Let the evil of the wicked come to an end,
but establish the righteous.
The One who examines the thoughts and emotions
is a righteous God.
My shield is with God,
who saves the upright in heart.
God is a righteous judge,
and a God who executes justice every day.

"The days are coming"—this is the LORD's declaration—"when I will raise up a righteous Branch of David. He will reign wisely as king and administer justice and righteousness in the land. In His days Judah will be saved, and Israel will dwell securely. This is what He will be named: The LORD Is Our Righteousness."

My little children, I am writing you these things so that you may not sin. But if anyone does sin, we have an advocate with the Father—Jesus Christ the righteous One. He Himself is the propitiation for our sins, and not only for ours, but also for those of the whole world.

PSALM 7:6-11; JEREMIAH 23:5-6; 1 JOHN 2:1-2

Related texts: EZRA 9; PSALM 36:5-10; 71; DANIEL 9:1-19;
MATTHEW 6:28-33; ACTS 3:12-16

Our Heavenly Father

For you are all sons of God through faith in Christ Jesus.

For as many of you as have been baptized into Christ have put on Christ. There is no Jew or Greek, slave or free, male or female; for you are all one in Christ Jesus. And if you are Christ's, then you are Abraham's seed, heirs according to the promise.

Now I say that as long as the heir is a child, he differs in no way from a slave, though he is the owner of everything. Instead, he is under guardians and stewards until the time set by his father. In the same way we also, when we were children, were in slavery under the elemental forces of the world. But when the completion of the time came, God sent His Son, born of a woman, born under the law, to redeem those under the law, so that we might receive adoption as sons. And because you are sons, God has sent the Spirit of His Son into our hearts, crying, "*Abba*, Father!" So you are no longer a slave, but a son; and if a son, then an heir through God.

My little children, I am writing you these things so that you may not sin. But if anyone does sin, we have an advocate with the Father—Jesus Christ the righteous One. He Himself is the propitiation for our sins, and not only for ours, but also for those of the whole world.

Galatians 3:26-29; 4:1-7; 1 John 3:1-2

Related texts: Deuteronomy 32:6; Psalm 2; Isaiah 9:1-7; John 1:12-13; Romans 8; Hebrews 12:1-14

Honor Your Father

Honor your father and your mother so that you may
have a long life in the land that the Lord your
God is giving you.

A man fathers a fool to his own sorrow;
the father of a fool has no joy.

My son, if your heart is wise,
my heart will indeed rejoice.
My innermost being will cheer
when your lips say what is right.

Listen, my son, and be wise;
keep your mind on the right course.

Let the message about the Messiah dwell richly
among you, teaching and admonishing one another in
all wisdom, and singing psalm, hymns, and spiritual
songs, with gratitude in your hearts to God. And whatever you do, in word or in deed, do everything in the
name of the Lord Jesus, giving thanks to God the Father
through Him.

Wives, be submissive to your husbands, as is fitting
in the Lord.
Husbands, love your wives and don't become bitter
against them.
Children, obey your parents in everything, for this is
pleasing in the Lord.
Fathers, do not exasperate your children, so they
won't become discouraged.

EXODUS 20:12; PROVERBS 17:21; 23:15-16,19;
COLOSSIANS 3:16-21

Related texts: EXODUS 21:15; LEVITICUS 19:3; PROVERBS
10:1; 23:22-25; EPHESIANS 6:1-3

A Father's Instruction

Listen, my sons, to a father's discipline,
and pay attention so that you may gain understanding,
for I am giving you good instruction.
Don't abandon my teaching.
When I was a son with my father,
tender and precious to my mother,
he taught me and said:
"Your heart must hold on to my words.
Keep my commands and live.
Get wisdom, get understanding;
don't forget or turn away from the words of my
    mouth.
Don't abandon wisdom, and she will watch over
    you;
love her, and she will guard you.
Wisdom is supreme—so get wisdom.
And whatever else you get, get understanding.
Cherish her, and she will exalt you;
if you embrace her, she will honor you.
She will place a garland of grace on your head;
she will give you a crown of beauty."
Listen, my son. Accept my words,
and you will live many years.
I am teaching you the way of wisdom;
I am guiding you on straight paths.
When you walk, your steps will not be hindered;
when you run, you will not stumble.

PROVERBS 4:1-12

A Father's Discipline

In struggling against sin, you have not yet resisted to the point of shedding your blood. And you have forgotten the exhortation that addresses you as sons:

My son, do not take the Lord's discipline lightly,
or faint when you are reproved by Him;
for the Lord disciplines the one He loves,
and punishes every son whom He receives.

Endure it as discipline: God is dealing with you as sons. For what son is there whom a father does not discipline? But if you are without discipline—which all receive—then you are illegitimate children and not sons. Furthermore, we had natural fathers discipline us, and we respected them. Shouldn't we submit even more to the Father of spirits and live? For they disciplined us for a short time based on what seemed good to them, but He does it for our benefit, so that we can share His holiness. No discipline seems enjoyable at the time, but painful. Later on, however, it yields the fruit of peace and righteousness to those who have been trained by it.

HEBREWS 12:4-11

Related texts: DEUTERONOMY 8:5; 1 SAMUEL 2:12-36; PROVERBS 3:11-12; 15:5; REVELATION 3:14-20

A Faithful Husband

My son, pay attention to my wisdom;
listen closely to my understanding
so that you may maintain discretion
and your lips safeguard knowledge.
Though the lips of the forbidden woman drip honey
and her words are smoother than oil,
in the end she's as bitter as wormwood
and as sharp as a double-edged sword.

Drink water from your own cistern,
water flowing from your own well.
Should your springs flow in the streets,
streams of water in the public squares?
They should be for you alone
and not for you to share with strangers.
Let your fountain be blessed,
and take pleasure in the wife of your youth.
A loving doe, a graceful fawn—
let her breasts always satisfy you;
be lost in her love forever.
Why, my son, would you be infatuated with a for-
    bidden woman
or embrace the breast of a stranger?
For a man's ways are before the LORD's eyes,
and He considers all his paths.
A wicked man's iniquities entrap him;
he is entangled in the ropes of his own sin.
He will die because there is no instruction,
and be lost because of his great stupidity.

PROVERBS 5:1-4,15-23

Related texts: EXODUS 20:14; LEVITICUS 20:10; PROVERBS
2:16-22; 6:23-35; 7; EPHESIANS 5:1-3

Love Song to a Husband

Like an apricot tree among the trees of the forest,
so is my love among the young men.
I delight to sit in his shade,
and his fruit is sweet to my taste.
He brought me to the banquet hall,
and he looked on me with love.

Listen! My love is approaching.
Look! Here he comes,
leaping over the mountains,
bounding over the hills.
My love is like a gazelle
or a young stag.
Look, he is standing behind our wall,
gazing through the windows,
peering through the lattice.
My love calls to me:
Arise, my darling.
Come away, my beautiful one.
For now the winter is past;
the rain has ended and gone away.
The blossoms appear in the countryside.
The time of singing has come,
and the turtledove's cooing is heard in our land.
The fig tree ripens its figs;
the blossoming vines give off their fragrance.
Arise, my darling.
Come away, my beautiful one.

SONG OF SONGS 2:3-4,8-13

Related texts: PSALM 45; SONG OF SONGS 1–8;
2 CORINTHIANS 11:2-3; 1 PETER 3:1-6

Husbands, Love Your Wives

Husbands, love your wives, just as also Christ loved the church and gave Himself for her, to make her holy, cleansing her in the washing of water by the word. He did this to present the church to Himself in splendor, without spot or wrinkle or any such thing, but holy and blameless. In the same way, husbands should love their wives as their own bodies. He who loves his wife loves himself. For no one ever hates his own flesh, but provides and cares for it, just as Christ does for the church, since we are members of His body.

Husbands, in the same way, live with your wives with understanding of their weaker nature yet showing them honor as co-heirs of the grace of life, so that your prayers will not be hindered.

EPHESIANS 5:25-33; 1 PETER 3:7

Related texts: GENESIS 2:18-25; HOSEA 3:1-3; MALACHI 2:13-16; COLOSSIANS 3:19; REVELATION 21:1-4

God's Daily Guidance for Israel

On the day the tabernacle was set up, the cloud covered the tabernacle, the tent of the testimony, and it appeared like fire above the tabernacle from evening until morning. It remained that way continuously: the cloud would cover it, appearing like fire at night. Whenever the cloud was lifted up above the tent, the Israelites would set out; at the place where the cloud stopped, there the Israelites camped. At the LORD's command the Israelites set out, and at the LORD's command they camped. As long as the cloud stayed over the tabernacle, they camped.

Even when the cloud stayed over the tabernacle many days, the Israelites carried out the LORD's requirement and did not set out. Sometimes the cloud remained over the tabernacle for only a few days. They would camp at the LORD's command and set out at the LORD's command. Sometimes the cloud remained only from evening until morning; when the cloud lifted in the morning, they set out. Or if it remained a day and a night, they moved out when the cloud lifted. Whether it was two days, a month, or longer, the Israelites camped and did not set out as long as the cloud stayed over the tabernacle. But when it was lifted, they set out. They camped at the LORD's command, and they set out at the LORD's command. They carried out the LORD's requirement according to His command through Moses.

NUMBERS 9:15-23

Related texts: EXODUS 13:22,33; 40:34-38; NUMBERS 14:11-14; 1 CORINTHIANS 10:1-2

Israel Puts God to the Test

They deliberately tested God,
demanding the food they craved.
Therefore, the LORD heard and became furious;
then fire broke out against Jacob,
and anger flared up against Israel
because they did not believe God
or rely on His salvation.
He gave a command to the clouds above
and opened the doors of heaven.
He rained manna for them to eat;
He gave them grain from heaven.
People ate the bread of angels.
He sent them an abundant supply of food.
He made the east wind blow in the skies
and drove the south wind by His might.
He rained meat on them like dust,
and winged birds like the sand of the seas.
He made them fall in His camp,
all around His tent.
They ate and were completely satisfied,
for He gave them what they craved.
Before they had satisfied their desire,
while the food was still in their mouths,
God's anger flared up against them,
and He killed some of their best men.
He struck down Israel's choice young men.
Despite all this, they kept sinning
and did not believe His wonderful works.
He made their days end in futility.

PSALM 78:18,21-32

Related texts: NUMBERS 11; PSALM 106:1-15; LUKE 4:1-13;
JAMES 4:1-4

Israel Rejects the Promised Land

The LORD spoke to Moses: "Send men to scout out the land of Canaan I am giving to the Israelites. Send one man who is a leader among them from each of their ancestral tribes."

The men went back to Moses, Aaron, and the entire Israelite community in the Wilderness of Paran at Kadesh. They brought back a report for them and the whole community, and they showed them the fruit of the land. They reported to Moses: "We went into the land where you sent us. Indeed it is flowing with milk and honey, and here is some of its fruit. However, the people living in the land are strong, and the cities are large and fortified. We also saw the descendants of Anak there."

Then Caleb quieted the people in the presence of Moses and said, "We must go up and take possession of the land because we can certainly conquer it!"

But the men who had gone up with him responded, "We can't go up against the people because they are stronger than we are!"

Then the whole community broke into loud cries, and the people wept that night. All the Israelites complained about Moses and Aaron, and the whole community told them, "If only we had died in the land of Egypt, or if only we had died in this wilderness! Why is the LORD bringing us into this land to die by the sword? Our wives and little children will become plunder. Wouldn't it be better for us to go back to Egypt?" So they said to one another, "Let's appoint a leader and go back to Egypt."

NUMBERS 13:1-2,26-28a,30-31; 14:1-4

Related texts: DEUTERONOMY 1:19-33; PSALM 106:24-27; PROVERBS 29:25; PHILIPPIANS 2:12-16

Forty Years in the Desert

Then Moses and Aaron fell down with their faces to the ground in front of the whole assembly of the Israelite community. Joshua son of Nun and Caleb son of Jephunneh, who were among those who scouted out the land, tore their clothes and said to the entire Israelite community: "The land we passed through and explored is an extremely good land. If the LORD is pleased with us, He will bring us into this land, a land flowing with milk and honey, and give it to us. Only don't rebel against the LORD, and don't be afraid of the people of the land, for we will devour them. Their protection has been removed from them, and the LORD is with us. Don't be afraid of them!"

Then the LORD spoke to Moses and Aaron: "How long must I endure this evil community that keeps complaining about Me? I have heard the Israelites' complaints that they make against Me. Tell them: As surely as I live, declares the LORD, I will do to you exactly as I heard you say. Your corpses will fall in this wilderness— all of you who were registered in the census, the entire number of you 20 years old or more—because you have complained about Me. I swear that none of you will enter the land I promised to settle you in, except Caleb son of Jephunneh and Joshua son of Nun.

"You will bear the consequences of your sins 40 years based on the number of the 40 days that you scouted the land, a year for each day. You will know My displeasure."

What then are we to say about these things? If God is for us, who is against us?

NUMBERS 14:5-9,26-30,34; ROMANS 8:31

Related texts: JOSHUA 5:1-6; JOHN 6:48-51; 1 CORINTHIANS 10:1-6; HEBREWS 3:7—4:7

Listen to God's Voice

Therefore, as the Holy Spirit says:
Today, if you hear His voice,
do not harden your hearts as in the rebellion,
on the day of testing in the desert,
where your fathers tested Me, tried Me,
and saw My works for 40 years.
Therefore I was provoked with this generation
and said, "They always go astray in their hearts,
and they have not known My ways."
So I swore in My anger,
"They will not enter My rest."

Watch out, brothers, so that there won't be in any of you an evil, unbelieving heart that departs from the living God. But encourage each other daily, while it is still called today, so that none of you is hardened by sin's deception. For we have become companions of the Messiah if we hold firmly until the end the reality that we had at the start. As it is said:

Today, if you hear His voice,
do not harden your hearts as in the rebellion.

For who heard and rebelled? Wasn't it really all who came out of Egypt under Moses? And with whom was He "provoked for 40 years"? Was it not with those who sinned, whose bodies fell in the desert? And to whom did He "swear that they would not enter His rest," if not those who disobeyed? So we see that they were unable to enter because of unbelief.

HEBREWS 3:7-19

Related texts: PSALM 95; MATTHEW 17:1-5; JOHN 14:15-24; ACTS 3:19-23; HEBREWS 4

God Crushes Rebellion

Now Korah son of Izhar, son of Kohath, son of Levi, with Dathan and Abiram, sons of Eliab, and On son of Peleth, sons of Reuben, took 250 prominent Israelite men who were leaders of the community and representatives in the assembly, and they rebelled against Moses. They came together against Moses and Aaron and told them, "You have gone too far! Everyone in the entire community is holy, and the LORD is among them. Why then do you exalt yourselves above the LORD's assembly?"

When Moses heard this, he fell facedown. Then he said to Korah and all his followers, "Tomorrow morning the LORD will reveal who belongs to Him, who is set apart, and the one He will let come near Him. He will let the one He chooses come near Him. Korah, you and all your followers are to do this: take firepans, and tomorrow place fire in them and put incense on them before the LORD. Then the man the LORD chooses will be the one who is set apart. It is you Levites who have gone too far!"

After Korah assembled the whole community against them at the entrance to the tent of meeting, the glory of the LORD appeared to the whole community. The earth opened its mouth and swallowed them and their households, all Korah's people, and all their possessions. They went down alive into Sheol with all that belonged to them. The earth closed over them, and they vanished from the assembly.

NUMBERS 16:1-7,19,32-33

Related texts: PSALM 106:16-17; HEBREWS 10:26-31; 12:23-29; 2 PETER 1:16–2:22; JUDE 11

Moses Disobeys God

The entire Israelite community entered the Wilderness of Zin in the first month, and they settled in Kadesh. Miriam died and was buried there.

There was no water for the community, so they assembled against Moses and Aaron. The people quarreled with Moses and said, "If only we had perished when our brothers perished before the LORD."

Then Moses and Aaron went from the presence of the assembly to the doorway of the tent of meeting. They fell down with their faces to the ground, and the glory of the LORD appeared to them. The LORD spoke to Moses, "Take the staff and assemble the community. You and your brother Aaron are to speak to the rock while they watch, and it will yield its water. You will bring out water for them from the rock and provide drink for the community and their livestock."

So Moses took the staff from the LORD's presence just as He had commanded him. Moses and Aaron summoned the assembly in front of the rock, and Moses said to them, "Listen, you rebels! Must we bring water out of this rock for you?" Then Moses raised his hand and struck the rock twice with his staff, so that a great amount of water gushed out, and the community and their livestock drank.

But the LORD said to Moses and Aaron, "Because you did not trust Me to show My holiness in the sight of the Israelites, you will not bring this assembly into the land I have given them."

NUMBERS 20:1-3,6-12

Related texts: EXODUS 7:19-21; 8:16-17; 17:1-6; DEUTERONOMY 4:20-22; ACTS 5:1-11

Look Up and Live

Then they set out from Mount Hor by way of the Red Sea to bypass the land of Edom, but the people became impatient because of the journey. The people spoke against God and Moses: "Why have you led us up from Egypt to die in the wilderness? There is no bread or water, and we detest this wretched food!" Then the LORD sent poisonous snakes among the people, and they bit them so that many Israelites died.

The people then came to Moses and said, "We have sinned by speaking against the LORD and against you. Intercede with the LORD so that He will take the snakes away from us." And Moses interceded for the people.

Then the LORD said to Moses, "Make a snake image and mount it on a pole. When anyone who is bitten looks at it, he will recover. So Moses made a bronze snake and mounted it on a pole. Whenever someone was bitten, and he looked at the bronze snake, he recovered.

Just as Moses lifted up the serpent in the wilderness, so the Son of Man must be lifted up, so that everyone who believes in Him will have eternal life.

"For God loved the world in this way: He gave His One and Only Son, so that everyone who believes in Him will not perish but have eternal life. For God did not send His Son into the world that He might judge the world, but that the world might be saved through Him."

NUMBERS 21:4-9; JOHN 3:14-17

Related texts: EXODUS 16:6-12; NUMBERS 14:26-37; 2 KINGS
18:1-4; LAMENTATIONS 3:25-40; 1 CORINTHIANS 10:1-11

Balaam Hired to Curse Israel

The Israelites traveled on and camped in the plains of Moab near the Jordan across from Jericho. Now Balak son of Zippor saw all that Israel had done to the Amorites. Moab was terrified of the people because they were numerous, and dreaded the Israelites.

Since Balak son of Zippor was Moab's king at that time, he sent messengers to Balaam son of Beor at Pethor, which is by the Euphrates in the land of his people. Balak said to him: "Look, a people has come out of Egypt; they cover the surface of the land and are living right across from me. Please come and put a curse on these people for me because they are more powerful than I am. I may be able to defeat them and drive them out of the land, for I know that those you bless are blessed and those you curse are cursed."

No Ammonite or Moabite may enter the LORD's assembly; none of their descendants, even to the tenth generation, may ever enter the LORD's assembly. This is because they did not meet you with food and water on the journey after you came out of Egypt, and because Balaam son of Beor from Pethor in Aram-naharaim was hired to curse you. Yet the LORD your God would not listen to Balaam, but He turned the curse into a blessing for you because the LORD your God loves you.

NUMBERS 22:1-3,4b-6; DEUTERONOMY 23:3-5

Related texts: GENESIS 12:1-3; NUMBERS 22–24; JOSHUA 24:8-10; 2 PETER 2:15-16

*This Bible is for the government
of the people, by the people,
and for the people.*

John Wycliffe (1328–1384)
ENGLISH THEOLOGIAN

*The more this Bible enters
into our national life the
grander and purer and better
will that life become.*

David Josiah Brewer (1837–1910)
UNITED STATES SUPREME COURT JUSTICE

*It is impossible to rightly
govern the world without
God and the Bible.*

George Washington (1732–1799)
UNITED STATES PRESIDENT

Balaam Blesses Israel

When Balaam looked up and saw Israel encamped tribe by tribe, the Spirit of God descended on him, and he proclaimed his poem:
The oracle of Balaam son of Beor,
the oracle of the man whose eyes are opened,
the oracle of one who hears the sayings of God,
who sees a vision from the Almighty,
who falls into a trance with his eyes uncovered:
How beautiful are your tents, Jacob,
your dwellings, Israel.
they stretch out like river valleys,
like gardens beside a stream,
like aloes the LORD has planted,
like cedars beside the water.
Water will flow from his buckets,
and his seed will be by abundant water.
His king will be greater than Agag,
and his kingdom will be exalted.
God brought him out of Egypt;
He is like the horns of a wild ox for them.
He will feed on enemy nations
and gnaw their bones;
he will strike them with his arrows.
He crouches, he lies down like a lion
or a lioness—who dares to rouse him?
Those who bless you will be blessed,
and those who curse you will be cursed.

NUMBERS 24:2-9

Related texts: GENESIS 12:1-3; 22:15-18; 27:26-29; DEUTERO-
NOMY 23:3-5; JOSHUA 13:22; 24:8-10; REVELATION 2:12-14

Judgment for Immorality

While Israel was staying in Acacia Grove, the people began to have sexual relations with the women of Moab. The women invited them to the sacrifices for their gods, and the people ate and bowed in worship to their gods. So Israel aligned itself with Baal of Peor, and the Lord's anger burned against Israel. The Lord said to Moses, "Take all the leaders of the people and execute them in broad daylight before the Lord so that His burning anger may turn away from Israel."

So Moses told Israel's judges, "Kill each of the men who aligned themselves with Baal of Peor."

An Israelite man came bringing a Midianite woman to his relatives in the sight of Moses and the whole Israelite community while they were weeping at the entrance to the tent of meeting. When Phinehas son of Eleazar, son of Aaron the priest, saw this, he got up from the assembly, took a spear in his hand, followed the Israelite man into the tent, and drove it through both the Israelite man and the woman—through her belly. Then the plague on the Israelites was stopped, but those who died in the plague numbered 24,000.

Flee from sexual immorality! "Every sin a person can commit is outside the body," but the person who is sexually immoral sins against his own body. Do you not know that your body is a sanctuary of the Holy Spirit who is in you, whom you have from God? You are not your own, for you were bought at a price; therefore glorify God in your body.

NUMBERS 25:1-9; 1 CORINTHIANS 6:18-20

Related texts: DEUTERONOMY 4:1-4; JOSHUA 22:16-20; PSALM 106:28-31; HOSEA 9:10; 1 CORINTHIANS 10:1-8

Vengeance Against Midian

The Lord spoke to Moses, "Execute vengeance for the Israelites against the Midianites. After that, you will be gathered to your people."

So Moses spoke to the people, "Equip some of your men for war. They will go against Midian to inflict the Lord's vengeance on them. Send 1,000 men to war from each Israelite tribe." So 1,000 were recruited from each Israelite tribe out of the thousands in Israel— 12,000 equipped for war.

They waged war against Midian, as the Lord had commanded Moses, and killed every male. Along with the others slain by them, they killed the Midianite kings—Evi, Rekem, Zur, Hur, and Reba, the five kings of Midian. They also killed Balaam son of Beor with the sword. The Israelites took the Midianite women and their children captive, and they plundered all their cattle, flocks, and property. Then they burned all the cities where the Midianites lived, as well as all their encampments.

Moses, Eleazar the priest, and all the leaders of the community went to meet them outside the camp. But Moses became furious with the officers, the commanders of thousands and commanders of hundreds, who were returning from the military campaign. "Have you let every female live?" he asked them. "Yet they are the ones who, at Balaam's advice, incited the Israelites to unfaithfulness against the Lord in the Peor incident, so that the plague came against the Lord's community."

NUMBERS 31:1-5,7-10,13-16

Related texts: NUMBERS 25; DEUTERONOMY 21:10-14; JOSHUA 13:16-22; JUDGES 6–8; ROMANS 12:16-21

Love the LORD Your God

This is the command—the statutes and ordinances—the LORD your God has instructed me to teach you, so that you may follow them in the land you are about to enter and possess. Do this so that you may fear the LORD your God all the days of your life by keeping all His statutes and commands I am giving you, your son, and your grandson, and so that you may have a long life. Listen, Israel, and be careful to follow them, so that you may prosper and multiply greatly, because the LORD, the God of your fathers, has promised you a land flowing with milk and honey.

Listen, Israel: The LORD our God, the LORD is One. Love the LORD your God with all your heart, with all your soul, and with all your strength. These words that I am giving you today are to be in your heart. Repeat them to your children. Talk about them when you sit in your house and when you walk along the road, when you lie down and when you get up. Bind them as a sign on your hand and let them be a symbol on your forehead. Write them on the doorposts of your house and on your gates.

How I love Your teaching!
It is my meditation all day long.

DEUTERONOMY 6:1-9; PSALM 119:97

Related texts: Deuteronomy 10:12-16; 11:18-21; Psalms 1; 119; Proverbs 22:6; Mark 12:28-34; Luke 10:25-28; 1 John 5:1-4

Joshua Succeeds Moses

Then Moses continued to speak these words to all Israel, saying, "I am now 120 years old; I can no longer act as your leader. The LORD has told me, 'You will not cross this Jordan.' The LORD your God is the One who will cross ahead of you. He will destroy these nations before you, and you will drive them out. Joshua is the one who will cross ahead of you, as the LORD has said. The LORD will deal with them as He did Sihon and Og, the kings of the Amorites, and their land when He destroyed them. The LORD will deliver them over to you, and you must do to them exactly as I have commanded you. Be strong and courageous; don't be terrified or afraid of them. For it is the LORD your God who goes with you; He will not leave you or forsake you."

Moses then summoned Joshua and said to him in the sight of all Israel, "Be strong and courageous, for you will go with this people into the land the LORD swore to give to their fathers. You will enable them to take possession of it. The LORD is the One who will go before you. He will be with you; He will not leave you or forsake you. Do not be afraid or discouraged."

Moses wrote down this law and gave it to the priests, the sons of Levi, who carried the ark of the LORD's covenant, and to all the elders of Israel.

DEUTERONOMY 31:1-9

Related texts: NUMBERS 21:21-35; DEUTERONOMY 2:24–3:17; 1 KINGS 8:54-57; HEBREWS 13:5-6

Be Strong and Courageous

After the death of Moses the LORD's servant, the LORD spoke to Joshua son of Nun, who had served Moses: "Moses My servant is dead. Now you and all the people prepare to cross over the Jordan to the land I am giving the Israelites. I have given you every place where the sole of your foot treads, just as I promised Moses. Your territory will be from the wilderness and Lebanon to the great Euphrates River—all the land of the Hittites—and west to the Mediterranean Sea. No one will be able to stand against you as long as you live. I will be with you, just as I was with Moses. I will not leave you or forsake you.

"Be strong and courageous, for you will distribute the land I swore to their fathers to give them as an inheritance. Above all, be strong and very courageous to carefully observe the whole instruction My servant Moses commanded you. Do not turn from it to the right or the left, so that you will have success wherever you go. This book of instruction must not depart from your mouth; you are to recite it day and night, so that you may carefully observe everything written in it. For then you will prosper and succeed in whatever you do. Haven't I commanded you: be strong and courageous? Do not be afraid or discouraged, for the LORD your God is with you wherever you go."

JOSHUA 1:1-9

Related texts: DEUTERONOMY 11:22-25; PSALMS 1; 119; 1 CORINTHIANS 16:13-14; HEBREWS 3:1-6

Rahab Hides the Israelite Spies

Joshua son of Nun secretly sent two men as spies from Acacia Grove, saying, "Go and scout the land, especially Jericho." So they left, and they came to the house of a woman, a prostitute named Rahab, and stayed there.

The king of Jericho was told, "Look, some of the Israelite men have come here tonight to investigate the land." Then the king of Jericho sent word to Rahab and said, "Bring out the men who came to you and entered your house, for they came to investigate the entire land."

But the woman had taken the two men and hidden them. So she said, "Yes, the men did come to me, but I didn't know where they were from. At nightfall, when the gate was about to close, the men went out, and I don't know where they were going. Chase after them quickly, and you can catch up with them!" But she had taken them up to the roof and hidden them among the stalks of flax that she had arranged on the roof.

So the two men went into the hill country and stayed there three days until the pursuers had returned. They searched all along the way, but did not find them. Then the men returned, came down from the hill country, and crossed the Jordan. They went to Joshua son of Nun and reported everything that had happened to them. They told Joshua, "The LORD has handed over the entire land to us. Everyone who lives in the land is also panicking because of us."

JOSHUA 2:1-6,22-24

Related texts: MATTHEW 1:1-6; HEBREWS 11:31; JAMES 2:25

The Israelites Conquer Jericho

Now Jericho was strongly fortified because of the Israelites—no one leaving or entering. The LORD said to Joshua, "Look, I have handed Jericho, its king, and its fighting men over to you. March around the city with all the men of war, circling the city one time. Do this for six days. Have seven priests carry seven ram's-horn trumpets in front of the ark. But on the seventh day, march around the city seven times, while the priests blow the trumpets. When there is a prolonged blast of the horn and you hear its sound, have all the people give a mighty shout. Then the city wall will collapse, and the people will advance, each man straight ahead."

So the people shouted, and the trumpets sounded. When they heard the blast of the trumpet, the people gave a great shout, and the wall collapsed. The people advanced into the city, each man straight ahead, and they captured the city. They completely destroyed everything in the city with the sword—every man and woman, both young and old, and every ox, sheep, and donkey.

But Joshua spared Rahab the prostitute, her father's household, and all who belonged to her, because she hid the men Joshua had sent to spy on Jericho, and she lives in Israel to this day.

JOSHUA 6:1-5,20-21,25

Related texts: NUMBERS 10:1-10; JUDGES 7:1-22; MATTHEW 1:1-6

Joshua Conquers the Land of Canaan

Just as the LORD had commanded His servant Moses, Moses commanded Joshua. That is what Joshua did, leaving nothing undone of all that the LORD had commanded Moses.

So Joshua took all this land—the hill country, all the Negev, all the land of Goshen, the Judean foothills, the plain, and the hill country of Israel with its Judean foothills—from Mount Halak, which ascends to Seir, as far as Baal-gad in the Valley of Lebanon at the foot of Mount Hermon. He captured all their kings and struck them down, putting them to death. Joshua waged war with all these kings for a long time. No city made peace with the Israelites except the Hivites who inhabited Gibeon; all of them were taken in battle. For it was the LORD's intention to harden their hearts, so that they would engage Israel in battle, be completely destroyed without mercy, and be annihilated, just as the LORD had commanded Moses.

So Joshua took the entire land, in keeping with all that the LORD had told Moses. Joshua then gave it as an inheritance to Israel according to their tribal allotments. After this, the land had rest from war.

JOSHUA 11:15-20,23

Related texts: DEUTERONOMY 7; 9:1-6; 18:9-14; 20:16-18;
JOSHUA 7–10

Joshua's Farewell Address

"Therefore, fear the LORD and worship Him in sincerity and truth. Get rid of the gods your ancestors worshiped beyond the Euphrates River and in Egypt, and worship the LORD. But if it doesn't please you to worship the LORD, choose for yourselves today the one you will worship: the gods your fathers worshiped beyond the Euphrates River, or the gods of the Amorites in whose land you are living. As for me and my family, we will worship the LORD."

The people replied, "We will certainly not abandon the LORD to worship other gods! For the LORD our God brought us and our fathers out of the land of Egypt, the place of slavery and performed these great signs before our eyes. He also protected us all along the way we went and among all the peoples whose lands we traveled through. The LORD drove out before us all the peoples, including the Amorites who lived in the land. We too will worship the LORD, because He is our God."

But Joshua told the people, "You will not be able to worship the LORD, because He is a holy God. He is a jealous God; He will not remove your transgressions and sins. If you abandon the LORD and worship foreign gods, He will turn against you, harm you, and completely destroy you, after He has been good to you."

"No!" the people answered Joshua. "We will worship the LORD."

JOSHUA 24:14-21

Related texts: EXODUS 24:3-8; LEVITICUS 26; ROMANS 6; HEBREWS 3–4

The Days of the Judges

The people worshiped the LORD throughout Joshua's lifetime and during the lifetimes of the elders who out-lived Joshua. They had seen all the LORD's great works He had done for Israel.

That whole generation was also gathered to their ancestors. After them another generation rose up who did not know the LORD or the works He had done for Israel. The Israelites did what was evil in the LORD's sight. They worshiped the Baals.

The Lord's anger burned against Israel, and He handed them over to marauders who raided them. He sold them to the enemies around them, so that they could no longer resist their enemies. Whenever the Israelites went out, the LORD was against them and brought disaster on them, just as He had promised and sworn to them. So they suffered greatly.

The LORD raised up judges, who saved them from the power of their marauders. Whenever the LORD raised up a judge for the Israelites, the LORD was with him and saved the people from the power of their ene-mies while the judge was still alive. The LORD was moved to pity whenever they groaned because of those who were oppressing and afflicting them. Whenever the judge died, the Israelites would act even more corruptly than their fathers, going after other gods to worship and bow down to them. They did not turn from their evil practices or their obstinate ways.

JUDGES 2:7,10-11,14-16,18-19

Related texts: DEUTERONOMY 4:1-10; 11:18-25; JUDGES 2:19-3:31; PSALM 78:1-6; EPHESIANS 2:1-10

Deborah: Prophetess and Judge

The Israelites again did what was evil in the sight of the LORD after Ehud had died. So the LORD sold them into the hand of Jabin king of Canaan, who reigned in Hazor. The commander of his forces was Sisera who lived in Harosheth of the Nations. Then the Israelites cried out to the LORD, because Jabin had 900 iron chariots, and he harshly oppressed them 20 years.

Deborah, a woman who was a prophet and the wife of Lappidoth, was judging Israel at that time. It was her custom to sit under the palm tree of Deborah between Ramah and Bethel in the hill country of Ephraim, and the Israelites went up to her for judgment.

She summoned Barak son of Abinoam from Kedesh in Naphtali and said to him, "Hasn't the LORD, the God of Israel, commanded you: 'Go, deploy the troops on Mount Tabor, and take with you 10,000 men from the Naphtalites and Zebulunites? Then I will lure Sisera commander of Jabin's forces, his chariots, and his army at the Wadi Kishon to fight against you, and I will hand him over to you.' "

Barak said to her, "If you will go with me, I will go. But if you will not go with me, I will not go."

"I will go with you," she said, "but you will receive no honor on the road you are about to take, because the LORD will sell Sisera into a woman's hand." So Deborah got up and went with Barak to Kedesh.

JUDGES 4:1-9a

Related texts: EXODUS 15:19-21; JUDGES 5:1-12; 2 KINGS 22:11-20; 2 CHRONICLES 34:19-28; LUKE 2:21-38

Jael Kills the Canaanite General

Then Deborah said to Barak, "Move on, for this is the day the LORD has handed Sisera over to you. Hasn't the LORD gone before you?" So Barak came down from Mount Tabor with 10,000 men following him.

The LORD threw Sisera, all his charioteers, and all his army into confusion before Barak. Sisera left his chariot and fled on foot. Barak pursued the chariots and the army as far as Harosheth of the Nations, and the whole army of Sisera fell by the sword; not a single man was left.

Meanwhile, Sisera had fled on foot to the tent of Jael, the wife of Heber the Kenite, because there was peace between Jabin king of Hazor and the family of Heber the Kenite. Jael went out to greet Sisera and said to him, "Come in, my lord. Come in with me. Don't be afraid." So he went into her tent, and she covered him with a rug. He said to her, "Please give me a little water to drink for I am thirsty." She opened a container of milk, gave him a drink, and covered him again. Then he said to her, "Stand at the entrance to the tent. If a man comes and asks you, 'Is there a man here?,' say, 'No.' " While he was sleeping from exhaustion, Heber's wife Jael took a tent peg, grabbed a hammer, and went silently to Sisera. She hammered the peg into his temple and drove it into the ground, and he died.

JUDGES 4:14-21

Related texts: JUDGES 3:12-30; 5:13-31; 1 SAMUEL 12:8-11;
HEBREWS 11:32-34

The Birth of Samson the Strongman

The Israelites again did what was evil in the LORD's sight, so the LORD handed them over to the Philistines 40 years. There was a certain man from Zorah, from the family of Dan, whose name was Manoah; his wife was barren and had no children. The Angel of the LORD appeared to the woman and said to her, "It is true that you are barren and have no children, but you will conceive and give birth to a son. Now please be careful not to drink wine or other alcoholic beverages, or to eat anything unclean; for indeed, you will conceive and give birth to a son. You must never cut his hair, because the boy will be a Nazirite to God from birth, and he will begin to save Israel from the power of the Philistines."

So the woman gave birth to a son and named him Samson. The boy grew, and the LORD blessed him. Then the Spirit of the LORD began to direct him in the Camp of Dan, between Zorah and Eshtaol.

And he judged Israel 20 years in the days of the Philistines.

JUDGES 13:1-5,24-25; 15:20

Related texts: GENESIS 25:21-24; NUMBERS 6:1-21; JUDGES 14–15; LUKE 1

Samson and Delilah

Samson went to Gaza, where he saw a prostitute and went to bed with her. When the Gazites heard that Samson was there, they surrounded the place and waited in ambush for him all that night at the city gate. While they were waiting quietly, they said, "Let us wait until dawn; then we will kill him." But Samson stayed in bed until midnight when he got up, took hold of the doors of the city gate along with the two gateposts, and pulled them out, bar and all. He put them on his shoulders and took them to the top of the mountain overlooking Hebron. Some time later, he fell in love with a woman named Delilah, who lived in the Sorek Valley. The Philistine leaders went to her and said, "Persuade him to tell you where his great strength comes from, so we can overpower him, tie him up, and make him helpless. Each of us will then give you 1,100 pieces of silver."

So Delilah said to Samson, "Please tell me, where does your great strength come from? How could someone tie you up and make you helpless?"

Samson told her, "If they tie me up with seven fresh bowstrings that have not been dried, I will become weak and be like any other man."

The Philistine leaders brought her seven fresh bowstrings that had not been dried, and she tied him up with them. While the men in ambush were waiting in her room, she called out to him, "Samson, the Philistines are here!" But he snapped the bowstrings as a strand of yarn snaps when it touches fire. The secret of his strength remained unknown.

JUDGES 16:1-9

JUDGES 14–15; PROVERBS 5; 6:20–7:27; 31:1-3; 2 TIMOTHY 2:20-23

The Philistines Blind Samson

"How can you say, 'I love you,' " she told him, "when your heart is not with me? This is the third time you have mocked me and not told me what makes your strength so great!"

Because she nagged him day after day and pled with him until she wore him out, he told her the whole truth and said to her, "My hair has never been cut, because I am a Nazirite to God from birth. If I am shaved, my strength will leave me, and I will become weak and be like any other man."

When Delilah realized that he had told her the whole truth, she sent this message to the Philistine leaders: "Come one more time, for he has told me the whole truth." The Philistine leaders came to her and brought the money with them.

Then she let him fall asleep on her lap and called a man to shave off the seven braids on his head. In this way, she rendered him helpless, and his strength left him. Then she cried, "Samson, the Philistines are here!" When he awoke from his sleep, he said, "I will escape as I did before and shake myself free." But he did not know that the Lord had left him.

The Philistines seized him and gouged out his eyes. They brought him down to Gaza and bound him with bronze shackles, and he was forced to grind grain in the prison.

JUDGES 16:15-21

Related texts: NUMBERS 6:2-21; 30:1-2; PROVERBS 11:13; 20:19; ECCLESIASTES 5:4-6; LUKE 12:47-48

Samson's Revenge

Now the Philistine leaders gathered together to offer a great sacrifice to their god Dagon. They rejoiced and said:

Our god has handed over our enemy Samson to us.

When they were drunk, they said, "Bring Samson here to entertain us." So they brought Samson from prison, and he entertained them. They had him stand between the pillars.

Samson said to the young man who was leading him by the hand, "Lead me where I can feel the pillars supporting the temple, so I can lean against them." The temple was full of men and women; all the leaders of the Philistines were there, and about 3,000 men and women were on the roof watching Samson entertain them. He called out to the LORD: "Lord GOD, please remember me. Strengthen me, God, just once more. With one act of vengeance, let me pay back the Philistines for my two eyes." 29 Samson took hold of the two middle pillars supporting the temple and leaned against them, one on his right hand and the other on his left. 30 Samson said, "Let me die with the Philistines." He pushed with all his might, and the temple fell on the leaders and all the people in it. And the dead he killed at his death were more than those he had killed in his life.

JUDGES 16:23,25-30

Related texts: PSALM 3; ISAIAH 1:24; JEREMIAH 5:7-9,29; 9:9; HEBREWS 11:32-34

Naomi and Ruth: Love and Loyalty

During the time of the judges, there was a famine in the land. A man left Bethlehem in Judah with his wife and two sons to live in the land of Moab for a while. The man's name was Elimelech, and his wife's name was Naomi. The names of his two sons were Mahlon and Chilion.

Naomi's husband Elimelech died, and she was left with her two sons. Her sons took Moabite women as their wives: one was named Orpah and the second was named Ruth. After they lived in Moab about 10 years, both Mahlon and Chilion also died, and Naomi was left without her two children and without her husband.

She said to them, "Each of you go back to your mother's home. May the Lord show faithful love to you as you have shown to the dead and to me. May the Lord enable each of you to find security in the house of your new husband."

But Ruth replied:

> Do not persuade me to leave you
> or go back and not follow you.
> For wherever you go, I will go,
> and wherever you live, I will live;
> your people will be my people,
> and your God will be my God.
> Where you die, I will die,
> and there I will be buried.
> May the Lord do this to me,
> and even more,
> if anything but death separates you and me.

So Naomi came back from the land of Moab with her daughter-in-law Ruth the Moabitess. They arrived in Bethlehem at the beginning of the barley harvest.

RUTH 1:1-2a,3-5,8-9a,16-17,22

Related texts: 2 SAMUEL 3:14-16; PROVERBS 20:6; SONG OF SONGS 8:6-7; 1 CORINTHIANS 13

Ruth Meets Boaz

Now Naomi had a relative on her husband's side named Boaz. He was a prominent man of noble character from Elimelech's family.

Ruth the Moabitess asked Naomi, "Will you let me go into the fields and gather fallen grain behind someone who allows me to?"

Naomi answered her, "Go ahead, my daughter." So Ruth left and entered the field to gather grain behind the harvesters. She happened to be in the portion of land belonging to Boaz, who was from Elimelech's family.

Then Boaz said to Ruth, "Listen, my daughter. Don't go and gather grain in another field, and don't leave this one, but stay here close to my young women."

She bowed with her face to the ground and said to him, "Why are you so kind to notice me, although I am a foreigner?"

Boaz answered her, "Everything you have done for your mother-in-law since your husband's death has been fully reported to me: how you left your father and mother, and the land of your birth, and how you came to a people you didn't previously know. May the LORD reward you for what you have done, and may you receive a full reward from the LORD God of Israel, under whose wings you have come for refuge."

RUTH 2:1-3,8,10-12

Related texts: LEVITICUS 25:25-27; PSALM 91; JEREMIAH 32:6-14

Ruth Proposes Marriage to Boaz

Ruth's mother-in-law Naomi said to her, "My daughter, shouldn't I find security for you, so that you will be taken care of? Now isn't Boaz our relative? Haven't you been working with his young women? This evening he will be winnowing barley on the threshing floor. Wash, put on perfumed oil, and wear your best clothes. Go down to the threshing floor, but don't let the man know you are there until he has finished eating and drinking. When he lies down, notice the place where he's lying, go in and uncover his feet, and lie down. Then he will explain to you what you should do."

After Boaz ate, drank, and was in good spirits, he went to lie down at the end of the pile of barley. Then she went in secretly, uncovered his feet, and lay down.

At midnight, Boaz was startled, turned over, and there lying at his feet was a woman! So he asked, "Who are you?"

"I am Ruth, your slave," she replied. "Spread your cloak over me, for you are a family redeemer."

Then he said, "May the LORD bless you, my daughter. You have shown more kindness now than before, because you have not pursued younger men, whether rich or poor. Now don't be afraid, my daughter. I will do for you whatever you say, since all the people in my town know that you are a woman of noble character."

RUTH 3:1-4,7-11

Related texts: GENESIS 38:8-10; DEUTERONOMY 25:5-10; HEBREWS 13:4

Ruth Marries Boaz

Boaz said to the elders and all the people, "You are witnesses today that I am buying from Naomi everything that belonged to Elimelech, Chilion, and Mahlon. I will also acquire Ruth the Moabitess, Mahlon's widow, as my wife, to perpetuate the deceased man's name on his property, so that his name will not disappear among his relatives or from the gate of his home. You are witnesses today."

The elders and all the people who were at the gate said, "We are witnesses. May the Lord make the woman who is entering your house like Rachel and Leah, who together built the house of Israel. May you be powerful in Ephrathah and famous in Bethlehem. May your house become like the house of Perez, the son Tamar bore to Judah, because of the offspring the Lord will give you by this young woman."

Boaz took Ruth and she became his wife. When he was intimate with her, the Lord enabled her to conceive, and she gave birth to a son. Then the women said to Naomi, "Praise the Lord, who has not left you without a family redeemer today. May his name be famous in Israel. He will renew your life and sustain you in your old age. Indeed, your daughter-in-law, who loves you and is better to you than seven sons, has given birth to him." Naomi took the child, placed him on her lap, and took care of him. The neighbor women said, "A son has been born to Naomi," and they named him Obed. He was the father of Jesse, the father of David.

RUTH 4:9-17

Related texts: GENESIS 29:31–30:4; 38; MICAH 5:2; MATTHEW 1:1-6

I AM: *The Bread of Life*

"Then what sign are You going to do so we may see and believe You?" they asked. "What are You going to perform? Our fathers ate the manna in the desert, just as it is written: He gave them bread from heaven to eat."

Jesus said to them, "I assure you: Moses didn't give you the bread from heaven, but My Father gives you the true bread from heaven. For the bread of God is the One who comes down from heaven and gives life to the world."

Then they said, "Sir, give us this bread always!"

"I am the bread of life," Jesus told them. "No one who comes to Me will ever be hungry, and no one who believes in Me will ever be thirsty again. But as I told you, you've seen Me, and yet you do not believe. Everyone the Father gives Me will come to Me, and the one who comes to Me I will never cast out. For I have come down from heaven, not to do My will, but the will of Him who sent Me. This is the will of Him who sent Me: that I should lose none of those He has given Me but should raise them up on the last day. For this is the will of My Father: that everyone who sees the Son and believes in Him may have eternal life, and I will raise him up on the last day."

JOHN 6:30-40

Related texts: DEUTERONOMY 8:2; PROVERBS 30:7-9; JOHN 6:25-29; 1 CORINTHIANS 10:16-17; REVELATION 2:17

I AM: *The Light of the World*

Then Jesus spoke to them again: "I am the light of the world. Anyone who follows Me will never walk in the darkness, but will have the light of life."

As He was passing by, He saw a man blind from birth. His disciples questioned Him: "Rabbi, who sinned, this man or his parents, that he was born blind?"

"Neither this man sinned nor his parents," Jesus answered. "This came about so that God's works might be displayed in him. We must do the works of Him who sent Me while it is day. Night is coming when no one can work. As long as I am in the world, I am the light of the world."

After He said these things He spit on the ground, made some mud from the saliva, and spread the mud on his eyes. "Go," He told him, "wash in the pool of Siloam" (which means "Sent"). So he left, washed, and came back seeing.

> In Him was life,
> and that life was the light of men.
> That light shines in the darkness,
> yet the darkness did not overcome it.

JOHN 8:12; 9:1-7; 1:4-5

I AM: *The Door for the Sheep*

[Jesus said,] "I assure you: Anyone who doesn't enter the sheep pen by the door, but climbs in some other way, is a thief and a robber. The one who enters by the door is the shepherd of the sheep. The doorkeeper opens it for him, and the sheep hear his voice. He calls his own sheep by name and leads them out. When he has brought all his own outside, he goes ahead of them. The sheep follow him because they recognize his voice. They will never follow a stranger; instead they will run away from him, because they don't recognize the voice of strangers."

Jesus gave them this illustration, but they did not understand what He was telling them.

So Jesus said again, "I assure you: I am the door of the sheep. All who came before Me are thieves and robbers, but the sheep didn't listen to them. I am the door. If anyone enters by Me, he will be saved, and will come in and go out and find pasture. A thief comes only to steal and to kill and to destroy. I have come that they may have life and have it in abundance."

JOHN 10:1-10

Related texts: PSALM 118:17-21; MATTHEW 7:13-14; 25:1-13; LUKE 13:23-29; JOHN 14

I AM: *The Good Shepherd*

[Jesus said,] "I am the good shepherd. The good shepherd lays down his life for the sheep. The hired man, since he's not the shepherd and doesn't own the sheep, leaves them and runs away when he sees a wolf coming. The wolf then snatches and scatters them. This happens because he is a hired man and doesn't care about the sheep.

"I am the good shepherd. I know My own sheep, and they know Me, as the Father knows Me, and I know the Father. I lay down My life for the sheep. But I have other sheep that are not of this fold; I must bring them also, and they will listen to My voice. Then there will be one flock, one shepherd. This is why the Father loves Me, because I am laying down My life that I may take it up again. No one takes it from Me, but I lay it down on My own. I have the right to lay it down, and I have the right to take it up again. I have received this command from My Father."

> He Himself bore our sins
> in His body on the tree,
> so that, having died to sins,
> we might live for righteousness;
> by **His wounding you have been healed.**
> For you **were like sheep going astray,**
> but you have now returned
> to the shepherd and guardian of your souls.

JOHN 10:11-18; 1 PETER 2:24-25

Related texts: PSALM 23; ISAIAH 40:10-11; ZECHARIAH 11:4-17; MATTHEW 25:31-46; LUKE 15:3-7; HEBREWS 13:20-21

I AM: *The Resurrection and the Life*

Now a man was sick, Lazarus, from Bethany, the village of Mary and her sister Martha.

When Jesus heard it, He said, "This sickness will not end in death, but is for the glory of God, so that the Son of God may be glorified through it."

When Jesus arrived, He found that Lazarus had already been in the tomb four days.

Then Martha said to Jesus, "Lord, if You had been here, my brother wouldn't have died. Yet even now I know that whatever You ask from God, God will give You."

"Your brother will rise again," Jesus told her.

Martha said, "I know that he will rise again in the resurrection at the last day."

Jesus said to her, "I am the resurrection and the life. The one who believes in Me, even if he dies, will live. Everyone who lives and believes in Me will never die— ever. Do you believe this?"

"Yes, Lord," she told Him, "I believe You are the Messiah, the Son of God, who was to come into the world."

After He said this, He shouted with a loud voice, "Lazarus, come out!" The dead man came out bound hand and foot with linen strips and with his face wrapped in a cloth. Jesus said to them, "Loose him and let him go."

JOHN 11:1,4,17,21-27,43-44

Related texts: DEUTERONOMY 32:39; JOHN 5:19-26; ROMANS 5–6; 2 TIMOTHY 1:8-10; 1 JOHN 1:1-3

I AM: *The Way and the Truth and the Life*

[Jesus said,] "Your heart must not be troubled. Believe in God; believe also in Me. In My Father's house are many dwelling places; if not, I would have told you. I am going away to prepare a place for you. If I go away and prepare a place for you, I will come back and receive you to Myself, so that where I am you may be also. You know the way where I am going."

"Lord," Thomas said, "we don't know where You're going. How can we know the way?"

Jesus told him, "I am the way, the truth, and the life. No one comes to the Father except through Me.

"If you know Me, you will also know My Father. From now on you do know Him and have seen Him."

"Lord," said Philip, "show us the Father, and that's enough for us."

Jesus said to him, "Have I been among you all this time without your knowing Me, Philip? The one who has seen Me has seen the Father.

JOHN 14:1-9a

Related texts: PSALM 96; JOHN 1:1-18; 3:13-16; HEBREWS 10:19-22

I AM: *The True Vine*

[Jesus said,] "I am the true vine, and My Father is the vineyard keeper. Every branch in Me that does not produce fruit He removes, and He prunes every branch that produces fruit so that it will produce more fruit. You are already clean because of the word I have spoken to you. Remain in Me, and I in you. Just as a branch is unable to produce fruit by itself unless it remains on the vine, so neither can you unless you remain in Me.

"I am the vine; you are the branches. The one who remains in Me and I in him produces much fruit, because you can do nothing without Me. If anyone does not remain in Me, he is thrown aside like a branch and he withers. They gather them, throw them into the fire, and they are burned. If you remain in Me and My words remain in you, ask whatever you want and it will be done for you. My Father is glorified by this: that you produce much fruit and prove to be My disciples.

"Just as the Father has loved Me, I also have loved you. Remain in My love. If you keep My commandments you will remain in My love, just as I have kept My Father's commandments and remain in His love.

"I have spoken these things to you so that My joy may be in you and your joy may be complete."

JOHN 15:1-11

Related texts: PSALM 80:8-19; ISAIAH 5:1-7; 27:2-6; LUKE 6:43-45; GALATIANS 5:22-23; COLOSSIANS 1:3-12

Hannah Prays for a Son

There was a man from Ramathaim-zophim in the hill country of Ephraim. His name was Elkanah son of Jeroham, son of Elihu, son of Tohu, son of Zuph, an Ephraimite. He had two wives, the first named Hannah and the second Peninnah. Peninnah had children, but Hannah was childless. This man would go up from his town every year to worship and to sacrifice to the LORD of Hosts at Shiloh, where Eli's two sons, Hophni and Phinehas, were the LORD's priests.

Whenever Elkanah offered a sacrifice, he always gave portions of the meat to his wife Peninnah and to each of her sons and daughters. But he gave a double portion to Hannah, for he loved her even though the LORD had kept her from conceiving. Her rival would taunt her severely just to provoke her, because the LORD had kept Hannah from conceiving.

Deeply hurt, Hannah prayed to the LORD and wept with many tears. Making a vow, she pleaded, "LORD of Hosts, if You will take notice of Your servant's affliction, remember and not forget me, and give Your servant a son, I will give him to the LORD all the days of his life, and his hair will never be cut."

1 SAMUEL 1:1-6,10-11

Related texts: GENESIS 11:29-30; 25:21; 29:31; PSALM 113:9;   *227*
ISAIAH 54:1; LUKE 1:4-22; 23:28-30; HEBREWS 11:11

SAMUEL: *Hannah's Firstborn*

The next morning Elkanah and Hannah got up early to bow and to worship the LORD. Afterwards, they returned home to Ramah. Then Elkanah was intimate with his wife Hannah, and the LORD remembered her. After some time, Hannah conceived and gave birth to a son. She named him Samuel, because she said, "I requested him from the LORD."

When Elkanah and all his household went up to make the annual sacrifice and his vow offering to the LORD, Hannah did not go and explained to her husband, "After the child is weaned, I'll take him to appear in the LORD's presence and to stay there permanently." When she had weaned him, she took him with her to Shiloh, as well as a three-year-old bull, two and one-half gallons of flour, and a jar of wine. Though the boy was still young, she took him to the LORD's house at Shiloh. Then they slaughtered the bull and brought the boy to Eli.

"Please, my lord," she said, "as sure as you live, my lord, I am the woman who stood here beside you praying to the LORD. I prayed for this boy, and since the LORD gave me what I asked Him for, I now give the boy to the Lord. For as long as he lives, he is given to the LORD." Then he bowed and worshiped the Lord there.

1 SAMUEL 1:19-22,24-28

Related texts: GENESIS 8:1; 19:29; 30:22; EXODUS 2:24; LUKE 1:23-45; ACTS 10:25-31; REVELATION 16:19; 18:5

SAMUEL: *Prophet and Judge*

Eli's sons were wicked men; they had no regard for the LORD.

The boy Samuel served in the LORD's presence and wore a linen ephod. Each year his mother made him a little robe and took it to him when she went with her husband to offer the annual sacrifice. Eli would bless Elkanah and his wife: "May the LORD give you children by this woman in place of the one she has given to the LORD." Then they would go home.

The LORD paid attention to Hannah's need, and she conceived and gave birth to three sons and two daughters. Meanwhile, the boy Samuel grew up in the presence of the LORD.

Samuel grew, and the LORD was with him and let nothing he said prove false. All Israel from Dan to Beersheba knew that Samuel was a confirmed prophet of the LORD. The LORD continued to appear in Shiloh, because there He revealed Himself to Samuel by His word.

Samuel judged Israel throughout his life. Every year he would go on a circuit to Bethel, Gilgal, and Mizpah and would judge Israel at all these locations. Then he would return to Ramah because his home was there, he judged Israel there, and he had built an altar to the LORD there.

1 SAMUEL 2:12,18-21; 3:19-21; 7:15-17

Related texts: GENESIS 4:25-26; DEUTERONOMY 18:15-19; JOSHUA 21:45; LUKE 1:13-17

Sin will keep you from this Book.
This Book will keep you from sin.

Dwight L. Moody (1837–1899)
AMERICAN EVANGELIST

The Bible is the greatest benefit which
the human race has ever experienced.
A single line in the Bible has consoled
me more than all the books I ever
read besides.

Immanuel Kant (1724–1804)
GERMAN PHILOSOPHER

The Bible is the one Book to which
any thoughtful man may go with
any honest question of life or destiny
and find the answer of God by
honest searching.

John Ruskin (1819–1900)
ENGLISH AUTHOR, REFORMER

Israel Asks for a King

When Samuel grew old, he appointed his sons as judges over Israel. However, his sons did not walk in his ways—they turned toward dishonest gain, took bribes, and perverted justice.

So all the elders of Israel gathered together and went to Samuel at Ramah. They said to him, "Look, you are old, and your sons do not follow your example. Therefore, appoint a king to judge us the same as all the other nations have."

When they said, "Give us a king to judge us," Samuel considered their demand sinful, so he prayed to the LORD. But the LORD told him, "Listen to the people and everything they say to you. They have rejected you; they have rejected Me as their king. They are doing the same thing to you that they have done to Me, since the day I brought them out of Egypt until this day, abandoning Me and worshiping other gods. Listen to them, but you must solemnly warn them and tell them about the rights of the king who will rule over them."

Samuel told all the LORD's words to the people who were asking him for a king.

1 SAMUEL 8:1,3-10,19,19-22a

SAUL: *The First King of Israel*

Samuel summoned the people to the LORD at Mizpah and said to the Israelites, "This is what the LORD, the God of Israel, says: 'I brought Israel out of Egypt, and I rescued you from the power of the Egyptians and all the kingdoms that were oppressing you.' But today you have rejected your God, who saves you from all your troubles and afflictions. You said to Him, 'You must set a king over us.' Now therefore present yourselves before the LORD by your tribes and clans."

Samuel had all the tribes of Israel come forward, and the tribe of Benjamin was selected. Then he had the tribe of Benjamin come forward by its clans, and the Matrite clan was selected. Finally, Saul son of Kish was selected. But when they searched for him, they could not find him. They again inquired of the LORD, "Has the man come here yet?"

The LORD replied, "There he is, hidden among the supplies."

They ran and got him from there. When he stood among the people, he stood a head taller than anyone else. Samuel said to all the people, "Do you see the one the LORD has chosen? There is no one like him among the entire population."

And all the people shouted, "Long live the king!"

Samuel proclaimed to the people the rights of kingship. He wrote them on a scroll, which he placed in the presence of the LORD. Then, Samuel sent all the people away, each to his home.

1 SAMUEL 10:17-25

Related texts: DEUTERONOMY 17:14-20; 1 SAMUEL 9:1–10:16; 11–14; JOHN 12:12-15

The LORD Rejects Saul as King

Samuel told Saul, "The LORD sent me to anoint you as king over His people Israel. Now, listen to the words of the LORD. This is what the LORD of Hosts says: 'I witnessed what the Amalekites did to the Israelites when they opposed them along the way as they were coming out of Egypt. Now go and attack the Amalekites and completely destroy everything they have. Do not spare them. Kill men and women, children and infants, oxen and sheep, camels and donkeys.' "

Then Saul struck down the Amalekites from Havilah all the way to Shur, which is next to Egypt. Saul and the troops spared Agag, and the best of the sheep, cattle, and fatlings, as well as the young rams and the best of everything else. They were not willing to destroy them, but they did destroy all the worthless and unwanted things.

Then the word of the LORD came to Samuel: "I regret that I made Saul king, for he has turned away from following Me and has not carried out My instructions." So Samuel became angry and cried out to the LORD all night.

When Samuel came to him, Saul said, "May the LORD bless you. I have carried out the LORD's instructions."

Then Samuel said:

Does the LORD take pleasure in burnt offerings and
    sacrifices
as much as in obeying the LORD?
Look: to obey is better than sacrifice,
to pay attention is better than the fat of rams.
For rebellion is like the sin of divination,
and defiance is like wickedness and idolatry.
Because you have rejected the word of the LORD,
He has rejected you as king.

1 SAMUEL 15:1-3a,7,9-11a,13,22-23

Related texts: EXODUS 17:8-16: DEUTERONOMY 25:17-19;   *235*
MICAH 6:6-8; LUKE 16:10-13

Samuel Anoints David as King

The LORD said to Samuel, "How long are you going to mourn for Saul, since I have rejected him as king over Israel? Fill your horn with oil and go. I am sending you to Jesse of Bethlehem because I have selected a king from his sons."

When they arrived, Samuel saw Eliab and said, "Certainly the LORD's anointed one is here before Him."

But the LORD said to Samuel, "Do not look at his appearance or his stature, because I have rejected him. Man does not see what the LORD sees, for man sees what is visible, but the LORD sees the heart."

After Jesse presented seven of his sons to him, Samuel told Jesse, "The LORD hasn't chosen any of these." Samuel asked him, "Are these all the sons you have?"

"There is still the youngest," he answered, "but right now he's tending the sheep." Samuel told Jesse, "Send for him. We won't sit down to eat until he gets here." So Jesse sent for him. He had beautiful eyes and a healthy, handsome appearance.

Then the LORD said, "Anoint him, for he is the one." So Samuel took the horn of oil, anointed him in the presence of his brothers, and the Spirit of the LORD took control of David from that day forward.

1 SAMUEL 16:1,6-7,10-13a

Related texts: PSALM 78:70-72; MATTHEW 5:8; 12:33-35; LUKE 6:43-45; ACTS 13:21-23

Goliath Challenges the Armies of Israel

The Philistines gathered their forces for war at Socoh in Judah and camped between Socoh and Azekah in Ephes-dammim. Saul and the men of Israel gathered and camped in the Valley of Elah; then they lined up in battle formation to face the Philistines.

The Philistines were standing on one hill, and the Israelites were standing on another hill with a ravine between them. Then a champion named Goliath, from Gath, came out from the Philistine camp. He was nine feet, nine inches tall and wore a bronze helmet and bronze scale armor that weighed 125 pounds. There was bronze armor on his shins, and a bronze sword was slung between his shoulders. His spear shaft was like a weaver's beam, and the iron point of his spear weighed 15 pounds. In addition, a shield-bearer was walking in front of him.

He stood and shouted to the battle formations: "Why do you come out to line up in battle formation?" He asked them, "Am I not a Philistine and are you not servants of Saul? Choose one of your men and have him come down against me. If he wins in a fight against me and kills me, we will be your servants. But if I win against him and kill him, then you will be our servants and serve us." Then the Philistine said, "I defy the ranks of Israel today. Send me a man so we can fight each other!" When Saul and all Israel heard these words from the Philistine, they lost their courage and were terrified.

1 SAMUEL 17:1-11

Related texts: NUMBERS 13:26-33; DEUTERONOMY 11:22-25; PSALM 15; PROVERBS 14:27; 15:33; 29:25

David Accepts Goliath's Challenge

David said to Saul, "Don't let anyone be discouraged by him; your servant will go and fight this Philistine!"

But Saul replied, "You can't go fight this Philistine. You're just a youth, and he's been a warrior since he was young."

David answered Saul, "Your servant has been tending his father's sheep. Whenever a lion or a bear came and carried off a lamb from the flock, I went after it, struck it down, and rescued the lamb from its mouth. If it reared up against me, I would grab it by its fur, strike it down, and kill it. Your servant has killed lions and bears; this uncircumcised Philistine will be like one of them, for he has defied the armies of the living God." Then David said, "The LORD who rescued me from the paw of the lion and the paw of the bear will rescue me from the hand of this Philistine."

Saul said to David, "Go, and may the LORD be with you."

Instead, he took his staff in his hand and chose five smooth stones from the wadi and put them in the pouch, in his shepherd's bag. Then, with his sling in his hand, he approached the Philistine.

1 SAMUEL 17:32-37,40

Related texts: PSALMS 31:11-18; 97:10; 144; EPHESIANS 6:10-18; 1 TIMOTHY 4:12

David Kills Goliath

The Philistine came closer and closer to David, with the shield-bearer in front of him. When the Philistine looked and saw David, he despised him because he was just a youth, healthy and handsome. He said to David, "Am I a dog that you come against me with sticks?" Then he cursed David by his gods.

David said to the Philistine, "You come against me with a dagger, spear, and sword, but I come against you in the name of the LORD of Hosts, the God of Israel's armies—you have defied Him. Today, the LORD will hand you over to me. Today, I'll strike you down, cut your head off, and give the corpses of the Philistine camp to the birds of the sky and the creatures of the earth. Then all the world will know that Israel has a God, and this whole assembly will know that it is not by sword or by spear that the LORD saves, for the battle is the LORD's. He will hand you over to us."

When the Philistine started forward to attack him, David ran quickly to the battle line to meet the Philistine. David put his hand in the bag, took out a stone, slung it, and hit the Philistine on his forehead. The stone sank into his forehead, and he fell on his face to the ground. David defeated the Philistine with a sling and a stone. Even though David had no sword, he struck down the Philistine and killed him.

1 SAMUEL 17:41-43,45-50

Related texts: 2 SAMUEL 21:15-22; PSALM 27; HEBREWS 11:32-34

Saul Becomes Jealous of David

When David had finished speaking with Saul, Jonathan committed himself to David, and loved him as much as he loved himself. Saul kept David with him from that day on and did not let him return to his father's house.

Jonathan made a covenant with David because he loved him as much as himself. Then Jonathan removed the robe he was wearing and gave it to David, along with his military tunic, his sword, his bow, and his belt.

David marched out with the army, and was successful in everything Saul sent him to do. Saul put him in command of the soldiers, which pleased all the people and Saul's servants as well.

As David was returning from killing the Philistine, the women came out from all the cities of Israel to meet King Saul, singing and dancing with tambourines, with shouts of joy, and with three-stringed instruments. As they celebrated, the women sang:

>Saul has killed his thousands,
>but David his tens of thousands.

Saul was furious and resented this song. "They credited tens of thousands to David," he complained, "but they only credited me with thousands. What more can he have but the kingdom?" So Saul watched David jealously from that day forward.

1 Samuel 18:1-9

Related texts: Proverbs 27:4; Acts 5:12-19; 7:9-10; Romans 13:12-14; 2 Corinthians 11:2; Galatians 5:19-22

Saul Tries to Kill David

Saul ordered his son Jonathan and all his servants to kill David. But Saul's son Jonathan liked David very much, so he told him: "My father Saul intends to kill you. Be on your guard in the morning and hide in a secret place and stay there. I'll go out and stand beside my father in the field where you are and talk to him about you. When I see what he says, I'll tell you."

Jonathan spoke well of David to his father Saul. He said to him: "The king should not sin against his servant David. He hasn't sinned against you; in fact, his actions have been a great advantage to you. He took his life in his hands when he struck down the Philistine, and the LORD brought about a great victory for all Israel. You saw it and rejoiced, so why would you sin against innocent blood by killing David for no reason?"

Saul listened to Jonathan's advice and swore an oath: "As surely as the LORD lives, David will not be killed." So Jonathan summoned David and told him all these words. Then Jonathan brought David to Saul, and he served him as he did before.

Now an evil spirit from the LORD came on Saul as he was sitting in his palace holding a spear. David was playing the harp, and Saul tried to pin David to the wall with the spear. As the spear struck the wall, David eluded Saul and escaped. That night he ran away.

1 SAMUEL 19:1-7,9-10

Related texts: 1 SAMUEL 19–30; PSALMS 52; 54; 59; JAMES 1:13-15

The Death of Saul and His Sons

The Philistines fought against Israel, and Israel's men fled from them and were killed on Mount Gilboa. The Philistines pursued Saul and his sons and killed Saul's sons Jonathan, Abinadab, and Malchishua. When the battle intensified against Saul, the archers found him and severely wounded him. Then Saul said to his armor-bearer, "Draw your sword and run me through with it, or these uncircumcised men will come and torture me!" But his armor-bearer wouldn't do it because he was terrified. Then Saul took his sword and fell on it. When his armor-bearer saw that Saul was dead, he also fell on his own sword and died. So Saul and his three sons died— his whole house died together.

When all the men of Israel in the valley saw that the army had run away and that Saul and his sons were dead, they abandoned their cities and fled. So the Philistines came and settled in them.

Saul died for his unfaithfulness to the LORD because he did not keep the LORD's word. He even consulted a medium for guidance, but he did not inquire of the LORD. So the LORD put him to death and turned the kingdom over to David son of Jesse.

1 CHRONICLES 10:1-7,13-14

Related texts: 1 SAMUEL 28:30-31; 2 SAMUEL 1; 16:15–17:23; MATTHEW 27:1-5; ACTS 16:22-28

The LORD Makes a Covenant with David

When the king had settled into his palace and the LORD had given him rest on every side from all his enemies, the king said to Nathan the prophet, "Look, I am living in a cedar house while the ark of God sits inside tent curtains."

So Nathan told the king, "Go and do all that is on your heart, for the LORD is with you."

But that night the word of the LORD came to Nathan:

"Now this is what you are to say to My servant David: 'This is what the LORD of Hosts says: I took you from the pasture and from following the sheep to be ruler over My people Israel. I have been with you wherever you have gone, and I have destroyed all your enemies before you. I will make a name for you like that of the greatest in the land.

"'The LORD declares to you: The LORD Himself will make a house for you. When your time comes and you rest with your fathers, I will raise up after you your descendant, who will come from your body, and I will establish his kingdom. He will build a house for My name, and I will establish the throne of his kingdom forever. I will be a father to him, and he will be a son to Me. When he does wrong, I will discipline him with a human rod and with blows from others. But My faithful love will never leave him as I removed it from Saul; I removed him from your way. Your house and kingdom will endure and your throne will be established forever.'"

2 SAMUEL 7:1-4,8-9,11b-16

Related texts: 1 CHRONICLES 17; PSALMS 2; 89; JEREMIAH 33:14-26; ROMANS 1:1-4

The LORD Is My Shepherd

The Lord is my shepherd;
there is nothing I lack.
He lets me lie down in green pastures;
He leads me beside quiet waters.
He renews my life;
He leads me along the right paths for His name's sake.
Even when I walk through the darkest valley,
I fear no danger,
for You are with me;
Your rod and Your staff —they comfort me.
You prepare a table before me
in the presence of my enemies;
You anoint my head with oil;
my cup overflows.
Only goodness andf aithful love will pursue me all the
    days of my life,
        and I will dwell in the house of the LORD as long as
        I live.

"I am the good shepherd. The good shepherd lays
down his life for the sheep."

PSALM 23; JOHN 10:11

Related texts: ISAIAH 40:10-11; MICAH 5:2-5; HEBREWS
13:20-21; 1 PETER 2:21-25; REVELATION 7:15-17

David Commits Adultery with Bathsheba

In the spring when kings march out to war, David sent Joab with his officers and all Israel. They destroyed the Ammonites and besieged Rabbah, but David remained in Jerusalem.

One evening David got up from his bed and strolled around on the roof of the palace. From the roof he saw a woman bathing—a very beautiful woman. So David sent someone to inquire about her, and he reported, "This is Bathsheba, daughter of Eliam and wife of Uriah the Hittite."

David sent messengers to get her, and when she came to him, he slept with her. Now she had just been purifying herself from her uncleanness. Afterwards, she returned home. The woman conceived and sent word to inform David: "I am pregnant."

David sent orders to Joab: "Send me Uriah the Hittite." So Joab sent Uriah to David. When Uriah came to him, David asked how Joab and the troops were doing and how the war was going. Then he said to Uriah, "Go down to your house and wash your feet." So Uriah left the palace, and a gift from the king followed him. But Uriah slept at the door of the palace with all his master's servants; he did not go down to his house.

2 SAMUEL 11:1-9

Related texts: DEUTERONOMY 5:18; JOB 31:1; PSALM 119:9-16; PROVERBS 5–6; 1 CORINTHIANS 6:9-11

David Arranges Uriah's Death

The next morning David wrote a letter to Joab and sent it with Uriah. In the letter he wrote: Put Uriah at the front of the fiercest fighting, then withdraw from him so that he is struck down and dies.

When Joab was besieging the city, he put Uriah in the place where he knew the best enemy soldiers were. Then the men of the city came out and attacked Joab, and some of the men from David's soldiers fell in battle; Uriah the Hittite also died.

When Uriah's wife heard that her husband Uriah had died, she mourned for him. When the time of mourning ended, David had her brought to his house. She became his wife and bore him a son. However, the LORD considered what David had done to be evil.

David responded to Nathan, "I have sinned against the Lord."

Then Nathan replied to David, "The LORD has taken away your sin; you will not die. However, because you treated the LORD with such contempt in this matter, the son born to you will die."

For the wages of sin is death, but the gift of God is eternal life in Christ Jesus our Lord.

2 SAMUEL 11:14-17,26-27; 12:13-14; ROMANS 6:23

Related texts: NUMBERS 32:23; 2 SAMUEL 12:15-25; PROVERBS 26:27; MATTHEW 1:1-6; HEBREWS 13:4

David's Prayer of Repentance

Be gracious to me, God, according to Your faithful love;
according to Your abundant compassion, blot out my
    rebellion.
Wash away my guilt,
and cleanse me from my sin.
For I am conscious of my rebellion,
and my sin is always before me.
Against You—You alone—I have sinned
and done this evil in Your sight.
So You are right when You pass sentence;
You are blameless when You judge.
Indeed, I was guilty when I was born;
I was sinful when my mother conceived me.
Surely You desire integrity in the inner self,
and You teach me wisdom deep within.
Purify me with hyssop, and I will be clean;
wash me, and I will be whiter than snow.
Let me hear joy and gladness;
let the bones You have crushed rejoice.
Turn Your face away from my sins
and blot out all my guilt.
God, create a clean heart for me
and renew a steadfast spirit within me.
Do not banish me from Your presence
or take Your Holy Spirit from me.
Restore the joy of Your salvation to me,
and give me a willing spirit.
Then I will teach the rebellious Your ways,
and sinners will return to You.

PSALM 51:1-13

Related texts: 2 SAMUEL 12; PSALM 32; ISAIAH 40:28-31;
HABAKKUK 3:2; TITUS 3:3-7

David Appoints Solomon as King

As the time approached for David to die, he instructed his son Solomon, "As for me, I am going the way of all of the earth. Be strong and brave, and keep your obligation to the LORD your God to walk in His ways and to keep His statutes, commandments, judgments, and testimonies. This is written in the law of Moses, so that you will have success in everything you do and wherever you turn, and so that the LORD will carry out His promise that He made to me: 'If your sons are careful to walk faithfully before Me with their whole mind and heart, you will never fail to have a man on the throne of Israel.'"

Solomon sat on the LORD's throne as king in place of his father David. He prospered, and all Israel obeyed him. All the leaders and the mighty men, and all of King David's sons as well, pledged their allegiance to King Solomon. The LORD highly exalted Solomon in the sight of all Israel and bestowed on him such royal majesty as had not been bestowed on any king over Israel before him.

Trust in the LORD with all your heart,
and do not rely on your own understanding;
think about Him in all your ways,
and He will guide you on the right paths.

1 KINGS 2:1-4; 1 CHRONICLES 29:23-25; PROVERBS 3:5-6

Related texts: 2 SAMUEL 7; 1 KINGS 1; 1 CHRONICLES 17; 23–29; MATTHEW 1:1-6; LUKE 12:22-31

Solomon Asks for Wisdom

At Gibeon the LORD appeared to Solomon in a dream at night. God said, "Ask. What should I give you?"

"LORD my God, You have now made Your servant king in my father David's place. Yet I am just a youth with no experience in leadership. Your servant is among Your people You have chosen, a people too numerous to be numbered or counted. So give Your servant an obedient heart to judge Your people and to discern between good and evil. For who is able to judge this great people of Yours?"

Now it pleased the Lord that Solomon had requested this. So God said to him, "Because you have requested this and did not ask for long life or riches for yourself, or the death of your enemies, but you asked discernment for yourself to understand justice, I will therefore do what you have asked. I will give you a wise and understanding heart, so that there has never been anyone like you before and never will be again. In addition, I will give you what you did not ask for: both riches and honor, so that no man in any kingdom will be your equal during your entire life. If you walk in My ways and keep My statutes and commandments just as your father David did, I will give you a long life."

1 KINGS 3:5,7-14

Related texts: 1 KINGS 3:16-28; 2 CHRONICLES 1:1-13; PROVERBS 1–4; 8:10-21; JAMES 1:5-8

The Wisdom of Solomon

Judah and Israel were as numerous as the sand by the sea; they were eating, drinking, and rejoicing. Solomon ruled over all the kingdoms from the Euphrates River to the land of the Philistines and as far as the border of Egypt. They offered tribute and served Solomon all the days of his life.

God gave Solomon wisdom, very great insight, and understanding as vast as the sand on the seashore. Solomon's wisdom was greater than the wisdom of all the people of the East, greater than all the wisdom of Egypt. He was wiser than anyone—wiser than Ethan the Ezrahite, and Heman, Calcol, and Darda, sons of Mahol. His reputation extended to all the surrounding nations.

Solomon composed 3,000 proverbs, and his songs numbered 1,005. He described trees, from the cedar in Lebanon to the hyssop growing out of the wall. He also taught about animals, birds, reptiles, and fish. People came from everywhere, sent by every king on earth who had heard of his wisdom, to listen to Solomon's wisdom.

1 Kings 4:20-21,29-34

Related texts: 1 Kings 10:1-13; Psalm 72; Proverbs 13:10; 16:16; 23:23; Matthew 12:38-42

The Proverbs of Solomon

The proverbs of Solomon son of David, king of
  Israel:
For gaining wisdom and being instructed;
for understanding insightful sayings;
for receiving wise instruction
in righteousness, justice, and integrity;
for teaching shrewdness to the inexperienced,
knowledge and discretion to a young man—
a wise man will listen and increase his learning,
and a discerning man will obtain guidance—
for understanding a proverb or a parable,
the words of the wise, and their riddles.
The fear of the LORD is the beginning of knowledge;
fools despise wisdom and instruction.

As the crowds were increasing, He began saying:
"This generation is an evil generation. It demands a
sign, but no sign will be given to it except the sign of
Jonah. For just as Jonah became a sign to the people of
Nineveh, so also the Son of Man will be to this generation. The queen of the south will rise up at the judgment with the men of this generation and condemn
them, because she came from the ends of the earth to
hear the wisdom of Solomon; and look—something
greater than Solomon is here!"

PROVERBS 1:1-7; LUKE 11:29-31

Related texts: 2 CHRONICLES 9:1-12; PROVERBS 10:1; 25:1;
SONG OF SONGS 1–8; JONAH 3; 1 CORINTHIANS 12:1-11

PARABLES OF JESUS: *The Sower*

As a large crowd was gathering, and people were flocking to Him from every town, He [Jesus] said in a parable: "A sower went out to sow his seed. As he was sowing, some fell along the path; it was trampled on, and the birds of the sky ate it up. Other seed fell on the rock; when it sprang up, it withered, since it lacked moisture. Other seed fell among thorns; the thorns sprang up with it and choked it. Still other seed fell on good ground; when it sprang up, it produced a crop: 100 times what was sown." As He said this, He called out, "Anyone who has ears to hear should listen!"

Then His disciples asked Him what this parable might mean. So He said, "To know the secrets of the kingdom of God has been granted to you, but to the rest it is in parables, so that

> Looking they may not see,
> and hearing they may not understand."

LUKE 8:4-10;

Related texts: PSALM 126; PROVERBS 11:18-21; ISAIAH 6:8-13; HOSEA 10:12-13; MATTHEW 13:1-7; MARK 4:1-12

PARABLES OF JESUS: *The Sower Explained*

[Jesus said,] "This is the meaning of the parable: The seed is the word of God. The seeds along the path are those who have heard. Then the Devil comes and takes away the word from their hearts, so that they may not believe and be saved. And the seeds on the rock are those who, when they hear, welcome the word with joy. Having no root, these believe for a while and depart in a time of testing. As for the seed that fell among thorns, these are the ones who, when they have heard, go on their way and are choked with worries, riches, and pleasures of life, and produce no mature fruit. But the seed in the good ground—these are the ones who, having heard the word with an honest and good heart, hold on to it and bear fruit with endurance.

"No one, after lighting a lamp, covers it with a basket or puts it under a bed, but puts it on a lampstand, so that those who come in may see the light. For nothing is concealed that won't be revealed, and nothing hidden that won't be made known and come to light. Therefore, take care how you listen. For whoever has, more will be given to him; and whoever does not have, even what he thinks he has will be taken away from him."

LUKE 8:11-18

Related texts: PROVERBS 11:30; MATTHEW 13:18-23; MARK 4:13-25; JOHN 15:1-17; GALATIANS 6:7-10

PARABLES OF JESUS: *The Kingdom*

He [Jesus] presented another parable to them: "The kingdom of heaven is like a mustard seed that a man took and sowed in his field. It's the smallest of all the seeds, but when grown, it's taller than the vegetables and becomes a tree, so that the birds of the sky come and nest in its branches."

He told them another parable: "The kingdom of heaven is like yeast that a woman took and mixed into three measures of flour until it spread through all of it.

"The kingdom of heaven is like treasure, buried in a field, that a man found and reburied. Then in his joy he goes and sells everything he has and buys that field.

"Again, the kingdom of heaven is like a merchant in search of fine pearls. When he found one priceless pearl, he went and sold everything he had, and bought it.

"Again, the kingdom of heaven is like a large net thrown into the sea. It collected every kind of fish, and when it was full, they dragged it ashore, sat down, and gathered the good fish into containers, but threw out the worthless ones. So it will be at the end of the age. The angels will go out, separate the evil who are among the righteous, and throw them into the blazing furnace. In that place there will be weeping and gnashing of teeth."

MATTHEW 13:31-33,44-50

Related texts: PSALM 45:6; MARK 1:1-15; 4:40-32; LUKE 13:18-19

PARABLES OF JESUS: *Lost and Found*

All the tax collectors and sinners were drawing near to listen to Him. And the Pharisees and scribes were complaining, "This man welcomes sinners and eats with them!"

So He [Jesus] told them this parable: "What man among you, who has 100 sheep and loses one of them, does not leave the 99 in the open field and go after the lost one until he finds it? When he has found it, he joyfully puts it on his shoulders, and coming home, he calls his friends and neighbors together, saying to them, 'Rejoice with me, because I have found my lost sheep!' I tell you, in the same way, there will be more joy in heaven over one sinner who repents than over 99 righteous people who don't need repentance.

"Or what woman who has 10 silver coins, if she loses one coin, does not light a lamp, sweep the house, and search carefully until she finds it? When she finds it, she calls her women friends and neighbors together, saying, 'Rejoice with me, because I have found the silver coin I lost!' I tell you, in the same way, there is joy in the presence of God's angels over one sinner who repents."

LUKE 15:1-10

PARABLES OF JESUS: *The Prodigal Son, Part 1*

He [Jesus] also said: "A man had two sons. The younger of them said to his father, 'Father, give me the share of the estate I have coming to me.' So he distributed the assets to them. Not many days later, the younger son gathered together all he had and traveled to a distant country, where he squandered his estate in foolish living. After he had spent everything, a severe famine struck that country, and he had nothing. Then he went to work for one of the citizens of that country, who sent him into his fields to feed pigs. He longed to eat his fill from the carob pods the pigs were eating, and no one would give him any. But when he came to his senses, he said, 'How many of my father's hired hands have more than enough food, and here I am dying of hunger! I'll get up, go to my father, and say to him, "Father, I have sinned against heaven and in your sight. I'm no longer worthy to be called your son. Make me like one of your hired hands."' So he got up and went to his father. But while the son was still a long way off, his father saw him and was filled with compassion. He ran, threw his arms around his neck, and kissed him. The son said to him, 'Father, I have sinned against heaven and in your sight. I'm no longer worthy to be called your son.'"

LUKE 15:11-21

Related texts: 2 CHRONICLES 7:13-14; PROVERBS 17:6,21; HOSEA 6:1-3; ACTS 3:19-20

PARABLES OF JESUS: *The Prodigal Son, Part 2*

"But the father told his slaves, 'Quick! Bring out the best robe and put it on him; put a ring on his finger and sandals on his feet. Then bring the fattened calf and slaughter it, and let's celebrate with a feast, because this son of mine was dead and is alive again; he was lost and is found!' So they began to celebrate.

"Now his older son was in the field; as he came near the house, he heard music and dancing. So he summoned one of the servants and asked what these things meant. 'Your brother is here,' he told him, 'and your father has slaughtered the fattened calf because he has him back safe and sound.'

"Then he became angry and didn't want to go in. So his father came out and pleaded with him. But he replied to his father, 'Look, I have been slaving many years for you, and I have never disobeyed your orders; yet you never gave me a young goat so I could celebrate with my friends. But when this son of yours came, who has devoured your assets with prostitutes, you slaughtered the fattened calf for him.'

"'Son,' he said to him, 'you are always with me, and everything I have is yours. But we had to celebrate and rejoice, because this brother of yours was dead and is alive again; he was lost and is found.'"

LUKE 15:22-32

Related texts: ISAIAH 55:6-7; MATTHEW 18:12-14; COLOSSIANS 1:1-14; 1 PETER 2:24-25

Solomon Builds the Temple

Hiram king of Tyre sent his servants to Solomon when he heard that he had been anointed king in his father's place, for Hiram had always been friends with David.

Solomon sent this message to Hiram: "You know my father David was not able to build a temple for the name of the LORD his God. This was because of the warfare all around him until the LORD put his enemies under his feet. The LORD my God has now given me rest all around; there is no enemy or crisis. So I plan to build a temple for the name of the LORD my God, according to what the LORD promised my father David: 'I will put your son on your throne in your place, and he will build the temple for My name.'

"Therefore, command that cedars from Lebanon be cut down for me. My servants will be with your servants, and I will pay your servants' wages according to whatever you say, for you know that not a man among us knows how to cut timber like the Sidonians."

When Hiram heard Solomon's words, he greatly rejoiced and said, "May the LORD be praised today! He has given David a wise son to be over this great people!"

1 KINGS 5:1-7

Related texts: 1 KINGS 5–9; 2 CHRONICLES 2–8; PSALM 127; MATTHEW 12:1-6; JOHN 2:13-21; EPHESIANS 2:11-22

The Wisdom of the Teacher

I, the Teacher, have been king over Israel in Jerusalem. I applied my mind to seek and explore through wisdom all that is done under heaven. God has given people this miserable task to keep them occupied. I have seen all the things that are done under the sun and have found everything to be futile, a pursuit of the wind.

> There is an occasion for everything,
> and a time for every activity under heaven:
> a time to give birth and a time to die;
> a time to plant and a time to uproot;
> a time to kill and a time to heal;
> a time to tear down and a time to build;
> a time to weep and a time to laugh;
> a time to mourn and a time to dance;
> a time to throw stones and a time to gather stones;
> a time to embrace and a time to avoid embracing;
> a time to search and a time to count as lost;
> a time to keep and a time to throw away;
> a time to tear and a time to sew;
> a time to be silent and a time to speak;
> a time to love and a time to hate;
> a time for war and a time for peace.

ECCLESIASTES 1:12-14; 3:1-8

Related texts: ECCLESIASTES 1:1-11; GALATIANS 4:4-5; 6:8-9; 1 TIMOTHY 2:3-6; 1 PETER 5:5-6

The Teacher's Proverbs and Conclusion

Two are better than one because they have a good reward for their efforts. For if either falls, his companion can lift him up; but pity the one who falls without another to lift him up. Also, if two lie down together, they can keep warm; but how can one person alone keep warm? And if somebody overpowers one person, two can resist him. A cord of three strands is not easily broken.

In addition to the Teacher being a wise man, he constantly taught the people knowledge; he weighed, explored, and arranged many proverbs. The Teacher sought to find delightful sayings and to accurately write words of truth. The sayings of the wise are like goads, and those from masters of collections are like firmly embedded nails. The sayings are given by one Shepherd.

But beyond these, my son, be warned: there is no end to the making of many books, and much study wearies the body. When all has been heard, the conclusion of the matter is: fear God and keep His commands, because this is for all humanity. For God will bring every act to judgment, including every hidden thing, whether good or evil.

Ecclesiastes 4:9-12; 12:9-14

Related texts: 1 SAMUEL 20:24-42; PSALM 37; PROVERBS 17:17; 27:6,10; 1 CORINTHIANS 4:5; REVELATION 20:11-15

The Sins of Solomon

King Solomon loved many foreign women in addition to Pharaoh's daughter: Moabite, Ammonite, Edomite, Sidonian, and Hittite women from the nations that the LORD had told the Israelites about, "Do not intermarry with them, and they must not intermarry with you, because they will turn you away from Me to their gods." Solomon was deeply attached to these women and loved them.

When Solomon was old, his wives seduced him to follow other gods. His heart was not completely with the LORD his God, as his father David's heart had been.

The LORD was angry with Solomon, because his heart had turned away from the LORD God of Israel, who had appeared to him twice. He had commanded him about this, so that he would not follow other gods, but Solomon did not do what the LORD had commanded.

Then the LORD said to Solomon, "Since you have done this and did not keep My covenant and My statues, which I commanded you, I will tear the kingdom away from you and give it to your servant. However, I will not do it during your lifetime because of your father David; I will tear it out of your son's hand. Yet, I will not tear the entire kingdom away from him. I will give one tribe to your son because of my servant David and because of Jerusalem that I chose."

1 KINGS 11:1-2,4,9-13

Related texts: DEUTERONOMY 7; EZRA; NEHEMIAH 13:23-27; 1 CORINTHIANS 7:39; 2 CORINTHIANS 6:14-16

The Kingdom Divides

The length of Solomon's reign in Jerusalem over all Israel totaled 40 years. Solomon rested with his fathers and was buried in the city of his father David. His son Rehoboam became king in his place.

Then Rehoboam went to Shechem, for all Israel had gone to Shechem to make him king. They summoned him, and Jeroboam and the whole assembly of Israel came and spoke to Rehoboam: "Your father made our yoke harsh. You, therefore, lighten your father's harsh service and the heavy yoke he put on us, and we will serve you."

Rehoboam replied, "Go home for three days and then return to me." So the people left.

Then the king answered the people harshly. He rejected the advice the elders had given him and spoke to them according to the young men's advice: "My father made your yoke heavy, but I will add to your yoke; my father disciplined you with whips, but I will discipline you with barbed whips."

When all Israel saw that the king had not listened to them, the people answered him:

> What portion do we have in David?
> We have no inheritance in the son of Jesse.
> Israel, return to your tents;
> David, now look after your own house!

So Israel went to their tents.

When all Israel heard that Jeroboam had come back, they summoned him to the assembly and made him king over all Israel. No one followed the house of David except the tribe of Judah alone.

1 KINGS 11:1-2,4,9-13; 11:42-43; 12:1,3-5,13-14,16,20

Related texts: 1 KINGS 11:26-40; 2 CHRONICLES 9:29–10:19; PROVERBS 15:1

The Sins of Jeroboam

Jeroboam built Shechem in the hill country of Ephraim and lived there. From there he went out and built Penuel. Jeroboam said to himself, "The way things are going now, the kingdom might return to the house of David. If these people regularly go to offer sacrifices in the LORD's temple in Jerusalem, the heart of these people will return to their lord, Rehoboam king of Judah. They will murder me and go back to the king of Judah." So the king sought advice.

Then he made two gold calves, and he said to the people, "Going to Jerusalem is too difficult for you. Israel, here is your God who brought you out of the land of Egypt." He set up one in Bethel, and put the other in Dan. This led to sin; the people walked in procession before one of the calves all the way to Dan.

Jeroboam also built shrines on the high places and set up priests from every class of people who were not Levites.

For the house of Jeroboam, this was the sin that caused it to be wiped out and annihilated from the face of the earth.

1 KINGS 12:25-31; 13:34

When you read God's word, you must
constantly be saying to yourself,
It is talking to me, and about me.

Soren Kierkegaard (1813–1855)
DANISH PHILOSOPHER

I must confess to you that the majesty
of the Scriptures astonishes me...
if it had been the invention of men,
the inventors would be greater than
the greatest heroes.

Jean Jacques Rousseau (1712–1778)
FRENCH PHILOSOPHER

After more than sixty years of almost
daily reading of the Bible, I never
fail to find it always new and marvelously
in tune with the changing needs of every day.

Cecil B. DeMille (1881–1959)
AMERICAN MOVIE PRODUCER

Elijah Confronts King Ahab

Ahab son of Omri became king over Israel in the thirty-eighth year of Judah's King Asa; Ahab son of Omri reigned over Israel in Samaria 22 years. But Ahab son of Omri did what was evil in the LORD's sight more than all who were before him. Then, as if following the sin of Jeroboam son of Nebat were a trivial matter, he married Jezebel, the daughter of Ethbaal king of the Sidonians, and then proceeded to serve Baal and worship him. He set up an altar for Baal in the temple of Baal that he had built in Samaria. Ahab also made an Asherah pole. Ahab did more to provoke the LORD God of Israel than all the kings of Israel who were before him.

Now Elijah the Tishbite, from the Gilead settlers, said to Ahab, "As the LORD God of Israel lives, I stand before Him, and there will be no dew or rain during these years except by my command!"

Then a revelation from the LORD came to him: "Leave here, turn eastward, and hide yourself at the Wadi Cherith where it enters the Jordan. You are to drink from the wadi. I have commanded the ravens to provide for you there."

So he did what the LORD commanded. Elijah left and lived by the Wadi Cherith where it enters the Jordan.

If I close the sky so there is no rain, or if I command the grasshopper to consume the land, or if I send pestilence on My people, and My people who are called by My name humble themselves, pray and seek My face, and turn from their evil ways, then I will hear from heaven, forgive their sin, and heal their land.

1 KINGS 16:29-33; 17:1-5; 2 CHRONICLES 7:13-14

Related texts: DEUTERONOMY 11:16-17; MARK 6:14-15; LUKE 1:11-17; 9:7-8; JAMES 5:17-18

Elijah Challenges the Prophets of Baal

After a long time, the word of the LORD came to Elijah in the third year: "Go and present yourself to Ahab. I will send rain on the surface of the land."

When Ahab saw Elijah, Ahab said to him, "Is that you, you destroyer of Israel?"

He replied, "I have not destroyed Israel, but you and your father's house have, because you have abandoned the LORD's commandments and followed the Baals. Now summon all Israel to meet me at Mount Carmel, along with the 450 prophets of Baal and the 400 prophets of Asherah who eat at Jezebel's table."

So Ahab summoned all the Israelites and gathered the prophets at Mount Carmel. Then Elijah approached all the people and said, "How long will you hesitate between two opinions? If Yahweh is God, follow Him. But if Baal, follow him." But the people didn't answer him a word.

Then Elijah said to the people, "I am the only remaining prophet of the LORD, but Baal's prophets are 450 men. Let two bulls be given to us. They are to choose one bull for themselves, cut it in pieces, and place it on the wood but not light the fire. I will prepare the other bull and place it on the wood but not light the fire. Then you call on the name of your god, and I will call on the name of Yahweh. The God who answers with fire, He is God."

All the people answered, "That sounds good."

1 KINGS 18:1,17-24

Related texts: DEUTERONOMY 12:28-31; 32:36-39; MARK 8:27-29; LUKE 9:28-36; JAMES 5:14-18

The LORD Defeats Baal

Then Elijah said to the prophets of Baal, "Since you are so numerous, choose for yourselves one bull and prepare it first. Then call on the name of your god but don't light the fire."

So they took the bull that he gave them, prepared it, and called on the name of Baal from morning till noon, saying, "Baal, answer us!" But there was no sound; no one answered. Then they did their lame dance around the altar they had made.

All afternoon, they kept on raving until the offering of the evening sacrifice, but there was no sound, no one answered, no one paid attention.

At the time for offering the evening sacrifice, Elijah the prophet approached the altar and said, "LORD God of Abraham, Isaac, and Israel, today let it be known that You are God in Israel and I am Your servant, and that at Your word I have done all these things. Answer me, LORD! Answer me so that this people will know that You, Yahweh, are God and that You have turned their hearts back."

Then Yahweh's fire fell and consumed the burnt offering, the wood, the stones, and the dust, and it licked up the water that was in the trench. When all the people saw it, they fell on their faces and said, "Yahweh, He is God! Yahweh, He is God!"

Then Elijah ordered them, "Seize the prophets of Baal! Do not let even one of them escape." So they seized them, and Elijah brought them down to the Wadi Kishon and slaughtered them there.

1 KINGS 18:25-26,29,36-40

Related texts: DEUTERONOMY 13; 17:2-5; 18:18-22; 1 KINGS 21–22; 2 KINGS 9:30–10:28; PHILIPPIANS 2:5-11

Jonah Disobeys the LORD

The word of the LORD came to Jonah son of Amittai: "Get up! Go to the great city of Nineveh and preach against it, because their wickedness has confronted Me." However, Jonah got up to flee to Tarshish away from the LORD's presence. He went down to Joppa and found a ship going to Tarshish. He paid the fare and went down into it to go with them to Tarshish, away from the LORD's presence.

Then the LORD hurled a violent wind onto the sea, and such a violent storm arose on the sea that the ship threatened to break apart. The sailors were afraid, and each cried out to his god.

"Come on!" the sailors said to each other. "Let's cast lots. Then we will know who is to blame for this trouble we're in." So they cast lots, and the lot singled out Jonah.

So they said to him, "What should we do to you to calm this sea that's against us?" For the sea was getting worse and worse.

He answered them, "Pick me up and throw me into the sea so it may quiet down for you, for I know that I'm to blame for this violent storm that is against you."

Then they picked up Jonah and threw him into the sea, and the sea stopped its raging. The men feared the LORD even more, and they offered a sacrifice to the LORD and made vows. Then the LORD appointed a great fish to swallow Jonah, and Jonah was in the fish three days and three nights.

JONAH 1:1-5a,7,11-12,15-17

Related texts: 2 KINGS 14:25; MATTHEW 12:38-41; 16:1-4; LUKE 11:29-32

Jonah Prays in the Belly of a Fish

Jonah prayed to the LORD his God from inside the fish:
    I called to the LORD in my distress,
    and He answered me.
    I cried out for help in the belly of Sheol;
    You heard my voice.
    You threw me into the depths,
    into the heart of the seas,
    and the current overcame me.
    All Your breakers and Your billows swept over me.
    But I said: I have been banished
    from Your sight,
    yet I will look once more
    toward Your holy temple.
    The waters engulfed me up to the neck;
    the watery depths overcame me;
    seaweed was wrapped around my head.
    I sank to the foundations of the mountains;
    the earth with its prison bars closed behind me
    forever!
    But You raised my life from the Pit, O LORD my God!
    As my life was fading away,
    I remembered the LORD.
    My prayer came toYou,
    to Your holy temple.
    Those who cling to worthless idols
    forsake faithful love,
    but as for me, I will sacrifice toYou
    with a voice of thanksgiving.
    I will fulfill what I have vowed.
    Salvation is from the LORD!
Then the LORD commanded the fish, and it vomited
Jonah onto dry land.

JONAH 2

Related texts: 2 KINGS 17:13-15; PSALMS 42; 69; ISAIAH
44:9-20; ACTS 27

The LORD Relents from Sending Disaster

Then the word of the LORD came to Jonah a second time: "Get up! Go to the great city of Nineveh and preach the message that I tell you." So Jonah got up and went to Nineveh according to the LORD's command.

Now Nineveh was an extremely large city, a three-day walk. Jonah set out on the first day of his walk in the city and proclaimed, "In 40 days Nineveh will be overthrown!" The men of Nineveh believed in God. They proclaimed a fast and dressed in sackcloth—from the greatest of them to the least.

When word reached the king of Nineveh, he got up from his throne, took off his royal robe, put on sackcloth, and sat in ashes. Then he issued a decree in Nineveh:

By order of the king and his nobles: No man or beast, herd or flock, is to taste anything at all. They must not eat or drink water. Furthermore, both man and beast must be covered with sackcloth, and everyone must call out earnestly to God. Each must turn from his evil ways and from the violence he is doing. Who knows? This God may turn and relent; He may turn from His burning anger so that we will not perish.

Then God saw their actions—that they had turned from their evil ways—so God relented from the disaster He had threatened to do to them. And He did not do it.

JONAH 3

Related texts: EXODUS 32:1-14; JEREMIAH 18:1-11; JOEL 2:12-14; LUKE 11:29-32

Joel Calls Israel to Repent

Even now—this is the LORD's declaration—
turn to Me with all your heart,
with fasting, weeping, and mourning.
Tear your hearts,
not just your clothes,
and return to the LORD your God.
For He is gracious and compassionate,
slow to anger, rich in faithful love,
and He relents from sending disaster.
Who knows? He may turn and relent
and leave a blessing behind Him,
so you can offer grain and wine
to the LORD your God.
Blow the horn in Zion!
Announce a sacred fast;
proclaim an assembly.
Gather the people;
sanctify the congregation;
assemble the aged;
gather the children,
even those nursing at the breast.
Let the bridegroom leave his bedroom,
and the bride her honeymoon chamber.
Let the priests, the LORD's ministers,
weep between the portico and the altar.
Let them say:
"Have pity on Your people, LORD,
and do not make Your inheritance a disgrace,
an object of scorn among the nations.
Why should it be said among the peoples,
'Where is their God?'"
Then the LORD became jealous for His land and
spared His people.

JOEL 2:12-18

Related texts: EXODUS 34:1-7; DEUTERONOMY 10:16;
JONAH 3; JAMES 4:6-8

Amos: Judgment and Hope

Look, the eyes of the Lord GOD
are on the sinful kingdom,
and I will destroy it
from the face of the earth.
However, I will not totally destroy
the house of Jacob—the Lord's declaration.

All the sinners among My people,
who say: Disaster will never overtake
or confront us,
will die by the sword.
In that day
I will restore the fallen booth of David:
I will repair its gaps,
restore its ruins,
and rebuild it as in the days of old,
so that they may possess
the remnant of Edom
and all the nations
that are called by My name—
this is the LORD's declaration—He will do this.
Hear this! The days are coming—the LORD's declaration—
when the plowman will overtake the reaper
and the one who treads grapes,
the sower of seed.
The mountains will drip with sweet wine,
and all the hills will flow with it.
I will restore the fortunes of My people Israel.
They will rebuild and occupy ruined cities,
plant vineyards and drink their wine,
make gardens and eat their produce.
I will plant them on their land,
and they will never again be uprooted
from the land that I have given them,
Yahweh your God has spoken.

AMOS 9:8,10-15

Related texts: 2 SAMUEL 7; ACTS 15:1-21; ROMANS 9–11

Hosea: The LORD's Anger and Compassion

When Israel was a child, I loved him,
and out of Egypt I called My son.
The more they called them,
the more they departed from Me.
They kept sacrificing to the Baals
and burning offerings to idols.
It was I who taught Ephraim to walk,
taking them in My arms;
but they never knew that I healed them.
I led them with human cords,
with ropes of kindness.
To them I was like one
who eases the yoke from their jaws;
I bent down to give them food.
Israel will not return to the land of Egypt
and Assyria will be his king,
because they refused to repent.

How can I give you up, Ephraim?
How can I surrender you, Israel?
How can I make you like Admah?
How can I treat you like Zeboiim?
I have had a change of heart;
My compassion is stirred!
I will not vent the full fury of My anger;
I will not turn back to destroy Ephraim.
For I am God and not man,
the Holy One among you;
I will not come in rage.
They will follow the Lord;
He will roar like a lion.
When He roars,
His children will come trembling from the west.
They will be roused like birds from Egypt
and like doves from the land of Assyria.
Then I will settle them in their homes.
This is the LORD's declaration.

HOSEA 11:1-5,8-11

Related texts: GENESIS 19:1-29; DEUTERONOMY 29:18-23; ZECHARIAH 10:6-12; 2 PETER 3:8-15

Isaiah Sees the Lord

In the year that King Uzziah died, I saw the Lord seated on a high and lofty throne, and His robe filled the temple. Seraphim were standing above Him; each one had six wings: with two he covered his face, with two he covered his feet, and with two he flew. And one called to another:

Holy, holy, holy is the LORD of Hosts;
His glory fills the whole earth.

The foundations of the doorways shook at the sound of their voices, and the temple was filled with smoke. Then I said:

Woe is me, for I am ruined,
because I am a man of unclean lips
and live among a people of unclean lips,
and because my eyes have seen the King,
the LORD of Hosts.

Then one of the seraphim flew to me, and in his hand was a glowing coal that he had taken from the altar with tongs. He touched my mouth with it and said:

Now that this has touched your lips,
your wickedness is removed,
and your sin is atoned for.

Then I heard the voice of the Lord saying:
Who should I send?
Who will go for Us?
I said:
Here I am. Send me.

ISAIAH 6:1-8

Related texts: EXODUS 3:1-6; 33:15-23; JOB 19:25-27; MATTHEW 5:8; 13:10-17; JOHN 12:37-41; REVELATION 4

MICAH: *The Sins of Israel*

The word of the Lord that came to Micah the
Moreshite—what he saw regarding Samaria and
Jerusalem in the days of Jotham, Ahaz, and Hezekiah,
kings of Judah.
Listen, all you peoples;
pay attention, earth and everyone in it!
The Lord GOD will be a witness against you,
the Lord, from His holy temple.
Look, the LORD is leaving His place
and coming down to trample
the heights of the earth.
The mountains will melt beneath Him,
and the valleys will split apart,
like wax near a fire,
like water cascading down a mountainside.
All this will happen because of Jacob's rebellion
and the sins of the house of Israel.
What is the rebellion of Jacob?
Isn't it Samaria?
And what is the high place of Judah?
Isn't it Jerusalem?
Therefore, I will make Samaria
a heap of ruins in the countryside,
a planting area for a vineyard.
I will roll her stones into the valley
and expose her foundations.
All her carved images will be smashed to pieces,
all her wages will be burned in the fire,
and I will destroy all her idols.
Since she collected the wages of a prostitute,
they will be used again for a prostitute.

MICAH 1:1-7

Related texts: DEUTERONOMY 5:6-10; JUDGES 10:11-16;   *277*
PSALMS 68:1-3; 97; JEREMIAH 26; ACTS 1:1-8

Israel Goes into Exile

In the ninth year of Hoshea, the king of Assyria captured Samaria. He deported the Israelites to Assyria and settled them in Halah and by the Habor, Gozan's river, and in the cities of the Medes.

This disaster happened because the people of Israel had sinned against the LORD their God who had brought them out of the land of Egypt from the power of Pharaoh king of Egypt and because they had worshiped other gods. They had lived according to the customs of the nations that the LORD had dispossessed before the Israelites and the customs the kings of Israel had introduced. The Israelites secretly did what was not right against the LORD their God. They built high places in all their towns from watchtower to fortified city. They set up for themselves sacred pillars and Asherah poles on every high hill and under every green tree. They burned incense on all the high places just like those nations that the LORD had driven out before them. They did evil things, provoking the LORD. They served idols, although the LORD had told them, "You must not do this." Still, the LORD warned Israel and Judah through every prophet and every seer, saying, "Turn from your evil ways and keep My commandments and statutes according to all the law I commanded your ancestors and sent to you through My servants the prophets."

But they would not listen. Instead, they became obstinate like their ancestors who did not believe the LORD their God.

2 KINGS 17:6-14

Related texts: DEUTERONOMY 28:14-68; 2 KINGS 15:16-20; ACTS 7:51-53

Good King Hezekiah

In the third year of Israel's King Hoshea son of Elah, Hezekiah son of Ahaz became king of Judah. He was 25 years old when he became king; he reigned 29 years in Jerusalem. His mother's name was Abi daughter of Zechariah. He did what was right in the LORD's sight just as his ancestor David had done. He removed the high places and shattered the sacred pillars and cut down the Asherah poles. He broke into pieces the bronze serpent that Moses made, for the Israelites burned incense to it up to that time. He called it Nehushtan.

Hezekiah trusted in the LORD God of Israel; not one of the kings of Judah was like him, either before him or after him. He held fast to the LORD and did not turn from following Him but kept the commandments the LORD had commanded Moses.

The LORD was with him, and wherever he went, he prospered. He rebelled against the king of Assyria and did not serve him. He defeated the Philistines as far as Gaza and its borders, from watchtower to fortified city.

In the fourth year of King Hezekiah, which was the seventh year of Israel's King Hoshea son of Elah, Shalmaneser king of Assyria marched against Samaria and besieged it. The Assyrians captured it at the end of three years. In the sixth year of Hezekiah, which was the ninth year of Israel's King Hoshea, Samaria was captured.

2 KINGS 18:1-10

Related texts: NUMBERS 21:1-9; DEUTERONOMY 28:1-14; 2 CHRONICLES 29–31; PROVERBS 25:1; MATTHEW 1:1-10

The LORD Delivers Judah from Assyria

In the fourteenth year of King Hezekiah, Sennacherib king of Assyria attacked all the fortified cities of Judah and captured them.

Then Hezekiah prayed before the LORD: "LORD God of Israel who is enthroned above the cherubim, You are God—You alone—of all the kingdoms of the earth. You made the heavens and the earth. Listen closely, LORD, and hear; open Your eyes, LORD, and see; hear the words that Sennacherib has sent to mock the living God. LORD, it is true that the kings of Assyria have devastated the nations and their lands. They have thrown their gods into the fire, for they were not gods but the work of human hands—wood and stone. So they have destroyed them. Now, LORD our God, please save us from his hand so that all the kingdoms of the earth may know that You are the LORD God—You alone."

Then Isaiah son of Amoz sent a message to Hezekiah: "The LORD, the God of Israel says: 'I have heard your prayer to Me about Sennacherib king of Assyria.'"

That night the angel of the LORD went out and struck down 185,000 in the camp of the Assyrians. When the people got up the next morning—there were all the dead bodies! So Sennacherib king of Assyria broke camp and left. He returned home and lived in Nineveh.

2 KINGS 18:13; 19:15-20,35-36

Related texts: 2 KINGS 19–20; 2 CHRONICLES 32; ISAIAH 36–39; ACTS 12

NAHUM: *God's Vengeance on Assyria*

The LORD is a jealous and avenging God;
the LORD takes vengeance
and is fierce in wrath.
The LORD takes vengeance against His foes;
He is furious with His enemies.
The LORD is slow to anger but great in power;
the LORD will never leave the guilty unpunished.
His path is in the whirlwind and storm,
and clouds are the dust beneath His feet.

Who can withstand His indignation?
Who can endure His burning anger?
His wrath is poured out like fire,
even rocks are shattered before Him.
The LORD is good,
a stronghold in a day of distress;
He cares for those who take refuge in Him.
But He will completely destroy Nineveh
with an overwhelming flood,
and He will chase His enemies into darkness.
Whatever you plot against the LORD,
He will bring it to complete destruction;
oppression will not rise up a second time.

King of Assyria, your shepherds slumber;
your officers sleep.
Your people are scattered across the mountains
with no one to gather them together.
There is no remedy for your injury;
your wound is severe.
All who hear the news about you
will clap their hands because of you,
for who has not experienced
your constant cruelty?

NAHUM 1:2-3,6-9; 3:18-19

Related texts: EXODUS 34:1-7; JONAH; JOHN 3:31-36;
ROMANS 1:18-19; EPHESIANS 5:5-6

ZEPHANIAH: *Jerusalem's Correction*

Woe to the city that is rebellious and defiled,
    the oppressive city!
She has not obeyed;
she has not accepted discipline.
She has not trusted in the LORD;
she has not drawn near to her God.
The princes within her are roaring lions;
her judges are wolves of the night,
which leave nothing for the morning.
Her prophets are reckless—treacherous men.
Her priests profane the sanctuary;
they do violence to instruction.
The righteous LORD is in her;
He does no wrong.
He applies His justice morning by morning;
He does not fail at dawn,
yet the one who does wrong knows no shame.

Sing for joy, Daughter Zion;
shout loudly, Israel!
Be glad and rejoice with all your heart,
Daughter Jerusalem!
The LORD has removed your punishment;
He has turned back your enemy.
The King of Israel, the LORD, is among you;
you need no longer fear harm.
On that day it will be said to Jerusalem:
"Do not fear;
Zion, do not let your hands grow weak.
The LORD your God is among you,
a warrior who saves.
He will rejoice over you with gladness.
He will bring you quietness with His love.
He will delight in you with shouts of joy."

ZEPHANIAH 3:1-5,14-17

Related texts: PSALMS 25; 34:1-5; ISAIAH 40; ROMANS 10:9-11

THE CALL OF JEREMIAH: *Part 1*

The words of Jeremiah, the son of Hilkiah, one of the priests living in Anathoth in the territory of Benjamin. The word of the LORD came to him in the thirteenth year of the reign of Josiah son of Amon, king of Judah. It also came throughout the days of Jehoiakim son of Josiah, king of Judah, until the fifth month of the eleventh year of Zedekiah son of Josiah, king of Judah, when the people of Jerusalem went into exile.

The word of the LORD came to me:
　　I chose you before I formed you in the womb;
　　I set you apart before you were born.
　　I appointed you a prophet to the nations.
But I protested, "Oh no, Lord God! Look, I don't know how to speak since I am only a youth."

Then the LORD said to me:
　　Do not say: I am only a youth,
　　for you will go to everyone I send you to
　　and speak whatever I tell you.
　　Do not be afraid of anyone,
　　for I will be with you to deliver you.
This is the LORD's declaration.

Then the LORD reached out His hand, touched my mouth, and told me:
　　Look, I have filled your mouth with My words.
　　See, today I have set you over nations and kingdoms
　　to uproot and tear down, to destroy and demolish,
　　to build and plant.

JEREMIAH 1:1-10

Related texts: EXODUS 4:10-12; PSALM 136; ISAIAH 6;
LUKE 1:13-16; 1 TIMOTHY 4:12

THE CALL OF JEREMIAH: *Part 2*

Again the word of the LORD came to me inquiring, "What do you see?"

And I replied, "I see a boiling pot, its mouth tilted from the north to the south."

Then the LORD said to me, "Disaster will be poured out from the north on all who live in the land. Indeed, I am about to summon all the clans and kingdoms of the north."

This is the LORD's declaration.

They will come, and each king will set up his throne
at the entrance to Jerusalem's gates.
They will attack all her surrounding walls
and all the other cities of Judah.

"I will pronounce My judgments against them for all the evil they did when they abandoned Me to burn incense to other gods and to worship the works of their own hands.

"Now, get ready. Stand up and tell them everything that I command you. Do not be intimidated by them or I will cause you to cower before them. Today, I am the One who has made you a fortified city, an iron pillar, and bronze walls against the whole land—against the kings of Judah, its officials, its priests, and the population. They will fight against you but never prevail over you, since I am with you to rescue you."

This is the LORD's declaration.

JEREMIAH 1:13-19

Related texts: DEUTERONOMY 28; JOSHUA 1; EZEKIEL 11; 24; 33:1-20, 1 JOHN 5:3-4

Jeremiah Is Saved by Micah's Prophecy

At the beginning of the reign of Jehoiakim son of Josiah, king of Judah, this word came from the LORD: "You are to say to them: This is what the LORD says: If you do not listen to Me by living according to My law that I set before you and by listening to the words of My servants the prophets I have been sending you time and time again, though you did not listen, I will make this temple like Shiloh. I will make this city an object of cursing for all the nations of the earth."

He finished the address the LORD had commanded him to deliver to all the people. Then the priests, the prophets, and all the people took hold of him, yelling, "You must surely die! How dare you prophesy in the name of the LORD, 'This temple will become like Shiloh and this city will become an uninhabited ruin'!" Then all the people assembled against Jeremiah at the LORD's temple.

Some of the elders of the land stood up and said to all the assembled people, "Micah the Moreshite prophesied in the days of Hezekiah king of Judah and said to all the people of Judah, 'This is what the LORD of Hosts says:

Zion will be plowed like a field,
Jerusalem will become ruins,
and the temple mount a forested hill.'

Did Hezekiah king of Judah and all the people of Judah put him to death? Did he not fear the LORD and plead for the LORD's favor, and did not the LORD relent concerning the disaster He had pronounced against them? We are about to bring great harm on ourselves!"

JEREMIAH 26:1,4-6,8-9,17-19

Related texts: JEREMIAH 18:1-11; 19:1–20:2; 38:1-13; *285*
LAMENTATIONS 3:52-57; MICAH 3:9-12; MATTHEW 16:13-14

Judah Goes into Exile

Zedekiah was 21 years old when he became king; he reigned 11 years in Jerusalem. He did what was evil in the sight of the LORD his God and did not humble himself before Jeremiah the prophet at the LORD's command.

But the LORD God of their ancestors sent word against them by the hand of his messengers, sending them time and time again, for He had compassion on His people and on His dwelling place. But they kept ridiculing God's messengers, despising His words, and scoffing at His prophets, until the LORD's wrath was so stirred up against His people that there was no remedy. So He brought up against them the king of the Chaldeans, who killed their choice young men with the sword in the house of their sanctuary. He had no pity on young man and virgin or elderly and aged; He handed them all over to him. He took everything to Babylon—all the articles of God's temple, large and small, the treasures of the LORD's temple, and the treasures of the king and his officials. Then the Chaldeans burned God's temple. They tore down Jerusalem's wall, burned down all its palaces, and destroyed all its valuable utensils.

Those who escaped from the sword he deported to Babylon, and they became servants to him and his sons until the rise of the Persian kingdom. This fulfilled the word of the LORD through Jeremiah and the land enjoyed its Sabbath rest all the days of the desolation until 70 years were fulfilled.

2 CHRONICLES 36:11-12,15-21

Related texts: LEVITICUS 26:1-43; 2 KINGS 20:12-18; 25; ISAIAH 39; JEREMIAH 25; 38; 52; MATTHEW 1:1-17

Lament over Fallen Jerusalem

How she sits alone,
the city once crowded with people!
She who was great among the nations
Has become like a widow.
The princess among the provinces
has become a slave.
She weeps aloud during the night,
With tears on her cheeks.
There is no one to offer her comfort,
Not one from all her lovers.
All her friends have betrayed her;
they have become her enemies.

I thought, My future is lost,
as well as my hope from the LORD.
Remember my affliction and homelessness,
The wormwood and the poison.
I continually remember them
And have become depressed.
Yet I call this to mind,
And therefore I have hope:
Because of the LORD's faithful love
we do not perish,
for His mercies never end.
They are new every morning;
great is Your faithfulness!
I say: The LORD is my portion,
therefore I will hope in Him.
The LORD is good to those who wait for Him,
to the person who seeks Him.
It is good to wait quietly
for deliverance from the LORD.

LAMENTATIONS 1:1-2; 3:18-26

Related texts: PSALM 137; EZEKIEL 19; 24; MATTHEW
23:33-39

The LORD Promises Vengeance on Babylon

Look, his ego is inflated;
he is without integrity.
But the righteous one will live by his faith.
Moreover, wine betrays;
an arrogant man is never at rest.
He enlarges his appetite like Sheol,
and like Death he is never satisfied.
He gathers all the nations to himself;
he collects all the peoples for himself.
Won't all of these take up a taunt against him,
with mockery and riddles about him?
They will say:
Woe to him who amasses what is not his—
how much longer?—
and loads himself with goods taken in pledge.

I heard, and I trembled within;
my lips quivered at the sound.
Rottenness entered my bones;
I trembled where I stood.
Now I must quietly wait for the day of distress
to come against the people invading us.
Though the fig tree does not bud
and there is no fruit on the vines,
though the olive crop fails
and the fields produce no food,
though there are no sheep in the pen
and no cattle in the stalls,
yet I will rejoice in the LORD;
I will rejoice in the God of my salvation!
Yahweh my Lord is my strength;
He makes my feet like those of a deer
and enables me to walk on mountain heights!

HABAKKUK 2:4-6; 3:16-19a

Related texts: GENESIS 9:5-6; 12:1-3; ROMANS 1:16-17;
GALATIANS 3:8-14; HEBREWS 10:32-39

OBADIAH: *The Day of the LORD*

In that day—the LORD's declaration—
will I not eliminate the wise ones of Edom
and those who understand
from the hill country of Esau?

You will be covered with shame
and destroyed forever
because of violence done to your brother Jacob.
On the day you stood aloof,
on the day strangers captured his wealth,
while foreigners entered his gate
and cast lots for Jerusalem,
you were just like one of them.
Do not gloat over your brother
in the day of his calamity;
do not rejoice over the people of Judah
in the day of their destruction;
do not boastfully mock
in the day of distress.

For the Day of the LORD is near,
against all the nations.
As you have done, so it will be done to you;
what you deserve will return on your own head.
For as you have drunk on My holy mountain,
so all the nations will drink continually.
They will drink and gulp down
and be as though they had never been.
But there will be a deliverance on Mount Zion,
and it will be holy;
the house of Jacob will dispossess them.

OBADIAH 8,10-12,15-17

Related texts: ISAIAH 13; JOEL 3; 2 PETER 3

Ezekiel Sees the Restoration of Israel

The hand of the LORD was on me, and He brought me out by His Spirit and set me down in the middle of a valley; it was full of bones.

He said to me, "Prophesy concerning these bones and say to them: Dry bones, hear the word of the LORD! This is what the Lord GOD says to these bones: Look, I will cause breath to enter you, and you shall live. I will put sinews on you, and make flesh come upon you, and spread skin over you; I will put breath in you, that you will come to life. Then you will know that I am the LORD."

So I prophesied as I had been commanded, and as I prophesied, there was a noise, a rattling sound, and the bones came together, bone to its bone.

He said to me, "Prophesy to the breath, prophesy, son of man. Say to the it: This is what the Lord GOD says: Breath, come from the four winds, Breath into these slain that they may live!" So I prophesied as He commanded me; the breath entered them, and they came to life and stood on their feet, a vast army.

Then He said to me, "Son of man, these bones are the whole house of Israel. Look how they say, Our bones are dried up, and our hope has perished; we are cut off." Therefore prophesy and say to them, This is what the Lord GOD says: I am going to open your graves, and bring you up, My people, and lead you into the land of Israel.

I will put My Spirit in you, and you will live, and I will settle you in your own land. Then you will know that I am the LORD. I have spoken, and I will do it." This is the declaration of the LORD.

EZEKIEL 37:1,4-7,9-12,14

Related texts: DEUTERONOMY 30:1-10; PSALM 80; ISAIAH 40; EZEKIEL 36; ACTS 17:24-25; 2 THESSALONIANS 2:7-8

The Writing on the Wall

King Belshazzar held a great feast for 1,000 of his nobles and drank wine in their presence. Under the influence of the wine, Belshazzar gave orders to bring in the gold and silver vessels that his predecessor Nebuchadnezzar had taken from the temple in Jerusalem, so that the king and his nobles, wives, and concubines could drink from them.

They drank the wine and praised their gods made of gold and silver, bronze, iron, wood, and stone. At that moment the fingers of a man's hand appeared and began writing on the plaster of the king's palace wall next to the lampstand. As the king watched the hand that was writing, his face turned pale, and his thoughts so terrified him that his hip joints shook and his knees knocked together.

Because of the outcry of the king and his nobles, the queen came to the banquet hall. "May the king live forever," she said. "Don't let your thoughts terrify you or your face be pale. There is a man in your kingdom who has the spirit of the holy gods in him. In the days of your predecessor he was found to have insight, intelligence, and wisdom like the wisdom of the gods. Your predecessor, King Nebuchadnezzar, appointed him chief of the diviners, mediums, Chaldeans, and astrologers. Your own predecessor, the king, did this because Daniel, the one the king named Belteshazzar, was found to have an extraordinary spirit, knowledge and perception, and the ability to interpret dreams, explain riddles, and solve problems. Therefore, summon Daniel, and he will give the interpretation."

Daniel 5:1-2,4-6,10-12

Related texts: Genesis 41; Daniel 1–4; Joel 2:28-32; Acts 2:1-21

Daniel Interprets the Writing

Then Daniel was brought before the king. The king said to him, "Are you Daniel, one of the Judean exiles that my predecessor the king brought from Judah? However, I have heard about you that you can give interpretations and solve problems. Therefore, if you can read this inscription and give me its interpretation, you will be clothed in purple, have a gold chain around your neck, and have the third highest position in the kingdom."

Then Daniel answered the king, "You may keep your gifts, and give your rewards to someone else; however, I will read the inscription for the king and make the interpretation known to him.

The vessels from His house were brought to you, and as you and your nobles, wives, and concubines drank wine from them, you praised the gods made of silver and gold, bronze, iron, wood, and stone, which do not see or hear or understand. But you have not glorified the God who holds your life-breath in His hand and who controls the whole course of your life. Therefore, He sent the hand, and this writing was inscribed.

"This is the writing that was inscribed:
MENE, MENE, TEKEL, PARSIN.

This is the interpretation of the message:

MENE means that God has numbered the days of your kingdom and brought it to an end.

TEKEL means that you have been weighed in the balance and found deficient.

PERES means that your kingdom has been divided and given to the Medes and Persians."

That very night Belshazzar the king of the Chaldeans was killed, and Darius the Mede received the kingdom at the age of 62.

Daniel 5:13,16-17,23b-28,30-31

Related texts: Isaiah 47; Daniel 4; Matthew 24:14-22; 1 Corinthians 12

Cyrus Sends Israel Home

In the first year of Cyrus king of Persia, the word of the LORD spoken through Jeremiah was fulfilled. The LORD put it into the mind of King Cyrus to issue a proclamation throughout his entire kingdom and to put it in writing:

This is what King Cyrus of Persia says: "The LORD, the God of heaven, has given me all the kingdoms of the earth and has appointed me to build Him a house at Jerusalem in Judah. Whoever is among His people, may his God be with him, and may he go to Jerusalem in Judah and build the house of the LORD, the God of Israel, the God who is in Jerusalem. Let every survivor, wherever he lives, be assisted by the men of that region with silver, gold, goods, and livestock, along with a freewill offering for the house of God in Jerusalem."

So the family leaders of Judah and Benjamin, along with the priests and Levites—everyone God had motivated—prepared to go up and rebuild the LORD's house in Jerusalem. All their neighbors supported them with silver articles, gold, goods, livestock, and valuables, in addition to all that was given as a freewill offering. King Cyrus also brought out the articles of the LORD's house that Nebuchadnezzar had taken from Jerusalem and had placed in the house of his gods.

EZRA 1:1-7

Haggai: Rebuild the Temple!

"The LORD of Hosts says this: These people say: The time has not come for the house of the LORD to be rebuilt."

The word of the LORD came through Haggai the prophet: "Is it time for you yourselves to live in your paneled houses, while this house lies in ruins?" Now, the LORD of Hosts says this: "Think carefully on your ways:
You have planted much but harvested little.
You eat but never have enough to be satisfied.
You drink but never have enough to become drunk.
You put on clothes but never have enough to get warm.
The wage earner puts his wages
Into a bag with a hole in it."

The LORD of Hosts says this: "Think carefully about your ways. Go up into the hills, bring down lumber, and build the house. Then I will be pleased with it and be glorified," says the LORD. "You expected much, but then it amounted to little. When you brought the harvest to your house, I ruined it. Why?" This is the declaration of the LORD of Hosts. "Because My house still lies in ruins, while each of you is busy with his own house.
So on your account, the skies have withheld the dew and the land its crops.
I have summoned a drought on the fields and the hills, on the grain, new wine, olive oil,
and whatever the ground yields,
on the people and animals,
and on all that your hands produce."

Then Zerubbabel son of Shealtiel, the high priest Joshua son of Jehozadak, and the entire remnant of the people obeyed the voice of the LORD their God and the words of the prophet Haggai, because the LORD their God had sent him. So the people feared the LORD.

HAGGAI 1:2-12

Related texts: HAGGAI 2; ZECHARIAH 1–6; 1 CORINTHIANS 3:19-17; 2 CORINTHIANS 6:14-16; EPHESIANS 2:11-22

Zechariah Encourages the Exiles

On the twenty-fourth day of the eleventh month, which is the month of Shebat, in the second year of Darius, the word of the LORD came to the prophet Zechariah son of Berechiah, son of Iddo:

I looked out in the night and saw a man riding on a red horse. He was standing among the myrtle trees in the valley. Behind him were red, sorrel, and white horses.

They reported to the Angel of the LORD standing among the myrtle trees, "We have patrolled the earth, and right now the whole earth is calm and quiet."

Then the Angel of the LORD responded, "How long, LORD of Hosts, will You withhold mercy from Jerusalem and the cities of Judah that You have been angry with these 70 years?" The LORD replied with kind and comforting words to the angel who was speaking with me.

So the angel who was speaking with me said, "Proclaim: The LORD of Hosts says: I am extremely jealous for Jerusalem and Zion. I am fiercely angry with the nations that are at ease, for I was a little angry, but they made it worse. Therefore, this is what the LORD says: I have graciously returned to Jerusalem; My house will be rebuilt within it"—the declaration of the LORD of Hosts— "and a measuring line will be stretched out over Jerusalem.

"Proclaim further: This is what the LORD of Hosts says: My cities will again overflow with prosperity; the LORD will once more comfort Zion and choose Jerusalem."

ZECHARIAH 1:7-8,11-17

Related texts: ISAIAH 40:1-2; ZECHARIAH 1–6; 1 CORINTHIANS 14:3; 2 CORINTHIANS 1:3-7

The Exiles Rebuild the Temple

When the enemies of Judah and Benjamin heard that the returned exiles were building a temple for the LORD, the God of Israel, they approached Zerubbabel and the leaders of the families and said to them, "Let us build with you, for we also worship your God and have been sacrificing to Him since the time King Esar-haddon of Assyria brought us here."

But Zerubbabel, Jeshua, and the other leaders of Israel's families answered them, "You may have no part with us in building a house for our God, since we alone must build it for the LORD, the God of Israel, as King Cyrus, the king of Persia has commanded us." Then the people who were already in the land discouraged the people of Judah and made them afraid to build. They also bribed officials to act against them to frustrate their plans throughout the reign of King Cyrus of Persia and until the reign of King Darius of Persia.

Then Tattenai governor of the region west of the Euphrates River, Shethar-bozenai, and their colleagues diligently carried out what King Darius had decreed. So the Jewish elders continued successfully with the building under the prophesying of Haggai the prophet and Zechariah son of Iddo. They finished the building according to the command of the God of Israel and the decrees of Cyrus, Darius, and King Artaxerxes of Persia. This house was completed on the third day of the month of Adar in the sixth year of the reign of King Darius.

EZRA 4:1-5; 6:13-15

Related texts: EZRA 3–6; EZEKIEL 40–48; HAGGAI 1–2; JOHN 2:13-21

The Bible is always ...with me. Indeed, I am not apt to dip pen in ink without first looking into the Book of Books.

Hayyhn Nahman Bialik (1873–1934)
HEBREW POET

This book ... is the best gift God has given to man... But for it we could not know right from wrong.

Abraham Lincoln (1809–1865)
UNITED STATES PRESIDENT

There is much in the Bible against which every instinct of my being rebels, so much that I regret the necessity which has compelled me to read it through from beginning to end.

Helen Keller (1880–1968)
US AUTHOR, LECTURER

Nehemiah Prays for the Exiles

The words of Nehemiah son of Hacaliah:

During the month of Chislev in the twentieth year, when I was in the fortress city of Susa, Hanani, one of my brothers, arrived with men from Judah, and I questioned them about Jerusalem and the Jewish remnant that had returned from exile. They said to me, "The survivors in the province, who returned from the exile, are in great trouble and disgrace. Jerusalem's wall has been broken down, and its gates have been burned down."

When I heard these words, I sat down and wept. I mourned for a number of days, fasting and praying before the God of heaven. I said,

"Lord God of heaven, the great and awe-inspiring God who keeps His gracious covenant with those who love Him and keep His commands, let Your eyes be open and Your ears be attentive to hear Your servant's prayer that I now pray to You day and night for Your servants, the Israelites. I confess the sins we have committed against You. Both I and my father's house have sinned. We have acted corruptly toward You and have not kept the commands, statutes, and ordinances You gave Your servant Moses. Please remember what You commanded Your servant Moses: 'If you are unfaithful, I will scatter you among the peoples. But if you return to Me and carefully observe My commands, even though your exiles were banished to the ends of the earth, I will gather them from there and bring them to the place where I chose to have My name dwell.'"

Nehemiah 1:1-9

Related texts: Leviticus 26:14-46; Deuteronomy 7:6-15; 28:15-68; Daniel 9:1-19; James 5:13-16

The Exiles Rebuild Jerusalem's Wall

So we rebuilt the wall until the entire wall was joined together up to half its height, for the people had the will to keep working.

When Sanballat, Tobiah, and the Arabs, Ammonites, and Ashdodites heard that the repair to the walls of Jerusalem was progressing and that the gaps were being closed, they became furious. They all plotted together to come and fight against Jerusalem and throw it into confusion. So we prayed to our God and stationed a guard because of them day and night.

From that day on, half of my men did the work while the other half held spears, shields, bows, and armor. The officers supported all the people of Judah, who were rebuilding the wall. The laborers who carried the loads worked with one hand and held a weapon with the other. Each of the builders had his sword strapped around his waist while he was building.

The wall was completed in 52 days, on the twenty-fifth day of the month Ellul. When all our enemies heard this, all the surrounding nations were intimidated and lost their confidence, for they realized that this task had been accomplished by our God.

NEHEMIAH 4:6-9,16-18a; 6:15-16

Related texts: NEHEMIAH 2–6; PSALMS 27; 51:18–19; 127:1; JOHN 16:33; 1 JOHN 4:4

Pray for the Peace of Jerusalem

I rejoiced with those who said to me,
"Let us go to the house of the LORD."
Our feet are standing
within your gates, Jerusalem—
Jerusalem, built as a city should be,
solidly joined together,
where the tribes, the tribes of the LORD, go up
to give thanks to the name of the LORD.
(This is an ordinance for Israel.)
There, thrones for judgment are placed,
thrones of the house of David.
Pray for the peace of Jerusalem:
"May those who love you prosper;
may there be peace within your walls,
prosperity within your fortresses."
Because of my brothers and friends,
I will say, "Peace be with you."
Because of the house of the LORD our God,
I will seek your good.

PSALM 122

Ezra Reads the Law to the Exiles

On the first day of the seventh month, Ezra the priest brought the law before the assembly of men, women, and all who could listen with understanding. While he was facing the square in front of the Water Gate, he read out of it from daybreak until noon before the men, the women, and those who could understand. All the people listened attentively to the book of the law.

Ezra opened the book in full view of all the people, since he was elevated above everyone. As he opened it, all the people stood up. Ezra blessed the LORD, the great God, and with their hands uplifted all the people said, "Amen, Amen!" Then they bowed down and worshiped the LORD with their faces to the ground.

Jeshua, Bani, Sherebiah, Jamin, Akkub, Shabbethai, Hodiah, Maaseiah, Kelita, Azariah, Jozabad, Hanan, and Pelaiah, who were Levites, explained the law to the people as they stood in their places. They read the book of the law of God, translating and giving the meaning so that the people could understand what was read. Nehemiah the governor, Ezra the priest and scribe, and the Levites who were instructing the people said to all of them, "This day is holy to the LORD your God. Do not mourn or weep." For all the people were weeping as they heard the words of the law. Then he said to them, "Go and eat what is rich, drink what is sweet, and send portions to those who have nothing prepared, since today is holy to our Lord. Do not grieve, because your strength comes from rejoicing in the LORD."

NEHEMIAH 8:2-3,5-10

Related texts: DEUTERONOMY 16:13-15; EZRA 6:19-22; ISAIAH 58; MATTHEW 13:18-23; ACTS 17:10-11

Persia Needs a New Queen

These events took place during the days of Ahasuerus, who ruled 127 provinces from India to Cush. In those days King Ahasuerus reigned from his royal throne in the fortress at Susa. He held a feast in the third year of his reign for all his officials and staff.

On the seventh day, when the king was feeling good from the wine, Ahasuerus commanded Mehuman, Biztha, Harbona, Bigtha, Abagtha, Zethar, and Carkas, the seven eunuchs who personally served him, to bring Queen Vashti before him with her royal crown. He wanted to show off her beauty to the people and the officials, because she was very beautiful. But Queen Vashti refused to come at the king's command that was delivered by his eunuchs. The king became furious and his anger burned within him.

Memucan said in the presence of the king and his officials, "Queen Vashti has defied not only the king, but all the officials and the peoples who are in every one of King Ahasuerus' provinces.

"If it meets the king's approval, he should personally issue a royal decree. Let it be recorded in the laws of Persia and Media, so that it cannot be revoked: Vashti is not to enter King Ahasuerus' presence, and her royal position is to be given to another woman who is more worthy than she. The decree the king issues will be heard throughout his vast kingdom, so all women will honor their husbands, from the least to the greatest."

ESTHER 1:1-3a,10-12,16,19-20

Related texts: EZRA 4:1-6; PROVERBS 31:1-9; DANIEL 9:1-2; 1 CORINTHIANS 6:9-10

Esther Becomes Queen of Persia

A Jewish man was in the fortress of Susa named Mordecai son of Jair, son of Shimei, son of Kish, a Benjaminite. He had been taken into exile from Jerusalem with the other captives when King Nebuchadnezzar of Babylon took King Jeconiah of Judah into exile. Mordecai was the legal guardian of his cousin Hadassah (that is, Esther), because she didn't have a father or mother. The young woman had a beautiful figure and was extremely good-looking. When her father and mother died, Mordecai had adopted her as his own daughter.

When the king's command and edict became public knowledge, many young women gathered at the fortress of Susa under Hegai's care. Esther was also taken to the palace and placed under the care of Hegai, who was in charge of the women. The young woman pleased him and gained his favor so that he accelerated the process of the beauty treatments and the special diet that she received. He assigned seven hand-picked female servants to her from the palace and transferred her and her servants to the harem's best quarters.

Esther did not reveal her ethnic background or her birthplace, because Mordecai had ordered her not to.

The king loved Esther more than all the other women. She won more favor and approval from him than did any of the other virgins. He placed the royal crown on her head and made her queen in place of Vashti.

ESTHER 2:5-10,17

Related texts: GENESIS 39; 41; NEHEMIAH 1:1-11; 1 PETER 3:1-6

Haman Plots to Kill the Jews

After all this took place, King Ahasuerus honored Haman, son of Hammedatha the Agagite. He promoted him in rank and gave him a higher position than all the other officials. The entire royal staff at the King's Gate bowed down and paid homage to Haman, because the king had commanded this to be done for him. But Mordecai would not bow down or pay homage.

When Haman saw that Mordecai was not bowing down or paying him homage, he was filled with rage. And when he learned of Mordecai's ethnic identity, Haman decided not to do away with Mordecai alone. He set out to destroy all of Mordecai's people, the Jews, throughout Ahasuerus' kingdom.

Then Haman informed King Ahasuerus, "There is one ethnic group, scattered throughout the peoples in every province of your kingdom, yet living in isolation. Their laws are different from everyone else's, so that they defy the king's laws. It is not in the king's best interest to tolerate them. If the king approves, let an order be drawn up authorizing their destruction, and I will pay 375 tons of silver to the accountants for deposit in the royal treasury."

The king removed his signet ring from his finger and gave it to Haman son of Hammedatha the Agagite, the enemy of the Jewish people. Then the king told Haman, "The money and people are given to you to do with as you see fit."

ESTHER 3:1-2,5-6,8-11

Related texts: GENESIS 12:1-3; DEUTERONOMY 30:1-7; ESTHER 4–6; PSALM 44:1-8; DANIEL 3; 6; ROMANS 9-11

Haman's Downfall

The king and Haman came to feast with Esther the queen. Once again, on the second day while drinking wine, the king asked Esther, "Queen Esther, whatever you ask will be given to you. Whatever you seek, even to half the kingdom, will be done."

Queen Esther answered, "If I have obtained your approval, my king, and if the king is pleased, let my life be given to me. This is my request and my people's, and it is what I seek. For my people and I have been sold out to destruction, death, and extermination. If we had merely been sold as male and female slaves, I would have kept silent. Indeed, the trouble wouldn't be worth burdening the king."

King Ahasuerus spoke up and asked Queen Esther, "Who is this, and where is the one who would devise such a scheme?"

Esther answered, "The adversary and enemy is this evil Haman."

Harbona, one of the royal eunuchs, said: "There is a gallows 75 feet tall at Haman's house that he made for Mordecai, who gave the report that saved the king."

The king commanded, "Hang him on it."

They hanged Haman on the gallows he had prepared for Mordecai. Then the king's anger subsided.

ESTHER 7:1-6,9-10

Related texts: DEUTERONOMY 23:3-5; ESTHER 8–10; JOEL 3:1-8; ODABIAH 15; REVELATION 19:11–20:10

MALACHI: *Messenger of the Covenant*

"See, I am going to send My messenger, and he will clear the way before Me. Then the Lord you seek will suddenly come to His temple, the Messenger of the covenant you desire—see, He is coming," says the Lord of Hosts. "But who can endure the day of His coming? And who will be able to stand when He appears? For He will be like a refiner's fire and like cleansing lye. He will be like a refiner and purifier of silver; He will purify the sons of Levi and refine them like gold and silver. Then they will present offerings to the LORD in righteousness. And the offerings of Judah and Jerusalem will please the LORD as in days of old and years gone by."

"For indeed, the day is coming, burning like a furnace, when all the arrogant and everyone who commits wickedness will become stubble. The coming day will consume them," says the LORD of Hosts, "not leaving them root or branches. But for you who fear My name, the sun of righteousness will rise with healing in its wings, and you will go out and playfully jump like calves from the stall. You will trample the wicked, for they will be ashes under the soles of your feet on the day I am preparing," says the LORD of Hosts.

"Look, I am going to send you Elijah the prophet before the great and awesome Day of the LORD comes. And he will turn the hearts of fathers to their children and the hearts of children to their fathers. Otherwise, I will come and strike the land with a curse."

MALACHI 3:1-4; 4:1-3,5-6

Related texts: ISAIAH 60; LUKE 11:1-17; MATTHEW 3:1-12; 17:10-13

The Promise of Jesus' Coming

And now, says the LORD,
who formed me from the womb to be His servant,
to bring Jacob back to Him
so that Israel might be gathered to Him;
for I am honored in the sight of the LORD,
and my God is my strength—
He says,
"It is not enough for you to be My servant
raising up the tribes of Jacob
and restoring the protected ones of Israel.
I will also appoint you as a light for the nations,
to be My salvation to the ends of the earth."

Bethlehem Ephrathah,
you are small among the clans of Judah;
One will come from you
to be ruler over Israel for Me.
His origin is from antiquity,
from eternity.
Therefore, He will abandon them until the time
when she who is in labor has given birth;
then the rest of His brothers will return
to the people of Israel.
He will stand and shepherd them
in the strength of Yahweh,
in the majestic name of Yahweh His God.
They will live securely,
for then His greatness will extend
to the ends of the earth.
There will be peace.

ISAIAH 49:5-6; MICAH 5:2-5a

Related texts: GENESIS 35:14-19; RUTH 4:10-17;
1 SAMUEL 17:12; MATTHEW 2:1-6

JESUS: *Son of God, Son of Man*

I continued watching in the night visions,
and I saw One like a son of man
coming with the clouds of heaven.
He approached the Ancient of Days
and was escorted before Him.
He was given authority to rule, and glory, and a
kingdom;
so that those of every people, nation, and language
should serve Him.
His dominion is an everlasting dominion
that will not pass away,
and His kingdom is one
that will not be destroyed.

Long ago God spoke to the fathers by the prophets
at different times and in different ways. In these last
days, He has spoken to us by His Son, whom He has
appointed heir of all things and through whom He
made the universe. He is the radiance of His glory, the
exact expression of His nature, and He sustains all
things by His powerful word. After making purification
for sins, He sat down at the right hand of the Majesty
on high. So He became higher in rank than the angels,
just as the name He inherited is superior to theirs.

For to which of the angels did He ever say, You are
My Son; today I have become Your Father, or again, I
will be His Father, and He will be My Son?

DANIEL 7:13-14; HEBREWS 1:1-5

Related texts: 2 SAMUEL 7:14; 1 CHRONICLES 17:13; PSALM 2:7;
MATTHEW 23:63-64; MARK 14:61-62; LUKE 22:67-70; JOHN 1:32-34

309

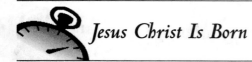

Jesus Christ Is Born

The birth of Jesus Christ came about this way: After His mother Mary had been engaged to Joseph, it was discovered before they came together that she was pregnant by means of the Holy Spirit. So Joseph, her husband, being a righteous man, and not wanting to disgrace her publicly, decided to divorce her secretly.

But after he had considered these things, an angel of the Lord suddenly appeared to him in a dream, saying, "Joseph, son of David, don't be afraid to take Mary as your wife, because what has been conceived in her is by the Holy Spirit. She will give birth to a son, and you are to name Him Jesus, because He will save His people from their sins."

Now all this took place to fulfill what was spoken by the Lord through the prophet:

See, the virgin will be with child and give birth to a son,

and they will name Him Immanuel,

which is translated "God is with us."

When Joseph woke up from his sleep, he did as the Lord's angel had commanded him. He took his wife home, but he did not know her intimately until she gave birth to a son. And he named Him Jesus.

MATTHEW 1:18-25

Related texts: ISAIAH 7:14; MATTHEW 2; LUKE 1–2; JOHN 4:1-42

The Boy Jesus in the Temple

Every year His parents traveled to Jerusalem for the Passover Festival. When He was 12 years old, they went up according to the custom of the festival. After those days were over, as they were returning, the boy Jesus stayed behind in Jerusalem, but His parents did not know it. Assuming He was in the traveling party, they went a day's journey. Then they began looking for Him among their relatives and friends. When they did not find Him, they returned to Jerusalem to search for Him. After three days, they found Him in the temple complex sitting among the teachers, listening to them and asking them questions. And all those who heard Him were astounded at His understanding and His answers. When His parents saw Him, they were astonished, and His mother said to Him, "Son, why have You treated us like this? Your father and I have been anxiously searching for You."

"Why were you searching for Me?" He asked them. "Didn't you know that I must be involved in My Father's interests?" But they did not understand what He said to them.

Then He went down with them and came to Nazareth, and was obedient to them. His mother kept all these things in her heart. And Jesus increased in wisdom and stature, and in favor with God and with people.

Luke 2:41-52

Related texts: 1 Samuel 2:21,26; Psalms 26:8; 27:4; 65; Matthew 2:13-23; John 2:13-17; 2 Corinthians 4:18–5:4

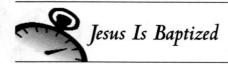

Jesus Is Baptized

The beginning of the gospel of Jesus Christ, the Son of God. As it is written in Isaiah the prophet:

> Look, I am sending My messenger ahead of You,
> who will prepare Your way.
> A voice of one crying out in the wilderness:
> "Prepare the way for the Lord;
> make His paths straight!"

John came baptizing in the wilderness and preaching a baptism of repentance for the forgiveness of sins. The whole Judean countryside and all the people of Jerusalem were flocking to him, and they were baptized by him in the Jordan River as they confessed their sins. John wore a camel-hair garment with a leather belt around his waist, and ate locusts and wild honey. He was preaching: "Someone more powerful than I will come after me. I am not worthy to stoop down and untie the strap of His sandals. I have baptized you with water, but He will baptize you with the Holy Spirit."

In those days Jesus came from Nazareth in Galilee and was baptized in the Jordan by John. As soon as He came up out of the water, He saw the heavens being torn open and the Spirit descending to Him like a dove. And a voice came from heaven:

> You are My beloved Son;
> In You I take delight!

MARK 1:1-11

Related texts: ISAIAH 40:3; MALACHI 3:1; MATTHEW 3; LUKE 3: JOHN 1:19-34

Jesus Is Tempted by the Devil

Then Jesus was led up by the Spirit into the wilderness to be tempted by the Devil. And after He had fasted 40 days and 40 nights, He was hungry. Then the tempter approached Him and said, "If You are the Son of God, tell these stones to become bread."

But He answered, "It is written:

> Man must not live on bread alone,
> but on every word that comes from the mouth of God."

Then the Devil took Him to the holy city, had Him stand on the pinnacle of the temple, and said to Him, "If You are the Son of God, throw Yourself down. For it is written:

> He will give His angels orders concerning you,
> and,
> they will support you with their hands,
> so that you will not strike your foot against a stone."

Jesus told him, "It is also written: You must not tempt the Lord your God."

Again, the Devil took Him to a very high mountain and showed Him all the kingdoms of the world and their splendor. And he said to Him, "I will give You all these things if You will fall down and worship me."

Then Jesus told him, "Go away, Satan! For it is written:

> You must worship the Lord your God,
> and you must serve Him only."

Then the Devil left Him, and immediately angels came and began to serve Him.

MATTHEW 4:1-11

Related texts: DEUTERONOMY 6:13,16; 8:3; PSALM 91:11-12; MARK 1:12-13; LUKE 4:1-13

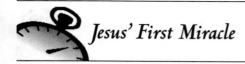

Jesus' First Miracle

On the third day a wedding took place in Cana of Galilee. Jesus' mother was there, and Jesus and His disciples were invited to the wedding as well. When the wine ran out, Jesus' mother told Him, "They don't have any wine."

"What has this concern of yours to do with Me, woman?" Jesus asked. "My hour has not yet come."

"Do whatever He tells you," His mother told the servants.

"Fill the jars with water," Jesus told them. So they filled them to the brim. Then He said to them, "Now draw some out and take it to the chief servant." And they did.

When the chief servant tasted the water (after it had become wine), he did not know where it came from—though the servants who had drawn the water knew. He called the groom and told him, "Everybody sets out the fine wine first, then, after people have drunk freely, the inferior. But you have kept the fine wine until now."

Jesus performed this first sign in Cana of Galilee. He displayed His glory, and His disciples believed in Him.

And there are also many other things that Jesus did, which, if they were written one by one, I suppose not even the world itself could contain the books that would be written.

JOHN 2:1-5,7-11; 21:25

Related texts: ISAIAH 55; JOEL 3:16-18; AMOS 9:11-15; JOHN 20:30-31

You Must Be Born Again

There was a man from the Pharisees named Nicodemus, a ruler of the Jews. This man came to Him at night and said, "Rabbi, we know that You have come from God as a teacher, for no one could perform these signs You do unless God were with him."

Jesus replied, "I assure you: Unless someone is born again, he cannot see the kingdom of God."

"But how can anyone be born when he is old?" Nicodemus asked Him. "Can he enter his mother's womb a second time and be born?"

Jesus answered, "I assure you: Unless someone is born of water and the Spirit, he cannot enter the kingdom of God.

"Are you a teacher of Israel and don't know these things?" Jesus replied.

"If I have told you about things that happen on earth and you don't believe, how will you believe if I tell you about things of heaven? No one has ascended into heaven except the One who descended from heaven—the Son of Man. Just as Moses lifted up the serpent in the wilderness, so the Son of Man must be lifted up, so that everyone who believes in Him will have eternal life.

"For God loved the world in this way: He gave His One and Only Son, so that everyone who believes in Him will not perish but have eternal life."

JOHN 3:1-5,9-10,12-16

Related texts: NUMBERS 21:1-9; JOHN 1:1-13; 1 PETER 1;
1 JOHN 2:28-29; 3:1-10; 4:7-8; 5

Jesus Calls His First Disciples

As the crowd was pressing in on Jesus to hear God's word, He was standing by Lake Gennesaret. He saw two boats at the edge of the lake; the fishermen had left them and were washing their nets. He got into one of the boats, which belonged to Simon, and asked him to put out a little from the land. Then He sat down and was teaching the crowds from the boat.

When He had finished speaking, He said to Simon, "Put out into deep water and let down your nets for a catch."

"Master," Simon replied, "we've worked hard all night long and caught nothing! But at Your word, I'll let down the nets."

When they did this, they caught a great number of fish, and their nets began to tear. So they signaled to their partners in the other boat to come and help them; they came and filled both boats so full that they began to sink.

When Simon Peter saw this, he fell at Jesus' knees and said, "Depart from me, because I'm a sinful man, Lord!" For he and all those with him were amazed at the catch of fish they took, and so were James and John, Zebedee's sons, who were Simon's partners.

"Don't be afraid," Jesus told Simon. "From now on you will be catching people!" Then they brought the boats to land, left everything, and followed Him.

LUKE 5:1-11

Related texts: PSALM 51:1-13; MATTHEW 4:18-22; MARK 1:16-20; JOHN 1:35-51

Healing Illness; Forgiving Sin

On one of those days while He was teaching, Pharisees and teachers of the law were sitting there who had come from every village of Galilee and Judea, and also from Jerusalem. And the Lord's power to heal was in Him. Just then some men came, carrying on a stretcher a man who was paralyzed. They tried to bring him in and set him down before Him. Since they could not find a way to bring him in because of the crowd, they went up on the roof and lowered him on the stretcher through the roof tiles into the middle of the crowd before Jesus.

Seeing their faith He said, "Friend, your sins are forgiven you."

Then the scribes and the Pharisees began to reason: "Who is this man who speaks blasphemies? Who can forgive sins but God alone?"

But perceiving their thoughts, Jesus replied to them, "Why are you reasoning this in your hearts? Which is easier: to say, 'Your sins are forgiven you,' or to say, 'Get up and walk'? But so you may know that the Son of Man has authority on earth to forgive sins"—He told the paralyzed man, "I tell you: get up, pick up your stretcher, and go home."

Immediately he got up before them, picked up what he had been lying on, and went home glorifying God. Then everyone was astounded, and they were giving glory to God. And they were filled with awe and said, "We have seen incredible things today!"

Luke 5:17-26

Related texts: Psalm 25:1-11; Micah 7:18; Matthew 9:1-8; Mark 2:1-12

Jesus Controls Storms and Spirits

As He got into the boat, His disciples followed Him. Suddenly, a violent storm arose on the sea, so that the boat was being swamped by the waves. But He was sleeping. So the disciples came and woke Him up, saying, "Lord, save us! We're going to die!"

But He said to them, "Why are you fearful, you of little faith?" Then He got up and rebuked the winds and the sea. And there was a great calm.

The men were amazed and said, "What kind of man is this?—even the winds and the sea obey Him!"

When He had come to the other side, to the region of the Gadarenes, two demon-possessed men met Him as they came out of the tombs. They were so violent that no one could pass that way. Suddenly they shouted, "What do You have to do with us, Son of God? Have You come here to torment us before the time?"

Now a long way off from them, a large herd of pigs was feeding. "If You drive us out," the demons begged Him, "send us into the herd of pigs."

"Go!" He told them. So when they had come out, they entered the pigs. And suddenly the whole herd rushed down the steep bank into the sea and perished in the water.

MATTHEW 8:23-32

Related texts: DEUTERONOMY 14:8; ISAIAH 65:1-4; JONAH 1; MARK 4:35–5:20; LUKE 8:22-39

Faith and Healing

As He was telling them these things, suddenly one of the leaders came and knelt down before Him, saying, "My daughter is near death, but come and lay Your hand on her, and she will live." So Jesus and His disciples got up and followed him.

Just then, a woman who had suffered from bleeding for 12 years approached from behind and touched the tassel on His robe, for she said to herself, "If I can just touch His robe, I'll be made well!"

But Jesus turned and saw her. "Have courage, daughter," He said. "Your faith has made you well." And the woman was made well from that moment.

When Jesus came to the leader's house, He saw the flute players and a crowd lamenting loudly. "Leave," He said, "because the girl isn't dead, but sleeping." And they started laughing at Him. But when the crowd had been put outside, He went in and took her by the hand, and the girl got up. And this news spread throughout that whole area.

Is anyone among you suffering? He should pray. Is anyone cheerful? He should sing praises. Is anyone among you sick? He should call for the elders of the church, and they should pray over him after anointing him with olive oil in the name of the Lord. The prayer of faith will save the sick person, and the Lord will raise him up; and if he has committed sins, he will be forgiven. Therefore, confess your sins to one another and pray for one another, so that you may be healed. The intense prayer of the righteous is very powerful.

MATTHEW 9:18-26; JAMES 5:13-16

Related texts: HABAKKUK 2:4; MATTHEW 9:27-30; MARK 5:21-43; LUKE 7:1-10,36-50; 8:22-25,40-56; 17:11-19; 18:35-43

Jesus Responds to Lack of Faith

Then He went into a house, and the crowd gathered again so that they were not even able to eat. When His family heard this, they set out to restrain Him, because they said, "He's out of His mind."

And the scribes who had come down from Jerusalem said, "He has Beelzebul in Him!" and, "He drives out demons by the ruler of the demons!"

So He summoned them and spoke to them in parables: "How can Satan drive out Satan? If a kingdom is divided against itself, that kingdom cannot stand. If a house is divided against itself, that house cannot stand. And if Satan rebels against himself and is divided, he cannot stand but is finished!

"On the other hand, no one can enter a strong man's house and rob his possessions unless he first ties up the strong man. Then he will rob his house. I assure you: People will be forgiven for all sins and whatever blasphemies they may blaspheme. But whoever blasphemes against the Holy Spirit never has forgiveness, but is guilty of an eternal sin" —because they were saying, "He has an unclean spirit."

MARK 3:20-30

Related texts: EXODUS 22:28; PSALM 106:1-37; MATTHEW 12:22-37; 13:53-58; MARK 6:1-6; LUKE 11:14-23; 12:10

Jesus Feeds Five Thousand

Therefore, when Jesus raised His eyes and noticed a huge crowd coming toward Him, He asked Philip, "Where will we buy bread so these people can eat?" He asked this to test him, for He Himself knew what He was going to do.

Philip answered, "Two hundred denarii worth of bread wouldn't be enough for each of them to have a little."

One of His disciples, Andrew, Simon Peter's brother, said to Him, "There's a boy here who has five barley loaves and two fish—but what are they for so many?"

Then Jesus said, "Have the people sit down."

There was plenty of grass in that place, so the men sat down, numbering about 5,000. Then Jesus took the loaves, and after giving thanks He distributed them to those who were seated; so also with the fish, as much as they wanted.

When they were full, He told His disciples, "Collect the leftovers so that nothing is wasted." So they collected them and filled 12 baskets with the pieces from the five barley loaves that were left over by those who had eaten.

When the people saw the sign He had done, they said, "This really is the Prophet who was to come into the world!"

JOHN 6:5-14

Related texts: DEUTERONOMY 8:2-3; MATTHEW 14:13-21; MARK 6:32-44; LUKE 9:10:17

Who Is Jesus?

When Jesus came to the region of Caesarea Philippi, He asked His disciples, "Who do people say that the Son of Man is?"

And they said, "Some say John the Baptist; others, Elijah; still others, Jeremiah or one of the prophets."

"But you," He asked them, "who do you say that I am?"

Simon Peter answered, "You are the Messiah, the Son of the living God!"

And Jesus responded, "Blessed are you, Simon son of Jonah, because flesh and blood did not reveal this to you, but My Father in heaven. And I also say to you that you are Peter, and on this rock I will build My church, and the forces of Hades will not overpower it. I will give you the keys of the kingdom of heaven, and whatever you bind on earth will have been bound in heaven, and whatever you loose on earth will have been loosed in heaven."

And He gave the disciples orders to tell no one that He was the Messiah.

From then on Jesus began to point out to His disciples that He must go to Jerusalem and suffer many things from the elders, chief priests, and scribes, be killed, and be raised the third day.

MATTHEW 16:13-21

Related texts: ISAIAH 52:14-15; MARK 8:27-33; LUKE 9:18-22; JOHN 6:67-71

The Transfiguration

After six days Jesus took Peter, James, and John, and led them up on a high mountain by themselves to be alone. He was transformed in front of them, and His clothes became dazzling, extremely white, as no launderer on earth could whiten them. Elijah appeared to them with Moses, and they were talking with Jesus.

Then Peter said to Jesus, "Rabbi, it is good for us to be here! Let us make three tabernacles: one for You, one for Moses, and one for Elijah"—because he did not know what he should say, since they were terrified.

A cloud appeared, overshadowing them, and a voice came from the cloud:

> This is My beloved Son;
> listen to Him!

Then suddenly, looking around, they no longer saw anyone with them except Jesus alone.

As they were coming down from the mountain, He ordered them to tell no one what they had seen until the Son of Man had risen from the dead. They kept this word to themselves, discussing what "rising from the dead" meant.

> The Word became flesh
> and took up residence among us.
> We observed His glory,
> the glory as the One and Only Son from the
>   Father,
> full of grace and truth.

MARK 9:2-10; JOHN 1:14

Related texts: EXODUS 40:33-35; MATTHEW 17:1-9; LUKE 9:28-36; ROMANS 16:25-27; 1 TIMOTHY 1:17; JUDE 24-25

Small Faith—Large Results

When they reached the crowd, a man approached and knelt down before Him. "Lord," he said, "have mercy on my son, because he has seizures and suffers severely. He often falls into the fire and often into the water. I brought him to Your disciples, but they couldn't heal him."

Jesus replied, "You unbelieving and rebellious generation! How long will I be with you? How long must I put up with you? Bring him here to Me." Then Jesus rebuked the demon, and it came out of him, and from that moment the boy was healed.

Then the disciples approached Jesus privately and said, "Why couldn't we drive it out?"

"Because of your little faith," He told them. "For I assure you: If you have faith the size of a mustard seed, you will tell this mountain, 'Move from here to there,' and it will move. Nothing will be impossible for you. [However, this kind does not come out except by prayer and fasting.]"

As they were meeting in Galilee, Jesus told them, "The Son of Man is about to be betrayed into the hands of men. They will kill Him, and on the third day He will be raised up." And they were deeply distressed.

"I assure you: The one who believes in Me will also do the works that I do. And he will do even greater works than these, because I am going to the Father. Whatever you ask in My name, I will do it, so that the Father may be glorified in the Son."

MATTHEW 17:14-23; JOHN 14:12-13

Related texts: 1 SAMUEL 16:14-23; MARK 9:14-32; LUKE 9:37-45; ROMANS 4:18-21; 11:1-23; HEBREWS 3:16-19

Jesus Teaches His Disciples to Pray

He was praying in a certain place, and when He finished, one of His disciples said to Him, "Lord, teach us to pray, just as John also taught his disciples."

He said to them, "Whenever you pray, say:

> Father, Your name be honored as holy.
> Your kingdom come.
> Give us each day our daily bread.
> And forgive us our sins,
> for we ourselves also forgive everyone in debt to us.
> And do not bring us into temptation."

He also said to them: "Suppose one of you has a friend and goes to him at midnight and says to him, 'Friend, lend me three loaves of bread, because a friend of mine on a journey has come to me, and I don't have anything to offer him.' Then he will answer from inside and say, 'Don't bother me! The door is already locked, and my children and I have gone to bed. I can't get up to give you anything.' I tell you, even though he won't get up and give him anything because he is his friend, yet because of his persistence, he will get up and give him as much as he needs.

"So I say to you, keep asking, and it will be given to you. Keep searching, and you will find. Keep knocking, and the door will be opened to you. For everyone who asks receives, and the one who searches finds, and to the one who knocks, the door will be opened."

LUKE 11:1-10

Related texts: PSALM 89:19-29; ISAIAH 9:6-7; MATTHEW 6:6-13; 7:7-11; REVELATION 3:14-22

Jesus Welcomes Little Children

Then an argument started among them about who would be the greatest of them. But Jesus, knowing the thoughts of their hearts, took a little child and had him stand next to Him. He told them, "Whoever welcomes this little child in My name welcomes Me. And whoever welcomes Me welcomes Him who sent Me. For whoever is least among you all—this one is great."

Some people were bringing little children to Him so He might touch them. But His disciples rebuked them. When Jesus saw it, He was indignant and said to them, "Let the little children come to Me; don't stop them, for the kingdom of God belongs to such as these. I assure you: Whoever does not welcome the kingdom of God like a little child will never enter it." After taking them in His arms, He laid His hands on them and blessed them.

In that same hour He rejoiced in the Holy Spirit and said, "I praise You, Father, Lord of heaven and earth, because You have hidden these things from the wise and the learned and have revealed them to infants. Yes, Father, because this was Your good pleasure. All things have been entrusted to Me by My Father. No one knows who the Son is except the Father, and who the Father is except the Son, and anyone to whom the Son desires to reveal Him."

LUKE 9:46-48; MARK 10:13-16; LUKE 10:21-22

Related texts: PSALM 127:3-5; MATTHEW 18:1-14; 19:13-15; MARK 9:33-37; LUKE 18:15-17

Jesus Heals on the Sabbath

As He was teaching in one of the synagogues on the Sabbath, a woman was there who had been disabled by a spirit for over 18 years. She was bent over and could not straighten up at all. When Jesus saw her, He called out to her, "Woman, you are free of your disability." Then He laid His hands on her, and instantly she was restored and began to glorify God.

But the leader of the synagogue, indignant because Jesus had healed on the Sabbath, responded by telling the crowd, "There are six days when work should be done; therefore come on those days and be healed, and not on the Sabbath day."

But the Lord answered him and said, "Hypocrites! Doesn't each one of you untie his ox or donkey from the manger on the Sabbath, and lead it to water? And this woman, a daughter of Abraham, whom Satan has bound for 18 years—shouldn't she be untied from this bondage on the Sabbath day?"

When He had said these things, all His adversaries were humiliated, but the whole crowd was rejoicing over all the glorious things He was doing.

Luke 13:10-17

Jesus Teaches on Divorce and Celibacy

Some Pharisees approached Him to test Him. They asked, "Is it lawful for a man to divorce his wife on any grounds?"

"Haven't you read," He replied, "that He who created them in the beginning made them male and female, and He also said:

For this reason a man will leave his father and mother
and be joined to his wife,
and the two will become one flesh?

So they are no longer two, but one flesh. Therefore what God has joined together, man must not separate."

"Why then," they asked Him, "did Moses command us to give divorce papers and to send her away?"

He told them, "Moses permitted you to divorce your wives because of the hardness of your hearts. But it was not like that from the beginning. And I tell you, whoever divorces his wife, except for sexual immorality, and marries another, commits adultery."

His disciples said to Him, "If the relationship of a man with his wife is like this, it's better not to marry!"

But He told them, "Not everyone can accept this saying, but only those to whom it has been given. For there are eunuchs who were born that way from their mother's womb, there are eunuchs who were made by men, and there are eunuchs who have made themselves that way because of the kingdom of heaven. Let anyone accept this who can."

MATTHEW 19:3-12

Related texts: GENESIS 1:27; 2:24; DEUTERONOMY 24:1-4; MALACHI 2:13-16; MARK 10:2-12; LUKE 16:18

Treasure in Heaven

A ruler asked Him, "Good Teacher, what must I do to inherit eternal life?"

"Why do you call Me good?" Jesus asked him. "No one is good but One—God. You know the commandments:

Do not commit adultery;
do not murder;
do not steal;
do not bear false witness;
honor your father and mother."

"I have kept all these from my youth," he said.

When Jesus heard this, He told him, "You still lack one thing: sell all that you have and distribute it to the poor, and you will have treasure in heaven. Then come, follow Me."

After he heard this, he became extremely sad, because he was very rich.

Seeing that he became sad, Jesus said, "How hard it is for those who have wealth to enter the kingdom of God! For it is easier for a camel to go through the eye of a needle than for a rich person to enter the kingdom of God."

Those who heard this asked, "Then who can be saved?"

He replied, "What is impossible with men is possible with God."

Then Peter said, "Look, we have left what we had and followed You."

So He said to them, " I assure you: There is no one who has left a house, wife or brothers, parents or children because of the kingdom of God, who will not receive many times more at this time, and eternal life in the age to come."

Luke 18:18-30

Related texts: Exodus 20:12-16; Deuteronomy 5:16-20; Matthew 19:16-30; Mark 10:17-31; 1 Corinthians 13:3

The Bible is alive, it speaks to me.
Martin Luther (1483–1546)
GERMAN THEOLOGIAN AND REFORMER

He rightly reads Scripture who turns words into deeds.
St. Bernard of Clairvaux (1090–1153)
FRENCH MONK

The Bible holds up before us ideals that are within sight of the weakest and the lowliest, and yet so high that the best and noblest are kept with their faces turned ever upward.
William Jennings Bryan (1860–1925)
AMERICAN ORATOR AND POLITICIAN

Jesus Visits a Sinner

He entered Jericho and was passing through. There was a man named Zacchaeus who was a chief tax collector, and he was rich. He was trying to see who Jesus was, but he was not able because of the crowd, since he was a short man. So running ahead, he climbed up a sycamore tree to see Jesus, since He was about to pass that way. When Jesus came to the place, He looked up and said to him, "Zacchaeus, hurry and come down, because today I must stay at your house."

So he quickly came down and welcomed Him joyfully. All who saw it began to complain, "He's gone to lodge with a sinful man!"

But Zacchaeus stood there and said to the Lord, "Look, I'll give half of my possessions to the poor, Lord! And if I have extorted anything from anyone, I'll pay back four times as much!"

"Today salvation has come to this house," Jesus told him, "because he too is a son of Abraham. For the Son of Man has come to seek and to save the lost."

And just as it is appointed for people to die once—and after this, judgment—so also the Messiah, having been offered once to bear the sins of many, will appear a second time, not to bear sin, but to bring salvation to those who are waiting for Him.

LUKE 19:1-10; HEBREWS 9:27-28

Related texts: EZEKIEL 34:7-16; MARK 2:14-17; LUKE 7:36-47

Jesus Anointed for Burial

Six days before the Passover, Jesus came to Bethany where Lazarus was, whom Jesus had raised from the dead. So they gave a dinner for Him there; Martha was serving them, and Lazarus was one of those reclining at the table with Him. Then Mary took a pound of fragrant oil—pure and expensive nard—anointed Jesus' feet, and wiped His feet with her hair. So the house was filled with the fragrance of the oil.

Then one of His disciples, Judas Iscariot (who was about to betray Him), said, "Why wasn't this fragrant oil sold for 300 denarii and given to the poor?" He didn't say this because he cared about the poor, but because he was a thief. He was in charge of the money-bag and would steal part of what was put in it.

Jesus answered, "Leave her alone; she has kept it for the day of My burial. For you always have the poor with you, but you do not always have Me."

Then a large crowd of the Jews learned that He was there. They came not only because of Jesus, but also to see Lazarus whom He had raised from the dead. Therefore the chief priests decided to kill Lazarus too, because he was the reason many of the Jews were deserting them and believing in Jesus.

John 12:1-11

Related texts: Psalm 16:9-11; Matthew 26:6-13; Mark 14:3-9; Luke 7:36-50; John 11

The Triumphal Entry

As He approached Bethphage and Bethany, at the place called the Mount of Olives, He sent two of the disciples and said, "Go into the village ahead of you. As you enter it, you will find a young donkey tied there, on which no one has ever sat. Untie it and bring it here. And if anyone asks you, 'Why are you untying it?' say this: 'The Lord needs it.'"

So those who were sent left and found it just as He had told them. As they were untying the young donkey, its owners said to them, "Why are you untying the donkey?"

"The Lord needs it," they said. Then they brought it to Jesus, and after throwing their robes on the donkey, they helped Jesus get on it. As He was going along, they were spreading their robes on the road. Now He came near the path down the Mount of Olives, and the whole crowd of the disciples began to praise God joyfully with a loud voice for all the miracles they had seen:

Blessed is the King who comes in the name of the Lord.

Peace in heaven and glory in the highest heaven!

And some of the Pharisees from the crowd told Him, "Teacher, rebuke Your disciples."

He answered, "I tell you, if they were to keep silent, the stones would cry out!"

LUKE 19:29-40

Related texts: PSALM 118: MATTHEW 21:1-9; MARK 11:1-10; JOHN 12:12-19

The Parable of the Vineyard

Then He began to tell the people this parable: "A man planted a vineyard, leased it to tenant farmers, and went away for a long time. At harvest time he sent a slave to the farmers so that they might give him some fruit from the vineyard. But the farmers beat him and sent him away empty-handed. He sent yet another slave, but they beat that one too, treated him shamefully, and sent him away empty-handed. And he sent yet a third, but they wounded this one too, and threw him out.

"Then the owner of the vineyard said, 'What should I do? I will send my beloved son. Perhaps they will respect him.'

"But when the tenant farmers saw him, they discussed it among themselves and said, 'This is the heir. Let's kill him, so that the inheritance may be ours!' So they threw him out of the vineyard and killed him.

"Therefore, what will the owner of the vineyard do to them? He will come and destroy those farmers and give the vineyard to others."

But when they heard this they said, "No—never!"

But He looked at them and said, "Then what is the meaning of this Scripture:

The stone that the builders rejected—
this has become the cornerstone?

Everyone who falls on that stone will be broken to pieces, and if it falls on anyone, it will grind him to powder!"

Then the scribes and the chief priests looked for a way to get their hands on Him that very hour, because they knew He had told this parable against them, but they feared the people.

Luke 20:9-19

Related texts: Psalm 118; Matthew 21:33-46; Mark 12:1-12

The Last Supper

Then one of the Twelve—the man called Judas Iscariot—went to the chief priests and said, "What are you willing to give me if I hand Him over to you?" So they weighed out 30 pieces of silver for him. And from that time he started looking for a good opportunity to betray Him.

On the first day of Unleavened Bread the disciples came to Jesus and asked, "Where do You want us to prepare the Passover so You may eat it?"

"Go into the city to a certain man," He said, "and tell him, 'The Teacher says: My time is near; I am celebrating the Passover at your place with My disciples.'" So the disciples did as Jesus had directed them and prepared the Passover. When evening came, He was reclining at the table with the Twelve. While they were eating, He said, "I assure you: One of you will betray Me."

Deeply distressed, each one began to say to Him, "Surely not I, Lord?"

He replied, "The one who dipped his hand with Me in the bowl—he will betray Me. The Son of Man will go just as it is written about Him, but woe to that man by whom the Son of Man is betrayed! It would have been better for that man if he had not been born."

Then Judas, His betrayer, replied, "Surely not I, Rabbi?"

"You have said it," He told him.

MATTHEW 26:14-25

Related texts: PSALM 41:9; PROVERBS 11:13; MARK 14:10-25; LUKE 22:3-23; JOHN 13–17

Faithless Friends

Then Jesus said to them, "All of you will fall, because it is written:

I will strike the shepherd,
and the sheep will be scattered.

But after I have been resurrected, I will go ahead of you to Galilee."

Peter told Him, "Even if everyone falls, yet I will not!"

"I assure you," Jesus said to him, "today, this very night, before the rooster crows twice, you will deny Me three times!"

But he kept insisting, "If I have to die with You, I will never deny You!" And they all said the same thing.

Then they came to a place named Gethsemane, and He told His disciples, "Sit here while I pray." He took Peter, James, and John with Him, and He began to be horrified and deeply distressed. Then He said to them, "My soul is swallowed up in sorrow—to the point of death. Remain here and stay awake." Then He went a little farther, fell to the ground, and began to pray that if it were possible, the hour might pass from Him. And He said, "*Abba*, Father! All things are possible for You. Take this cup away from Me. Nevertheless, not what I will, but what You will."

Then He came and found them sleeping. "Simon, are you sleeping?" He asked Peter. "Couldn't you stay awake one hour? Stay awake and pray, so that you won't enter into temptation. The spirit is willing, but the flesh is weak."

MARK 14:27-38

Related texts: ZECHARIAH 13:7; MARK 14:26-42; LUKE 22:31-46; JOHN 13:36-38

Betrayal and Denial

While He was still speaking, suddenly a mob was there, and one of the Twelve named Judas was leading them. He came near Jesus to kiss Him, but Jesus said to him, "Judas, are you betraying the Son of Man with a kiss?"

They seized Him, led Him away, and brought Him into the high priest's house. Meanwhile Peter was following at a distance. When they had lit a fire in the middle of the courtyard and sat down together, Peter sat among them. When a servant saw him sitting in the firelight, and looked closely at him, she said, "This man was with Him too."

But he denied it: "Woman, I don't know Him!"

After a little while, someone else saw him and said, "You're one of them too!"

"Man, I am not!" Peter said.

About an hour later, another kept insisting, "This man was certainly with Him, since he's also a Galilean."

But Peter said, "Man, I don't know what you're talking about!" Immediately, while he was still speaking, a rooster crowed. Then the Lord turned and looked at Peter. So Peter remembered the word of the Lord, how He had said to him, "Before the rooster crows today, you will deny Me three times." And he went outside and wept bitterly.

Luke 22:47-48,54-62

Related texts: Psalm 42; Matthew 26:47-56,69-75; Mark 14:43-53,66-72; John 18:2-12,25-27

Jesus Is Sentenced to Death

The chief priests and the whole Sanhedrin were looking for testimony against Jesus to put Him to death. But they could find none. For many were giving false testimony against Him, but the testimonies did not agree. Some stood up and were giving false testimony against Him, stating, "We heard Him say, 'I will demolish this sanctuary made by hands, and in three days I will build another not made by hands.' " But not even on this did their testimony agree.

Then the high priest stood up before them all and questioned Jesus, "Don't You have an answer to what these men are testifying against You?" But He kept silent and did not answer anything. Again the high priest questioned Him, "Are You the Messiah, the Son of the Blessed One?"

"I am," said Jesus, "and all of you will see the Son of Man seated at the right hand of the Power and coming with the clouds of heaven."

Then the high priest tore his robes and said, "Why do we still need witnesses? You have heard the blasphemy! What is your decision?"

And they all condemned Him to be deserving of death. Then some began to spit on Him, to blindfold Him, and to beat Him, saying, "Prophesy!" Even the temple police took Him and slapped Him.

Mark 14:55-65

Related texts: Exodus 20:16; Daniel 7:13-14; Matthew 26:59-67; Luke 23:63-71; John 18:19-24

Jesus Is Crucified

When they arrived at the place called The Skull, they crucified Him there, along with the criminals, one on the right and one on the left. Then Jesus said, "Father, forgive them, because they do not know what they are doing." And they divided His clothes and cast lots.

The people stood watching, and even the leaders kept scoffing: "He saved others; let Him save Himself if this is God's Messiah, the Chosen One!"

Then one of the criminals hanging there began to yell insults at Him: "Aren't You the Messiah? Save Yourself and us!"

But the other answered, rebuking him: "Don't you even fear God, since you are undergoing the same punishment? We are punished justly, because we're getting back what we deserve for the things we did, but this man has done nothing wrong." Then he said, "Jesus, remember me when You come into Your kingdom!"

And He said to him, " I assure you: Today you will be with Me in paradise."

It was now about noon, and darkness came over the whole land until three, because the sun's light failed. The curtain of the sanctuary was split down the middle. And Jesus called out with a loud voice, "Father, into Your hands I entrust My spirit." Saying this, He breathed His last.

When the centurion saw what happened, he began to glorify God, saying, "This man really was righteous!"

LUKE 23:33-35,39-47

Related texts: PSALM 22; MATTHEW 27; MARK 15; LUKE 23; JOHN 18:28–19:42

The Resurrection

On the first day of the week Mary Magdalene came to the tomb early, while it was still dark. She saw that the stone had been removed from the tomb. So she ran to Simon Peter and to the other disciple, whom Jesus loved, and said to them, "They have taken the Lord out of the tomb, and we don't know where they have put Him!"

At that, Peter and the other disciple went out, heading for the tomb. The two were running together, but the other disciple outran Peter and got to the tomb first. Stooping down, he saw the linen cloths lying there, yet he did not go in. Then, following him, Simon Peter came also. He entered the tomb and saw the linen cloths lying there. The wrapping that had been on His head was not lying with the linen cloths but folded up in a separate place by itself. The other disciple, who had reached the tomb first, then entered the tomb, saw, and believed. For they still did not understand the Scripture that He must rise from the dead.

In the evening of that first day of the week, the disciples were gathered together with the doors locked because of their fear of the Jews. Then Jesus came, stood among them, and said to them, "Peace to you!"

Having said this, He showed them His hands and His side. So the disciples rejoiced when they saw the Lord.

And there are also many other things that Jesus did, which, if they were written one by one, I suppose not even the world itself could contain the books that would be written.

JOHN 20:1-9,19-20

Related texts: PSALM 16:9-11; ISAIAH 53:9-12; MATTHEW 28; MARK 16; LUKE 24; JOHN 20–21

Alive in Christ

Be careful that no one takes you captive through philosophy and empty deceit based on human tradition, based on the elemental forces of the world, and not based on Christ. For in Him the entire fullness of God's nature dwells bodily, and you have been filled by Him, who is the head over every ruler and authority. In Him you were also circumcised with a circumcision not done with hands, by putting off the body of flesh, in the circumcision of the Messiah. Having been buried with Him in baptism, you were also raised with Him through faith in the working of God, who raised Him from the dead. And when you were dead in trespasses and in the uncircumcision of your flesh, He made you alive with Him and forgave us all our trespasses. He erased the certificate of debt, with its obligations, that was against us and opposed to us, and has taken it out of the way by nailing it to the cross. He disarmed the rulers and authorities and disgraced them publicly; He triumphed over them by Him.

Therefore don't let anyone judge you in regard to food and drink or in the matter of a festival or a new moon or a sabbath day. These are a shadow of what was to come; the substance is the Messiah.

COLOSSIANS 2:8-17

Related texts: ISAIAH 1:11-14; ACTS 2:22-36; ROMANS 6:1-11; 1 CORINTHIANS 15:12-58

Jesus Returns to the Father

I wrote the first narrative, Theophilus, about all that Jesus began to do and teach until the day He was taken up, after He had given orders through the Holy Spirit to the apostles whom He had chosen. After He had suffered, He also presented Himself alive to them by many convincing proofs, appearing to them during 40 days and speaking about the kingdom of God.

While He was together with them, He commanded them not to leave Jerusalem, but to wait for the Father's promise. "This," He said, "is what you heard from Me; for John baptized with water, but you will be baptized with the Holy Spirit not many days from now."

So when they had come together, they asked Him, "Lord, at this time are You restoring the kingdom to Israel?"

He said to them, "It is not for you to know times or periods that the Father has set by His own authority. But you will receive power when the Holy Spirit has come upon you, and you will be My witnesses in Jerusalem, in all Judea and Samaria, and to the ends of the earth."

After He had said this, He was taken up as they were watching, and a cloud received Him out of their sight. While He was going, they were gazing into heaven, and suddenly two men in white clothes stood by them. They said, "Men of Galilee, why do you stand looking up into heaven? This Jesus, who has been taken from you into heaven, will come in the same way that you have seen Him going into heaven."

Acts 1:1-11

Related texts: 1 Chronicles 16:8,23-31; Psalms 67; 72; Isaiah 45:22-23; 49:6; Luke 24:50-53

The Gift of the Holy Spirit

When the day of Pentecost had arrived, they were all together in one place. Suddenly a sound like that of a violent rushing wind came from heaven, and it filled the whole house where they were staying. And tongues, like flames of fire that were divided, appeared to them and rested on each one of them. Then they were all filled with the Holy Spirit and began to speak in different languages, as the Spirit gave them ability for speech.

There were Jews living in Jerusalem, devout men from every nation under heaven. When this sound occurred, the multitude came together and was confused because each one heard them speaking in his own language. And they were astounded and amazed, saying, "Look, aren't all these who are speaking Galileans? How is it that we hear, each of us, in our own native language? Parthians, Medes, Elamites; those who live in Mesopotamia, in Judea and Cappadocia, Pontus and Asia, Phrygia and Pamphylia, Egypt and the parts of Libya near Cyrene; visitors from Rome, both Jews and proselytes, Cretans and Arabs—we hear them speaking in our own languages the magnificent acts of God." And they were all astounded and perplexed, saying to one another, "What could this be?" But some sneered and said, "They're full of new wine!"

ACTS 2:1-13

Related texts: LEVITICUS 23:4-16; MATTHEW 3:1-12; JOHN 14:15-26; 16:12-15

Peter's First Sermon

But Peter stood up with the Eleven, raised his voice, and proclaimed to them: "Jewish men and all you residents of Jerusalem, let this be known to you and pay attention to my words. For these people are not drunk, as you suppose, since it's only nine in the morning. On the contrary, this is what was spoken through the prophet Joel:

> And it will be in the last days, says God,
> that I will pour out My Spirit on all humanity;
> then your sons and your daughters will prophesy,
> your young men will see visions,
> and your old men will dream dreams.
> I will even pour out My Spirit
> on My male and female slaves in those days,
> and they will prophesy.
> Then whoever calls on the name of the Lord
> will be saved.

"Men of Israel, listen to these words: This Jesus the Nazarene was a man pointed out to you by God with miracles, wonders, and signs that God did among you through Him, just as you yourselves know. Though He was delivered up according to God's determined plan and foreknowledge, you used lawless people to nail Him to a cross and kill Him. God raised Him up, ending the pains of death, because it was not possible for Him to be held by it.

"Repent," Peter said to them, "and be baptized, each of you, in the name of Jesus the Messiah for the forgiveness of your sins, and you will receive the gift of the Holy Spirit."

ACTS 2:14-18,21-24,38

Related texts: EZEKIEL 36:16-28; 39:21-29; JOEL 2:28-32; ROMANS 10:1-13

Peter Heals a Crippled Beggar

Now Peter and John were going up together to the temple complex at the hour of prayer at three in the afternoon. And a man who was lame from his mother's womb was carried there and placed every day at the temple gate called Beautiful, so he could beg from those entering the temple complex. When he saw Peter and John about to enter the temple complex, he asked for help. Peter, along with John, looked at him intently and said, "Look at us." So he turned to them, expecting to get something from them. But Peter said, "I have neither silver nor gold, but what I have, I give to you: In the name of Jesus Christ the Nazarene, get up and walk!" Then, taking him by the right hand he raised him up, and at once his feet and ankles became strong. So he jumped up, stood, and started to walk, and he entered the temple complex with them—walking, leaping, and praising God. All the people saw him walking and praising God, and they recognized that he was the one who used to sit and beg at the Beautiful Gate of the temple complex. So they were filled with awe and astonishment at what had happened to him.

Now as they were speaking to the people, the priests, the commander of the temple guard, and the Sadducees confronted them, because they were provoked that they were teaching the people and proclaiming in the person of Jesus the resurrection from the dead. So they seized them and put them in custody until the next day, since it was already evening. But many of those who heard the message believed, and the number of the men came to about 5,000.

ACTS 3:1-10; 4:1-4

Related texts: JEREMIAH 37:15; 38:6; MATTHEW 15:29-31; 21:1-16; JOHN 5; 14:12-14

Obey God before People

When they observed the boldness of Peter and John and realized that they were uneducated and untrained men, they were amazed and knew that they had been with Jesus. And since they saw the man who had been healed standing with them, they had nothing to say in response. After they had ordered them to leave the Sanhedrin, they conferred among themselves, saying, "What should we do with these men? For an obvious sign, evident to all who live in Jerusalem, has been done through them, and we cannot deny it! But so this does not spread any further among the people, let's threaten them against speaking to anyone in this name again." So they called for them and ordered them not to preach or teach at all in the name of Jesus.

But Peter and John answered them, "Whether it's right in the sight of God for us to listen to you rather than to God, you decide; for we are unable to stop speaking about what we have seen and heard."

After threatening them further, they released them. They found no way to punish them, because the people were all giving glory to God over what had been done; for the man was over 40 years old on whom this sign of healing had been performed.

After they were released, they went to their own fellowship and reported all that the chief priests and the elders had said to them.

ACTS 4:13-23

Related texts: JEREMIAH 20:9; MATTHEW 5:10-12; ACTS 5:17-42

Stephen Is Martyred for His Testimony

So the preaching about God flourished, the number of the disciples in Jerusalem multiplied greatly, and a large group of priests became obedient to the faith.

Stephen, full of grace and power, was performing great wonders and signs among the people. Then some from what is called the Freedmen's Synagogue, composed of both Cyrenians and Alexandrians, and some from Cilicia and Asia, came forward and disputed with Stephen. But they were unable to stand up against the wisdom and the Spirit by whom he spoke.

Then they induced men to say, "We heard him speaking blasphemous words against Moses and God!" They stirred up the people, the elders, and the scribes; so they came up, dragged him off, and took him to the Sanhedrin.

But Stephen, filled by the Holy Spirit, gazed into heaven. He saw God's glory, with Jesus standing at the right hand of God, and he said, "Look! I see the heavens opened and the Son of Man standing at the right hand of God!"

Then they screamed at the top of their voices, stopped their ears, and rushed together against him. They threw him out of the city and began to stone him. And the witnesses laid their robes at the feet of a young man named Saul. They were stoning Stephen as he called out: "Lord Jesus, receive my spirit!" Then he knelt down and cried out with a loud voice, "Lord, do not charge them with this sin!" And saying this, he fell asleep.

Saul agreed with putting him to death.

ACTS 6:7-12; 7:55–8:1a

Related texts: LEVITICUS 24:10-16; MARK 13:9-13; JOHN 16:1-4; ACTS 7:1-54; 8:1-4

Saul Meets Jesus

On that day a severe persecution broke out against the church in Jerusalem, and all except the apostles were scattered throughout the land of Judea and Samaria. But devout men buried Stephen and mourned deeply over him. Saul, however, was ravaging the church, and he would enter house after house, drag off men and women, and put them in prison.

So those who were scattered went on their way proclaiming the message of good news.

Meanwhile Saul, still breathing threats and murder against the disciples of the Lord, went to the high priest and requested letters from him to the synagogues in Damascus, so that if he found any who belonged to the Way, either men or women, he might bring them as prisoners to Jerusalem. As he traveled and was nearing Damascus, a light from heaven suddenly flashed around him. Falling to the ground, he heard a voice saying to him, "Saul, Saul, why are you persecuting Me?"

"Who are You, Lord?" he said.

"I am Jesus, whom you are persecuting," He replied. "But get up and go into the city, and you will be told what you must do."

The men who were traveling with him stood speechless, hearing the sound but seeing no one. Then Saul got up from the ground, and though his eyes were open, he could see nothing. So they took him by the hand and led him into Damascus. He was unable to see for three days, and did not eat or drink.

ACTS 8:1b-4; 9:1-9

Related texts: DANIEL 8:26-27; LUKE 1:18-20; ACTS 22:1-21; 26:1-29

Saul Begins to Preach about Jesus

Now in Damascus there was a disciple named Ananias. And the Lord said to him in a vision, "Ananias!"

"Here I am, Lord!" he said.

"Get up and go to the street called Straight," the Lord said to him, "to the house of Judas, and ask for a man from Tarsus named Saul, since he is praying there. In a vision he has seen a man named Ananias coming in and placing his hands on him so he may regain his sight."

"Lord," Ananias answered, "I have heard from many people about this man, how much harm he has done to Your saints in Jerusalem. And he has authority here from the chief priests to arrest all who call on Your name."

But the Lord said to him, "Go! For this man is My chosen instrument to carry My name before Gentiles, kings, and the sons of Israel."

So Ananias left and entered the house. Then he placed his hands on him and said, "Brother Saul, the Lord Jesus, who appeared to you on the road you were traveling, has sent me so you may regain your sight and be filled with the Holy Spirit."

At once something like scales fell from his eyes, and he regained his sight. Then he got up and was baptized. And after taking some food, he regained his strength.

Saul was with the disciples in Damascus for some days. Immediately he began proclaiming Jesus in the synagogues: "He is the Son of God."

Acts 9:10-15,17-20

Related texts: Genesis 20; Numbers 12; 1 Corinthians 15:1-11; Galatians 1:11-24

The First Missionary Journey

In the local church at Antioch there were prophets and teachers: Barnabas, Simeon who was called Niger, Lucius the Cyrenian, Manaen, a close friend of Herod the tetrarch, and Saul.

As they were ministering to the Lord and fasting, the Holy Spirit said, "Set apart for Me Barnabas and Saul for the work that I have called them to." Then, after they had fasted, prayed, and laid hands on them, they sent them off.

Being sent out by the Holy Spirit, they came down to Seleucia, and from there they sailed to Cyprus. Arriving in Salamis, they proclaimed God's message in the Jewish synagogues. They also had John as their assistant. When they had gone through the whole island as far as Paphos, they came across a sorcerer, a Jewish false prophet named Bar-Jesus. He was with the proconsul, Sergius Paulus, an intelligent man. This man summoned Barnabas and Saul and desired to hear God's message. But Elymas, the sorcerer, which is how his name is translated, opposed them and tried to turn the proconsul away from the faith.

Then Saul—also called Paul—filled with the Holy Spirit, stared straight at the sorcerer and said, "You son of the Devil, full of all deceit and all fraud, enemy of all righteousness! Won't you ever stop perverting the straight paths of the Lord? Now, look! The Lord's hand is against you: you are going to be blind, and will not see the sun for a time." Suddenly a mist and darkness fell on him, and he went around seeking someone to lead him by the hand.

Then the proconsul, seeing what happened, believed and was astonished at the teaching about the Lord.

ACTS 13:1-12

Related texts: NUMBERS 27:22-23; MATTHEW 19:13-15; LUKE 4:40; ACTS 6:1-6; 8:5-25; 1 TIMOTHY 4:11-14

Paul and Barnabas among the Gentiles

In Lystra a man without strength in his feet, lame from birth, and who had never walked, sat and heard Paul speaking. After observing him closely and seeing that he had faith to be healed, Paul said in a loud voice, "Stand up straight on your feet!" And he jumped up and started to walk around.

Then some Jews came from Antioch and Iconium, and when they had won over the crowds and stoned Paul, they dragged him out of the city, thinking he was dead. After the disciples surrounded him, he got up and went into the town. The next day he left with Barnabas for Derbe.

After they had evangelized that town and made many disciples, they returned to Lystra, to Iconium, and to Antioch, strengthening the hearts of the disciples by encouraging them to continue in the faith, and by telling them, "It is necessary to pass through many troubles on our way into the kingdom of God."

When they had appointed elders in every church and prayed with fasting, they committed them to the Lord in whom they had believed.

From there they sailed back to Antioch where they had been entrusted to the grace of God for the work they had completed. After they arrived and gathered the church together, they reported everything God had done with them, and that He had opened the door of faith to the Gentiles. And they spent a considerable time with the disciples.

ACTS 14:8-10,19-23,26-28

Related texts: EXODUS 17:1-4; NUMBERS 14:1-10; JOHN 8:31-59; ACTS 7:52-60; 14:1-7; ROMANS 1:1-17; EPHESIANS 2:11-22

In Everything Give Thanks

Give thanks to the LORD; call on His name;
proclaim His deeds among the peoples.
Sing to Him; sing praise to Him;
tell about all His wonderful works!

Come, let us shout joyfully to the LORD,
shout triumphantly to the rock of our salvation!
Let us enter His presence with thanksgiving;
let us shout triumphantly to Him in song.
For the LORD is a great God,
a great King above all gods.
The depths of the earth are in His hand,
and the mountain peaks are His.
The sea is His; He made it.
His hands formed the dry land.
Come, let us worship and bow down;
let us kneel before the LORD our Maker.
For He is our God,
and we are the people of His pasture, the sheep under His care.

Rejoice always!
Pray constantly.
Give thanks in everything,
for this is God's will for you in Christ Jesus.

1 CHRONICLES 16:8-9; PSALM 95:1-7a; 1 THESSALONIANS
5:16-18

Related texts: NEHEMIAH 12:27-43; PSALMS 77; 135:1-7;
148; LUKE 22:14-19

Give Thanks for God's Provision

Give thanks to the LORD, for He is good;
His faithful love endures forever.
Let the redeemed of the LORD proclaim
that He has redeemed them from the hand of the foe
and has gathered them from the lands—
from the east and the west,
from the north and the south.
Some wandered in the desolate wilderness,
finding no way to a city where they could live.
They were hungry and thirsty;
their spirits failed within them.
Then they cried out to the LORD in their trouble;
He rescued them from their distress.
He led them by the right path
to go to a city where they could live.
Let them give thanks to the LORD for His faithful love
and His wonderful works for the human race.
For He has satisfied the thirsty
and filled the hungry with good things.

Let them give thanks to the LORD for His faithful love
and His wonderful works for the human race.
Let them offer sacrifices of thanksgiving
and announce His works with shouts of joy.

PSALM 107:1-9,21-22

Related texts: 2 CHRONICLES 20:14-26; PSALMS 104; 118;
145; MATTHEW 6:25-34

Give Thanks to God among His People

Shout triumphantly to the LORD, all the earth.
Serve the LORD with gladness;
come before Him with joyful songs.
Acknowledge that the LORD is God.
He made us, and we are His—
His people, the sheep of His pasture.
Enter His gates with thanksgiving
and His courts with praise.
Give thanks to Him and praise His name.
For the LORD is good, and His love is eternal;
His faithfulness endures through all generations.

And let the peace of the Messiah, to which you were also called in one body, control your hearts. Be thankful. Let the message about the Messiah dwell richly among you, teaching and admonishing one another in all wisdom, and singing psalms, hymns, and spiritual songs, with gratitude in your hearts to God. And whatever you do, in word or in deed, do everything in the name of the Lord Jesus, giving thanks to God the Father through Him.

PSALM 100; COLOSSIANS 3:15-17

Related texts: 2 CHRONICLES 6:41; PSALMS 65; 84; 96;
EPHESIANS 5:18-20; 3 JOHN 11

Give Thanks to God for His Enduring Love

Give thanks to the L ORD, for He is good.
His love is eternal.
Give thanks to the God of gods.
His love is eternal.
Give thanks to the Lord of lords.
His love is eternal.

We always thank God, the Father of our Lord Jesus Christ, when we pray for you, for we have heard of your faith in Christ Jesus and of the love you have for all the saints because of the hope reserved for you in heaven. You have already heard about this hope in the message of truth, the gospel that has come to you. It is bearing fruit and growing all over the world, just as it has among you since the day you heard it and recognized God's grace in the truth.

I always thank my God when I mention you in my prayers, because I hear of your love and faith toward the Lord Jesus and for all the saints. I pray that your participation in the faith may become effective through knowing every good thing that is in us for the glory of Christ. For I have great joy and encouragement from your love, because the hearts of the saints have been refreshed through you, brother.

P SALM 136:1-3; C OLOSSIANS 1:3-6; P HILEMON 4-7

Related texts: 1 C HRONICLES 16:34-36; 2 C HRONICLES 5–7; P SALMS 118:1-4; 136:4-26; 2 C ORINTHIANS 9:10-15

Receive God's Good Gifts with Thanksgiving

Now the Spirit explicitly says that in the latter times some will depart from the faith, paying attention to deceitful spirits and the teachings of demons, through the hypocrisy of liars whose consciences are seared. They forbid marriage and demand abstinence from foods that God created to be received with gratitude by those who believe and know the truth. For everything created by God is good, and nothing should be rejected if it is received with thanksgiving, since it is sanctified by the word of God and by prayer.

If you point these things out to the brothers, you will be a good servant of Christ Jesus, nourished by the words of the faith and of the good teaching that you have followed. But have nothing to do with irreverent and silly myths. Rather, train yourself in godliness, for,

> the training of the body has a limited benefit,
> but godliness is beneficial in every way,
> since it holds promise for the present life
> and also for the life to come.

This saying is trustworthy and deserves full acceptance. In fact, we labor and strive for this, because we have put our hope in the living God, who is the Savior of everyone, especially of those who believe.

Command and teach these things.

1 TIMOTHY 4:1-11

Related texts: 1 CHRONICLES 16:4-14; ROMANS 8:18-28; 14; 1 CORINTHIANS 10

Give Thanks to God in Heaven

Immediately I was in the Spirit, and there in heaven a throne was set. One was seated on the throne and the One seated looked like jasper and carnelian stone. A rainbow that looked like an emerald surrounded the throne. Around that throne were 24 thrones, and on the thrones sat 24 elders dressed in white clothes, with gold crowns on their heads. From the throne came flashes of lightning, rumblings, and thunder. Burning before the throne were seven fiery torches, which are the seven spirits of God. Also before the throne was something like a sea of glass, similar to crystal. In the middle and around the throne were four living creatures covered with eyes in front and in back.

Day and night they never stop, saying:
Holy, holy, holy,
Lord God, the Almighty,
who was, who is, and who is coming.
Whenever the living creatures give glory, honor, and thanks to the One seated on the throne, the One who lives forever and ever, the 24 elders fall down before the One seated on the throne, worship the One who lives forever and ever, cast their crowns before the throne, and say:
Our Lord and God,
You are worthy to receive
glory and honor and power,
because You have created all things,
and because of Your will
they exist and were created.

REVELATION 4:2-6,8b-11

Related texts: EXODUS 24:1-11; ISAIAH 6; PSALMS 103:20-22;
148; MARK 10:17-18

Let Everything Praise the LORD!

Hallelujah!
Praise God in His sanctuary.
Praise Him in His mighty heavens.
Praise Him for His powerful acts;
praise Him for His abundant greatness.
Praise Him with trumpet blast;
praise Him with harp and lyre.
Praise Him with tambourine and dance;
praise Him with flute and strings.
Praise Him with resounding cymbals;
praise Him with clashing cymbals.
Let everything that breathes praise the LORD.
Hallelujah!

And don't get drunk with wine, which leads to
reckless actions, but be filled with the Spirit:
    speaking to one another in psalms, hymns, and
       spiritual songs,
    singing and making music to the Lord in your heart,
    giving thanks always for everything
    to God the Father in the name of our Lord Jesus
       Christ.

PSALM 150; EPHESIANS 5:18-20

Related texts: EXODUS 15:1-21; 1 CHRONICLES 15–16;
COLOSSIANS 3:16-17

Jews and Gentiles Are One in Christ

You have heard, haven't you, about the administration of God's grace that He gave to me for you? The mystery was made known to me by revelation, as I have briefly written above. By reading this you are able to understand my insight about the mystery of the Messiah. This was not made known to people in other generations as it is now revealed to His holy apostles and prophets by the Spirit: the Gentiles are co-heirs, members of the same body, and partners of the promise in Christ Jesus through the gospel. I was made a servant of this gospel by the gift of God's grace that was given to me by the working of His power.

This grace was given to me—the least of all the saints!—to proclaim to the Gentiles the incalculable riches of the Messiah, and to shed light for all about the administration of the mystery hidden for ages in God who created all things. This is so that God's multi-faceted wisdom may now be made known through the church to the rulers and authorities in the heavens. This is according to the purpose of the ages, which He made in the Messiah, Jesus our Lord, in whom we have boldness, access, and confidence through faith in Him.

EPHESIANS 3:2-12

Related texts: ISAIAH 49:1-6; ACTS 15; GALATIANS 3:25-29; EPHESIANS 2:11-22

Spiritual Gifts

About matters of the spirit: brothers, I do not want you to be unaware. You know how, when you were pagans, you were led to dumb idols—being led astray. Therefore I am informing you that no one speaking by the Spirit of God says, "Jesus is cursed," and no one can say, "Jesus is Lord," except by the Holy Spirit.

Now there are different gifts, but the same Spirit. There are different ministries, but the same Lord. And there are different activities, but the same God is active in everyone and everything. A manifestation of the Spirit is given to each person to produce what is beneficial:

> to one is given a message of wisdom through the Spirit,
>
> to another, a message of knowledge by the same Spirit,
>
> to another, faith by the same Spirit,
>
> to another, gifts of healing by the one Spirit,
>
> to another, the performing of miracles,
>
> to another, prophecy,
>
> to another, distinguishing between spirits,
>
> to another, different kinds of languages,
>
> to another, interpretation of languages.

But one and the same Spirit is active in all these, distributing to each one as He wills.

For as the body is one and has many parts, and all the parts of that body, though many, are one body—so also is Christ. For we were all baptized by one Spirit into one body—whether Jews or Greeks, whether slaves or free—and we were all made to drink of one Spirit.

1 CORINTHIANS 12:1-13

Related texts: ROMANS 12:1-8; 1 CORINTHIANS 13–14; EPHESIANS 4:1-16; HEBREWS 2:1-4; 1 PETER 4:7-11

I believe that the intention of Holy Writ was to persuade men of the truths necessary to salvation; such as neither science nor other means could render credible, but only the voice of the Holy Spirit.

Galileo (1564–1642)
ITALIAN ASTRONOMER

I feel that a comprehensive study of the Bible is a liberal education for anyone. Nearly all of the great men of our country have been well versed in the teachings of the Bible.

Franklin D. Roosevelt (1882–1945)
UNITED STATES PRESIDENT

I have found in the Bible words for my inmost thoughts, songs for my joy, utterance for my hidden griefs and pleading for My shame and feebleness.

Samuel Taylor Coleridge (1772–1834)
ENGLISH POET

Future Hope, Future Reward

For we know that if our earthly house, a tent, is destroyed, we have a building from God, a house not made with hands, eternal in the heavens. And, in fact, we groan in this one, longing to put on our house from heaven, since, when we are clothed, we will not be found naked. Indeed, we who are in this tent groan, burdened as we are, because we do not want to be unclothed but clothed, so that mortality may be swallowed up by life. And the One who prepared us for this very thing is God, who gave us the Spirit as a down payment.

Therefore, though we are always confident and know that while we are at home in the body we are away from the Lord—for we walk by faith, not by sight—yet we are confident and satisfied to be out of the body and at home with the Lord. Therefore, whether we are at home or away, we make it our aim to be pleasing to Him. For we must all appear before the judgment seat of Christ, so that each may be repaid for what he has done in the body, whether good or bad.

2 CORINTHIANS 5:1-10

Related texts: ECCLESIASTES 12; JOHN 11:20-27; ROMANS 14:1-13; PHILIPPIANS 1:20-26; 1 CORINTHIANS 15:35-54

Sealed for Salvation

Blessed be the God and Father of our Lord Jesus Christ, who has blessed us with every spiritual blessing in the heavens, in Christ; for He chose us in Him, before the foundation of the world, to be holy and blameless in His sight. In love He predestined us to be adopted through Jesus Christ for Himself, according to His favor and will, to the praise of His glorious grace that He favored us with in the Beloved.

In Him we have redemption through His blood, the forgiveness of our trespasses, according to the riches of His grace that He lavished on us with all wisdom and understanding. He made known to us the mystery of His will, according to His good pleasure that He planned in Him for the administration of the days of fulfillment—to bring everything together in the Messiah, both things in heaven and things on earth in Him.

In Him we were also made His inheritance, predestined according to the purpose of the One who works out everything in agreement with the decision of His will, so that we who had already put our hope in the Messiah might bring praise to His glory.

In Him you also, when you heard the word of truth, the gospel of your salvation—in Him when you believed—were sealed with the promised Holy Spirit. He is the down payment of our inheritance, for the redemption of the possession, to the praise of His glory.

EPHESIANS 1:3-14

Related texts: PSALM 113; ROMANS 8:29-39; EPHESIANS 2:4-10; REVELATION 3:5; 13:8; 17:8; 20:15

Humility and Glory

If then there is any encouragement in Christ, if any consolation of love, if any fellowship with the Spirit, if any affection and mercy, fulfill my joy by thinking the same way, having the same love, sharing the same feelings, focusing on one goal. Do nothing out of rivalry or conceit, but in humility consider others as more important than yourselves. Everyone should look out not only for his own interests, but also for the interests of others. Make your own attitude that of Christ Jesus,

> who, existing in the form of God, did not
> consider equality with God
> as something to be used for His own advantage.
> Instead He emptied Himself by assuming the
> form of a slave,
> taking on the likeness of men.
> And when He had come as a man in His
> external form,
> He humbled Himself by becoming obedient
> to the point of death—even to death on a cross.
> For this reason God also highly exalted Him
> and gave Him the name that is above every
> name,
> so that at the name of Jesus every knee should
> bow—
> of those who are in heaven and on earth and
> under the earth—
> and every tongue should confess that Jesus
> Christ is Lord,
> to the glory of God the Father.

PHILIPPIANS 2:1-11

Related texts: ISAIAH 45:22-25; JOHN 13:1-15; ROMANS 14:11-12; 1 CORINTHIANS 15:20-28; PHILIPPIANS 2:19-21; 1 PETER 5:5-6

To Know Christ

If anyone else thinks he has grounds for confidence in the flesh, I have more: circumcised the eighth day; of the nation of Israel, of the tribe of Benjamin, a Hebrew born of Hebrews; as to the law, a Pharisee; as to zeal, persecuting the church; as to the righteousness that is in the law, blameless.

But everything that was a gain to me, I have considered to be a loss because of Christ. More than that, I also consider everything to be a loss in view of the surpassing value of knowing Christ Jesus my Lord. Because of Him I have suffered the loss of all things and consider them filth, so that I may gain Christ and be found in Him, not having a righteousness of my own from the law, but one that is through faith in Christ—the righteousness from God based on faith. My goal is to know Him and the power of His resurrection and the fellowship of His sufferings, being conformed to His death, assuming that I will somehow reach the resurrection from among the dead.

Not that I have already reached the goal or am already fully mature, but I make every effort to take hold of it because I also have been taken hold of by Christ Jesus. Brothers, I do not consider myself to have taken hold of it. But one thing I do: forgetting what is behind and reaching forward to what is ahead, I pursue as my goal the prize promised by God's heavenly call in Christ Jesus.

PHILIPPIANS 3:4b-14

Related texts: PSALM 18:30-33; MATTHEW 5:43-48; MARK 8:34-37; ACTS 22:1-21; COLOSSIANS 1:24; HEBREWS 12:1-3a

The Supremacy of Christ

He is the image of the invisible God,
the firstborn over all creation;
because by Him everything was created,
in heaven and on earth, the visible and the
invisible,
whether thrones or dominions or rulers or
authorities—
all things have been created through Him and
for Him.
He is before all things, and by Him all things
hold together.
He is also the head of the body, the church;
He is the beginning, the firstborn from the dead,
so that He might come to have first place in
everything.
For God was pleased to have all His fullness
dwell in Him,
and through Him to reconcile everything to
Himself
by making peace through the blood of His cross—
whether things on earth or things in heaven.

And you were once alienated and hostile in mind
because of your evil actions. But now He has reconciled
you by His physical body through His death, to present
you holy, faultless, and blameless before Him—if indeed
you remain grounded and steadfast in the faith, and are
not shifted away from the hope of the gospel that you
heard. This gospel has been proclaimed in all creation
under heaven, and I, Paul, have become a minister of it.

COLOSSIANS 1:15-23

Related texts: GENESIS 1:26; JOHN 1:1-18; ROMANS 5:9-11;
2 CORINTHIANS 5:17-21; COLOSSIANS 2:9-10; HEBREWS 1:1-3

Meeting the Lord in the Air

We do not want you to be uninformed, brothers, concerning those who are asleep, so that you will not grieve like the rest, who have no hope. Since we believe that Jesus died and rose again, in the same way God will bring with Him those who have fallen asleep through Jesus. For we say this to you by a revelation from the Lord: We who are still alive at the Lord's coming will certainly have no advantage over those who have fallen asleep. For the Lord Himself will descend from heaven with a shout, with the archangel's voice, and with the trumpet of God, and the dead in Christ will rise first. Then we who are still alive will be caught up together with them in the clouds to meet the Lord in the air; and so we will always be with the Lord. Therefore encourage one another with these words.

About the times and the seasons: brothers, you do not need anything to be written to you. For you yourselves know very well that the Day of the Lord will come just like a thief in the night. When they say, "Peace and security," then sudden destruction comes on them, like labor pains on a pregnant woman, and they will not escape. But you, brothers, are not in the dark, so that this day would overtake you like a thief.

1 THESSALONIANS 4:13–5:4

Related texts: DANIEL 12:1-3; MATTHEW 24; 2 PETER 3; REVELATION 3:1-6

Work Is Good

Now we command you, brothers, in the name of our Lord Jesus Christ, to keep away from every brother who walks irresponsibly and not according to the tradition received from us. For you yourselves know how you must imitate us: we were not irresponsible among you; we did not eat anyone's bread free of charge; instead, we labored and toiled, working night and day, so that we would not be a burden to any of you. It is not that we don't have the right to support, but we did it to make ourselves an example to you so that you would imitate us. In fact, when we were with you, this is what we commanded you: "If anyone isn't willing to work, he should not eat." For we hear that there are some among you who walk irresponsibly, not working at all, but interfering with the work of others. Now we command and exhort such people, by the Lord Jesus Christ, that quietly working, they may eat their own bread. Brothers, do not grow weary in doing good.

And if anyone does not obey our instruction in this letter, take note of that person; don't associate with him, so that he may be ashamed. Yet don't treat him as an enemy, but warn him as a brother.

2 THESSALONIANS 3:6-15

Godliness and Contentment

If anyone teaches other doctrine and does not agree with the sound teaching of our Lord Jesus Christ and with the teaching that promotes godliness, he is conceited, understanding nothing, but having a sick interest in disputes and arguments over words. From these come envy, quarreling, slanders, evil suspicions, and constant disagreement among men whose minds are depraved and deprived of the truth, who imagine that godliness is a way to material gain. But godliness with contentment is a great gain.

> For we brought nothing into the world, and we can take nothing out.
> But if we have food and clothing, we will be content with these.

But those who want to be rich fall into temptation, a trap, and many foolish and harmful desires, which plunge people into ruin and destruction. For the love of money is a root of all kinds of evil, and by craving it, some have wandered away from the faith and pierced themselves with many pains.

Instruct those who are rich in the present age not to be arrogant or to set their hope on the uncertainty of wealth, but on God, who richly provides us with all things to enjoy. Instruct them to do good, to be rich in good works, to be generous, willing to share, storing up for themselves a good foundation for the age to come, so that they may take hold of life that is real.

1 TIMOTHY 6:3-10,17-19

Related texts: PSALM 112:4; PROVERBS 11:24-26; 14:31; 19:17; 22:9; 28:8; LUKE 12:13-34; 16:1-15; PHILIPPIANS 4:10-14

The Profit of the Scriptures

But know this: difficult times will come in the last days. For people will be lovers of self, lovers of money, boastful, proud, blasphemers, disobedient to parents, ungrateful, unholy, unloving, irreconcilable, slanderers, without self-control, brutal, without love for what is good, traitors, reckless, conceited, lovers of pleasure rather than lovers of God, holding to the form of religion but denying its power. Avoid these people!

But you have followed my teaching, conduct, purpose, faith, patience, love, and endurance, along with the persecutions and sufferings that came to me in Antioch, Iconium, and Lystra. What persecutions I endured! Yet the Lord rescued me from them all. In fact, all those who want to live a godly life in Christ Jesus will be persecuted. Evil people and imposters will become worse, deceiving and being deceived. But as for you, continue in what you have learned and firmly believed, knowing those from whom you learned, and that from childhood you have known the sacred Scriptures, which are able to instruct you for salvation through faith in Christ Jesus. All Scripture is inspired by God and is profitable for teaching, for rebuking, for correcting, for training in righteousness, so that the man of God may be complete, equipped for every good work.

2 TIMOTHY 3:1-5,10-17

JESUS: *Our High Priest*

Therefore since we have a great high priest who has passed through the heavens—Jesus the Son of God—let us hold fast to the confession. For we do not have a high priest who is unable to sympathize with our weaknesses, but One who has been tested in every way as we are, yet without sin. Therefore let us approach the throne of grace with boldness, so that we may receive mercy and find grace to help us at the proper time.

During His earthly life, He offered prayers and appeals, with loud cries and tears, to the One who was able to save Him from death, and He was heard because of His reverence. Though a Son, He learned obedience through what He suffered. After He was perfected, He became the source of eternal salvation to all who obey Him, and He was declared by God a high priest "in the order of Melchizedek."

Therefore He had to be like His brothers in every way, so that He could become a merciful and faithful high priest in service to God, to make propitiation for the sins of the people. For since He Himself was tested and has suffered, He is able to help those who are tested.

HEBREWS 4:14-16; 5:7-10; 2:17-18

Related texts: GENESIS 14:18-20; PSALM 110; MATTHEW 4:1-11

HEROES OF FAITH: *Part 1*

Now faith is the reality of what is hoped for, the proof of what is not seen. For by it our ancestors were approved.

By faith we understand that the universe was created by the word of God, so that what is seen has been made from things that are not visible.

By faith Abel offered to God a better sacrifice than Cain did. By this he was approved as a righteous man, because God approved his gifts, and even though he is dead, he still speaks through this.

By faith, Enoch was taken away so that he did not experience death, and he was not to be found because God took him away. For prior to his transformation he was approved, having pleased God. Now without faith it is impossible to please God, for the one who draws near to Him must believe that He exists and rewards those who seek Him.

By faith Noah, after being warned about what was not yet seen, in reverence built an ark to deliver his family. By this he condemned the world and became an heir of the righteousness that comes by faith.

By faith Abraham, when he was called, obeyed and went out to a place he was going to receive as an inheritance; he went out, not knowing where he was going.

HEBREWS 11:1-8

Related texts: GENESIS 1; 4:1-16; 5:23-24; 6–8; 12; JUDE 14-15

HEROES OF FAITH: *Part 2*

By faith even Sarah herself, when she was barren, received power to conceive offspring, even though she was past the age, since she considered that the One who had promised was faithful. And therefore from one man—in fact, from one as good as dead—came offspring as numerous as the stars of heaven and as innumerable as the grains of sand by the seashore.

By faith Abraham, when he was tested, offered up Isaac; he who had received the promises was offering up his unique son, about whom it had been said, In Isaac your seed will be called. He considered God to be able even to raise someone from the dead, from which he also got him back as an illustration.

By faith Moses, when he had grown up, refused to be called the son of Pharaoh's daughter and chose to suffer with the people of God rather than to enjoy the short-lived pleasure of sin. For he considered reproach for the sake of the Messiah to be greater wealth than the treasures of Egypt, since his attention was on the reward.

By faith he left Egypt behind, not being afraid of the king's anger, for he persevered, as one who sees Him who is invisible.

All these were approved through their faith, but they did not receive what was promised, since God had provided something better for us, so that they would not be made perfect without us.

HEBREWS 11:11-12,17-19,24-27,39-40

Related texts: GENESIS 21–22; EXODUS 2–3; HEBREWS 10:36-39

Wisdom in Trials

Consider it a great joy, my brothers, whenever you experience various trials, knowing that the testing of your faith produces endurance. But endurance must do its complete work, so that you may be mature and complete, lacking nothing.

Now if any of you lacks wisdom, he should ask God, who gives to all generously and without criticizing, and it will be given to him. But let him ask in faith without doubting. For the doubter is like the surging sea, driven and tossed by the wind. That person should not expect to receive anything from the Lord. An indecisive man is unstable in all his ways.

Blessed is a man who endures trials, because when he passes the test he will receive the crown of life that He has promised to those who love Him.

No one undergoing a trial should say, "I am being tempted by God." For God is not tempted by evil, and He Himself doesn't tempt anyone. But each person is tempted when he is drawn away and enticed by his own evil desires. Then after desire has conceived, it gives birth to sin, and when sin is fully grown, it gives birth to death.

JAMES 1:2-8,12-15

Related texts: JOB 1–42; MATTHEW 6:9-13; 21:18-22; 1 CORINTHIANS 10:12-13

Controlling the Tongue

Not many should become teachers, my brothers, knowing that we will receive a stricter judgment; for we all stumble in many ways. If anyone does not stumble in what he says, he is a mature man who is also able to control his whole body.

Now when we put bits into the mouths of horses to make them obey us, we also guide the whole animal. And consider ships: though very large and driven by fierce winds, they are guided by a very small rudder wherever the will of the pilot directs. So too, though the tongue is a small part of the body, it boasts great things. Consider how large a forest a small fire ignites. And the tongue is a fire. The tongue, a world of unrighteousness, is placed among the parts of our bodies; it pollutes the whole body, sets the course of life on fire, and is set on fire by hell.

For every creature—animal or bird, reptile or fish— is tamed and has been tamed by man, but no man can tame the tongue. It is a restless evil, full of deadly poison. With it we bless our Lord and Father, and with it we curse men who are made in God's likeness. Out of the same mouth come blessing and cursing. My brothers, these things should not be this way. Does a spring pour out sweet and bitter water from the same opening? Can a fig tree produce olives, my brothers, or a grapevine produce figs? Neither can a saltwater spring yield fresh water.

JAMES 3:1-12

Related texts: PSALM 12; PROVERBS 6:16-19; 10:18-21, 31-32; 12:17-19,22

The Promise of Salvation

Blessed be the God and Father of our Lord Jesus Christ. According to His great mercy, He has given us a new birth into a living hope through the resurrection of Jesus Christ from the dead, and into an inheritance that is imperishable, uncorrupted, and unfading, kept in heaven for you, who are being protected by God's power through faith for a salvation that is ready to be revealed in the last time. You rejoice in this, though now for a short time you have had to be distressed by various trials so that the genuineness of your faith—more valuable than gold, which perishes though refined by fire—may result in praise, glory, and honor at the revelation of Jesus Christ. You love Him, though you have not seen Him. And though not seeing Him now, you believe in Him and rejoice with inexpressible and glorious joy, because you are receiving the goal of your faith, the salvation of your souls.

Concerning this salvation, the prophets who prophesied about the grace that would come to you searched and carefully investigated. They inquired into what time or what circumstances the Spirit of Christ within them was indicating when He testified in advance to the messianic sufferings and the glories that would follow. It was revealed to them that they were not serving themselves but you concerning things that have now been announced to you through those who preached the gospel to you by the Holy Spirit sent from heaven. Angels desire to look into these things.

1 PETER 1:3-12

Related texts: ISAIAH 52:13–53:12; ZECHARIAH 13:7-9; HEBREWS 1–2; JAMES 1

Living Stones and the Cornerstone

So rid yourselves of all wickedness, all deceit, hypocrisy, envy, and all slander. Like newborn infants, desire the unadulterated spiritual milk, so that you may grow by it in your salvation, since you have tasted that the Lord is good. Coming to Him, a living stone—rejected by men but chosen and valuable to God—you yourselves, as living stones, are being built into a spiritual house for a holy priesthood to offer spiritual sacrifices acceptable to God through Jesus Christ. For it stands in Scripture:

> Look! I lay a stone in Zion,
> a chosen and valuable cornerstone,
> and the one who believes in Him
> will never be put to shame!

So the honor is for you who believe; but for the unbelieving,

> The stone that the builders rejected—
> this One has become the cornerstone,

and

> A stone that causes men to stumble,
> and a rock that trips them up.

They stumble by disobeying the message; they were destined for this.

> But you are a chosen race, a royal priesthood,
> a holy nation, a people for His possession,
> so that you may proclaim the praises
> of the One who called you out of darkness
> into His marvelous light.
> Once you were not a people,
> but now you are God's people;
> you had not received mercy,
> but now you have received mercy.

1 PETER 2:1-10

Related texts: PSALMS 34; 118:22-29; ISAIAH 28:16-17; MATTHEW 16:13-19; LUKE 20:9-19; HEBREWS 5:11-14

The Morning Star

For we did not follow cleverly contrived myths when we made known to you the power and coming of our Lord Jesus Christ; instead, we were eyewitnesses of His majesty. For when He received honor and glory from God the Father, a voice came to Him from the Majestic Glory:

This is My beloved Son.

I take delight in Him!

And we heard this voice when it came from heaven while we were with Him on the holy mountain. So we have the prophetic word strongly confirmed. You will do well to pay attention to it, as to a lamp shining in a dismal place, until the day dawns and the morning star arises in your hearts. First of all, you should know this: no prophecy of Scripture comes from one's own inter- pretation, because no prophecy ever came by the will of man; instead, moved by the Holy Spirit, men spoke from God.

Your word is a lamp for my feet

and a light on my path.

"I, Jesus, have sent My angel to attest these things to you for the churches. I am the Root and the Offspring of David, the Bright Morning Star."

2 Peter 1:16-21; Psalm 119:105; Revelation 22:16

Related texts: Jeremiah 26; Amos 3:1-8; Isaiah 61; Mark 9:2-9; Luke 1:1-4

Love One Another

My little children, I am writing you these things so that you may not sin. But if anyone does sin, we have an advocate with the Father—Jesus Christ the righteous One. He Himself is the propitiation for our sins, and not only for ours, but also for those of the whole world.

This is how we are sure that we have come to know Him: by keeping His commands. The one who says, "I have come to know Him," without keeping His commands, is a liar, and the truth is not in him. But whoever keeps His word, truly in him the love of God is perfected. This is how we know we are in Him: the one who says he remains in Him should walk just as He walked.

Dear friends, I am not writing you a new command, but an old command that you have had from the beginning. The old command is the message you have heard. Yet I am writing you a new command, which is true in Him and in you, because the darkness is passing away and the true light is already shining.

"I give you a new commandment: that you love one another. Just as I have loved you, you should also love one another. By this all people will know that you are My disciples, if you have love for one another."

1 John 2:1-8; John 13:34-35

Related texts: 1 Kings 8:46-51; Psalm 119:9-11; John 14:15; Hebrews 2:17-18; 4:14-16; 1 John 3:11-24

The Love of the Father

Do not love the world or the things that belong to the world. If anyone loves the world, love for the Father is not in him. Because everything that belongs to the world—the lust of the flesh, the lust of the eyes, and the pride in one's lifestyle—is not from the Father, but is from the world. And the world with its lust is passing away, but the one who does God's will remains forever.

Look at how great a love the Father has given us, that we should be called God's children. And we are! The reason the world does not know us is that it didn't know Him.

Everyone who believes that Jesus is the Messiah has been born of God, and everyone who loves the parent also loves his child. This is how we know that we love God's children when we love God and obey His commands. For this is what love for God is: to keep His commands. Now His commands are not a burden, because whatever has been born of God conquers the world. This is the victory that has conquered the world: our faith. And who is the one who conquers the world but the one who believes that Jesus is the Son of God?

1 JOHN 2:15-17; 3:1; 5:1-5

Related texts: DEUTERONOMY 30:11-16; JOHN 15:17-25; 1 JOHN 4:7-21

Antichrists

Children, it is the last hour. And as you have heard, "Antichrist is coming," even now many antichrists have come. We know from this that it is the last hour. They went out from us, but they did not belong to us; for if they had belonged to us, they would have remained with us. However, they went out so that it might be made clear that none of them belongs to us.
But you have an anointing from the Holy One, and you all have knowledge. I have not written to you because you don't know the truth, but because you do know it, and because no lie comes from the truth. Who is the liar, if not the one who denies that Jesus is the Messiah? He is the antichrist, the one who denies the Father and the Son. No one who denies the Son can have the Father; he who confesses the Son has the Father as well.

Many deceivers have gone out into the world; they do not confess the coming of Jesus Christ in the flesh. This is the deceiver and the antichrist. Watch yourselves so that you don't lose what we have worked for, but you may receive a full reward. Anyone who does not remain in the teaching about Christ, but goes beyond it, does not have God. The one who remains in that teaching, this one has both the Father and the Son. If anyone comes to you and does not bring this teaching, do not receive him into your home, and don't say, "Welcome," to him; for the one who says, "Welcome," to him shares in his evil works.

1 John 2:18-23; 2 John 7-11

Related texts: Proverbs 13:5; Isaiah 44:24-25; Jeremiah 14:14-15; 2 Timothy 3; 2 Peter 2–3

The Salvation We Share

Dear friends, although I was eager to write you about our common salvation, I found it necessary to write and exhort you to contend for the faith that was delivered to the saints once for all. For certain men, who were designated for this judgment long ago, have come in by stealth; they are ungodly, turning the grace of our God into promiscuity and denying our only Master and Lord, Jesus Christ.

But you, dear friends, remember the words foretold by the apostles of our Lord Jesus Christ; they told you, "In the end time there will be scoffers walking according to their own ungodly desires." These people create divisions and are merely natural, not having the Spirit.

But you, dear friends, building yourselves up in your most holy faith and praying in the Holy Spirit, keep yourselves in the love of God, expecting the mercy of our Lord Jesus Christ for eternal life. Have mercy on some who doubt; save others by snatching them from the fire; on others have mercy in fear, hating even the garment defiled by the flesh.

Now to Him who is able to protect you from stumbling and to make you stand in the presence of His glory, blameless and with great joy, to the only God our Savior, through Jesus Christ our Lord, be glory, majesty, power, and authority before all time, now, and forever. Amen.

Jude 3-4,17-25

Related texts: Amos 4:11; Zechariah 3; Acts 20:28-31; 1 Timothy 4:1-6; 2 Peter 3

December 22

The LORD's Anointed King

Why do the nations rebel
and the peoples plot in vain?
The kings of the earth take their stand
and the rulers conspire together
against the LORD and His Anointed One:
"Let us tear off their chains
and free ourselves from their restraints."
The One enthroned in heaven laughs;
the Lord ridicules them.
Then He speaks to them in His anger
and terrifies them in His wrath:
"I have consecrated My King
on Zion, My holy mountain."
I will declare the LORD's decree:
He said to Me, "You are My Son;
today I have become Your Father.
Ask of Me, and I will make the nations Your
    inheritance
and the ends of the earth Your possession.
You will break them with a rod of iron;
You will shatter them like pottery."
So now, kings, be wise;
receive instruction, you judges of the earth.
Serve the LORD with reverential awe,
and rejoice with trembling.
Pay homage to the Son, or He will be angry,
and you will perish in your rebellion,
for His anger may ignite at any moment.
All those who take refuge in Him are happy.

PSALM 2

Related texts: 2 SAMUEL 7; 1 CHRONICLES 17; MARK 1:1-11; REVELATION 2:18-29

David's Son and Lord

The LORD declared to my Lord:
"Sit at My right hand
until I make Your enemies Your footstool."
The LORD will extend Your mighty scepter from Zion.
Rule over Your surrounding enemies.
Your people will volunteer on Your day of battle.
In holy splendor, from the womb of the dawn,
the dew of Your youth belongs to You.
The LORD has sworn an oath and will not take it back:
"Forever, You are a priest like Melchizedek."
The Lord is at Your right hand;
He will crush kings on the day of His anger.
He will judge the nations, heaping up corpses;
He will crush leaders over the entire world.
He will drink from the brook by the road;
therefore, He will lift up His head.

Now many have become Levitical priests, since they are prevented by death from remaining in office. But because He remains forever, He holds His priesthood permanently. Therefore He is always able to save those who come to God through Him, since He always lives to intercede for them.

For this is the kind of high priest we need: holy, innocent, undefiled, separated from sinners, and exalted above the heavens.

PSALM 110; HEBREWS 7:23-26

Related texts: GENESIS 14:18-20; MATTHEW 22:41-46; HEBREWS 5:1-10; 7

Christ Is Born

And Joseph also went up from the town of Nazareth in Galilee, to Judea, to the city of David, which is called Bethlehem, because he was of the house and family line of David, to be registered along with Mary, who was engaged to him and was pregnant. While they were there, it happened that the days were completed for her to give birth. Then she gave birth to her firstborn Son, and she wrapped Him snugly in cloth and laid Him in a manger—because there was no room for them at the inn.

In the same region, shepherds were living out in the fields and keeping watch at night over their flock. Then an angel of the Lord stood before them, and the glory of the Lord shone around them, and they were terrified. But the angel said to them, "Do not be afraid, for you see, I announce to you good news of great joy that will be for all the people: because today in the city of David was born for you a Savior, who is Christ the Lord. This will be the sign for you: you will find a baby wrapped snugly in cloth and lying in a manger."

Suddenly there was a multitude of the heavenly host with the angel, praising God and saying:

> Glory to God in the highest heaven,
> and peace on earth to people He favors!

Luke 2:4-14

Related texts: 2 Samuel 7:8-17; Psalm 89:20-37; Isaiah 9:6-7; Matthew 1:18-25; Luke 1–2

The Gifts of the Magi

After Jesus was born in Bethlehem of Judea in the days of King Herod, wise men from the east arrived unexpectedly in Jerusalem, saying, "Where is He who has been born King of the Jews? For we saw His star in the east and have come to worship Him."

When King Herod heard this, he was deeply disturbed, and all Jerusalem with him. So he assembled all the chief priests and scribes of the people and asked them where the Messiah would be born.

"In Bethlehem of Judea," they told him, "because this is what was written through the prophet:

And you, Bethlehem, in the land of Judah,
are by no means least among the leaders of Judah:
because out of you will come a Leader
who will shepherd My people Israel."

Then Herod secretly summoned the wise men and learned from them the time when the star appeared. He sent them to Bethlehem and said, "Go and search carefully for the child. When you find Him, report back to me so that I too can go and worship Him."

After hearing the king, they went on their way. And there it was—the star they had seen in the east! It led them until it came and stopped above the place where the child was. When they saw the star, they were overjoyed beyond measure. Entering the house, they saw the child with Mary His mother, and falling to their knees, they worshiped Him. Then they opened their treasures and presented Him with gifts: gold, frankincense, and myrrh. And being warned in a dream not to go back to Herod, they returned to their own country by another route.

MATTHEW 2:1-12

Related texts: EXODUS 30:22-33; MICAH 5:2-5; MARK 15:16-24; LUKE 1–2; JOHN 12:1-7; HEBREWS 13:15-21

New Heavens and a New Earth

"For I will create a new heaven and a new earth;
the past events will not be remembered or come to mind.
Then be glad and rejoice forever
in what I am creating;
for I will create Jerusalem to be a joy,
and its people to be a delight.
I will rejoice in Jerusalem
and be glad in My people.
The sound of weeping and crying
will no longer be heard in her.
In her, a nursing infant will no longer live
only a few days,
or an old man not live out his days.
Indeed, the youth will die at a hundred years,
and the one who misses a hundred years will be cursed.

They will not labor without success
or bear children destined for disaster,
for they will be a people blessed by the Lord
along with their descendants.
Even before they call, I will answer;
while they are still speaking, I will hear.
The wolf and the lamb will feed together,
and the lion will eat straw like the ox,
but the serpent's food will be dust!
They will not do evil or destroy
on My entire holy mountain,"
says the Lord.

ISAIAH 65:17-20,23-25

Related texts: GENESIS 3:1-14; ISAIAH 66:22-24; 2 PETER 3:1-14; REVELATION 21:1-5

Ezekiel Sees the Glory Return to Jerusalem

He led me to the gate, the one that faces east, and I saw the glory of the God of Israel coming from the east. His voice sounded like the roar of mighty waters, and the earth shone with His glory. The vision I saw was like the one I had seen when He came to destroy the city, and like the ones I had seen by the Chebar Canal. I fell facedown. The glory of the Lord entered the temple by way of the gate that faced east. Then the Spirit lifted me up and brought me to the inner court, and the glory of the Lord filled the temple.

While the man was standing beside me, I heard someone speaking to me from the temple. He said to me: "Son of man, this is the place of My throne and the place for the soles of My feet, where I will dwell among the Israelites forever. The house of Israel and their kings will no longer defile My holy name by their religious prostitution and by the corpses of their kings at their high places. Whenever they placed their threshold next to My threshold and their doorposts beside My doorposts, with only a wall between Me and them, they were defiling My holy name by the abominations they committed. So I destroyed them in My anger. Now let them remove their prostitution and the corpses of their kings far from Me, and I will dwell among them forever."

EZEKIEL 43:1-9

Related texts: EZEKIEL 1; 3; 8–11; ZECHARIAH 14;
REVELATION 21:1-4

His Face Was Like the Sun

I, John, your brother and partner in the tribulation, kingdom, and perseverance in Jesus, was on the island called Patmos because of God's word and the testimony about Jesus. I was in the Spirit on the Lord's day, and I heard behind me a loud voice like a trumpet saying, "Write on a scroll what you see and send it to the seven churches: Ephesus, Smyrna, Pergamum, Thyatira, Sardis, Philadelphia, and Laodicea."

I turned to see the voice that was speaking to me. When I turned I saw seven gold lampstands, and among the lampstands was One like the Son of Man, dressed in a long robe, and with a gold sash wrapped around His chest. His head and hair were white like wool—white as snow, His eyes like a fiery flame, His feet like fine bronze fired in a furnace, and His voice like the sound of cascading waters. In His right hand He had seven stars; from His mouth came a sharp two-edged sword; and His face was shining like the sun at midday.

When I saw Him, I fell at His feet like a dead man. He laid His right hand on me, and said, "Don't be afraid! I am the First and the Last, and the Living One. I was dead, but look—I am alive forever and ever, and I hold the keys of death and Hades. Therefore write what you have seen, what is, and what will take place after this."

REVELATION 1:9-19

Related texts: PSALM 149; DANIEL 7; 2 TIMOTHY 3; HEBREWS 4:12-13; REVELATION 2–11; 19:11-21

The Saints and the Serpent

Then I saw an angel coming down from heaven with the key to the abyss and a great chain in his hand. He seized the dragon, that ancient serpent who is the Devil and Satan, and bound him for 1,000 years. He threw him into the abyss, closed it, and put a seal on it so that he would no longer deceive the nations until the 1,000 years were completed. After that, he must be released for a short time.

Then I saw thrones, and people seated on them who were given authority to judge. I also saw the souls of those who had been beheaded because of their testimony about Jesus and because of God's word, who had not worshiped the beast or his image, and who had not accepted the mark on their foreheads or their hands. They came to life and reigned with the Messiah for 1,000 years. The rest of the dead did not come to life until the 1,000 years were completed. This is the first resurrection. Blessed and holy is the one who shares in the first resurrection! The second death has no power over these, but they will be priests of God and the Messiah, and they will reign with Him for 1,000 years.

When the 1,000 years are completed, Satan will be released from his prison and will go out to deceive the nations at the four corners of the earth, Gog and Magog, to gather them for battle. Their number is like the sand of the sea. They came up over the surface of the earth and surrounded the encampment of the saints, the beloved city. Then fire came down from heaven and consumed them. The Devil who deceived them was thrown into the lake of fire and sulfur where the beast and the false prophet are, and they will be tormented day and night forever and ever.

REVELATION 20:1-10

Related texts: GENESIS 3:1-15; EZEKIEL 38–39; 1 CORINTHIANS 6:1-3; REVELATION 12–13; 17–19

Judgment Day

Then I saw a great white throne and One seated on it. Earth and heaven fled from His presence, and no place was found for them. I also saw the dead, the great and the small, standing before the throne, and books were opened. Another book was opened, which is the book of life, and the dead were judged according to their works by what was written in the books.

Then the sea gave up its dead, and Death and Hades gave up their dead; all were judged according to their works. Death and Hades were thrown into the lake of fire. This is the second death, the lake of fire. And anyone not found written in the book of life was thrown into the lake of fire.

Then I saw a new heaven and a new earth, for the first heaven and the first earth had passed away, and the sea existed no longer. I also saw the Holy City, new Jerusalem, coming down out of heaven from God, prepared like a bride adorned for her husband.

Then I heard a loud voice from the throne:

> Look! God's dwelling is with men,
> and He will live with them.
> They will be His people,
> and God Himself will be with them and be their
> God.
> He will wipe away every tear from their eyes.
> Death will exist no longer;
> grief, crying, and pain will exist no longer,
> because the previous things have passed away.

REVELATION 20:11–21:4

Related texts: ISAIAH 65:17-25; 66:22-24; DANIEL 12:1-3; JOHN 1:14-18; 2 PETER 3:1-14

Jesus Is Coming Soon!

"Look, I am coming quickly! Blessed is the one who keeps the prophetic words of this book."

"Look! I am coming quickly, and My reward is with Me to repay each person according to what he has done. I am the Alpha and the Omega, the First and the Last, the Beginning and the End.

"Blessed are those who wash their robes, so that they may have the right to the tree of life and may enter the city by the gates. Outside are the dogs, the sorcerers, the sexually immoral, the murderers, the idolaters, and everyone who loves and practices lying.

"I, Jesus, have sent My angel to attest these things to you for the churches. I am the Root and the Offspring of David, the Bright Morning Star."

Both the Spirit and the bride say, "Come!" Anyone who hears should say, "Come!" And the one who is thirsty should come. Whoever desires should take the living water as a gift.

He who testifies about these things says, "Yes, I am coming quickly."

Amen! Come, Lord Jesus!

The grace of the Lord Jesus be with all the saints. Amen.

REVELATION 22:7,12-17,20-21

Related texts: PSALMS 1; 37; MATTHEW 16:24-27; LUKE 12:35-40; 1 THESSALONIANS 4:13–5:11; REVELATION 1:1-3

Daily Bible Reading Plan I

Day	Date	AM	PM	Day	Date	AM	PM
1	Jan 1	Gn 1-2	Mt 1	61	Mar 1	Nm 26-27	Mk 8:22-38
2	Jan 2	Gn 3-5	Mt 2	62	Mar 2	Nm 28-29	Mk 9:1-29
3	Jan 3	Gn 6-8	Mt 3	63	Mar 3	Nm 30-31	Mk 9:30-50
4	Jan 4	Gn 9-11	Mt 4	64	Mar 4	Nm 32-33	Mk 10:1-31
5	Jan 5	Gn 12-14	Mt 5:1-26	65	Mar 5	Nm 34-36	Mk 10:32-52
6	Jan 6	Gn 15-17	Mt 5:27-48	66	Mar 6	Dt 1-2	Mk 11:1-19
7	Jan 7	Gn 18-19	Mt 6	67	Mar 7	Dt 3-4	Mk 11:20-33
8	Jan 8	Gn 20-22	Mt 7	68	Mar 8	Dt 5-7	Mk 12:1-27
9	Jan 9	Gn 23-24	Mt 8	69	Mar 9	Dt 8-10	Mk 12:28-44
10	Jan 10	Gn 25-26	Mt 9:1-17	70	Mar 10	Dt 11-13	Mk 13:1-13
11	Jan 11	Gn 27-28	Mt 9:18-38	71	Mar 11	Dt 14-16	Mk 13:14-37
12	Jan 12	Gn 29-30	Mt 10:1-23	72	Mar 12	Dt 17-19	Mk 14:1-25
13	Jan 13	Gn 31-32	Mt 10:24-42	73	Mar 13	Dt 20-22	Mk 14:26-50
14	Jan 14	Gn 33-35	Mt 11	74	Mar 14	Dt 23-25	Mk 14:51-72
15	Jan 15	Gn 36-37	Mt 12:1-21	75	Mar 15	Dt 26-27	Mk 15:1-26
16	Jan 16	Gn 38-40	Mt 12:22-50	76	Mar 16	Dt 28	Mk 15:27-47
17	Jan 17	Gn 41	Mt 13:1-32	77	Mar 17	Dt 29-30	Mk 16
18	Jan 18	Gn 42-43	Mt 13:33-58	78	Mar 18	Dt 31-32	Lk 1:1-23
19	Jan 19	Gn 44-45	Mt 14:1-21	79	Mar 19	Dt 33-34	Lk 1:24-56
20	Jan 20	Gn 46-48	Mt 14:22-36	80	Mar 20	Jos 1-3	Lk 1:57-80
21	Jan 21	Gn 49-50	Mt 15:1-20	81	Mar 21	Jos 4-6	Lk 2:1-24
22	Jan 22	Ex 1-3	Mt 15:21-39	82	Mar 22	Jos 7-8	Lk 2:25-52
23	Jan 23	Ex 4-6	Mt 16	83	Mar 23	Jos 9-10	Lk 3
24	Jan 24	Ex 7-8	Mt 17	84	Mar 24	Jos 11-13	Lk 4:1-32
25	Jan 25	Ex 9-10	Mt 18:1-20	85	Mar 25	Jos 14-15	Lk 4:33-44
26	Jan 26	Ex 11-12	Mt 18:21-35	86	Mar 26	Jos 16-18	Lk 5:1-16
27	Jan 27	Ex 13-15	Mt 19:1-15	87	Mar 27	Jos 19-20	Lk 5:17-39
28	Jan 28	Ex 16-18	Mt 19:16-30	88	Mar 28	Jos 21-22	Lk 6:1-26
29	Jan 29	Ex 19-21	Mt 20:1-16	89	Mar 29	Jos 23-24	Lk 6:27-49
30	Jan 30	Ex 22-24	Mt 20:17-34	90	Mar 30	Jdg 1-2	Lk 7:1-30
31	Jan 31	Ex 25-26	Mt 21:1-22	91	Mar 31	Jdg 3-5	Lk 7:31-50
32	Feb 1	Ex 27-28	Mt 21:23-46	92	Apr 1	Jdg 6-7	Lk 8:1-21
33	Feb 2	Ex 29-30	Mt 22:1-22	93	Apr 2	Jdg 8-9	Lk 8:22-56
34	Feb 3	Ex 31-33	Mt 22:23-46	94	Apr 3	Jdg 10-11	Lk 9:1-36
35	Feb 4	Ex 34-36	Mt 23:1-22	95	Apr 4	Jdg 12-14	Lk 9:37-62
36	Feb 5	Ex 37-38	Mt 23:23-39	96	Apr 5	Jdg 15-17	Lk 10:1-24
37	Feb 6	Ex 39-40	Mt 24:1-22	97	Apr 6	Jdg 18-19	Lk 10:25-42
38	Feb 7	Lv 1-3	Mt 24:23-51	98	Apr 7	Jdg 20-21	Lk 11:1-28
39	Feb 8	Lv 4-6	Mt 25:1-30	99	Apr 8	Ru	Lk 11:29-54
40	Feb 9	Lv 7-9	Mt 25:31-46	100	Apr 9	1 Sm 1-3	Lk 12:1-34
41	Feb 10	Lv 10-12	Mt 26:1-19	101	Apr 10	1 Sm 4-6	Lk 12:35-59
42	Feb 11	Lv 13	Mt 26:20-54	102	Apr 11	1 Sm 7-9	Lk 13:1-21
43	Feb 12	Lv 14	Mt 26:55-75	103	Apr 12	1 Sm 10-12	Lk 13:22-35
44	Feb 13	Lv 15-17	Mt 27:1-31	104	Apr 13	1 Sm 13-14	Lk 14:1-24
45	Feb 14	Lv 18-19	Mt 27:32-66	105	Apr 14	1 Sm 15-16	Lk 14:25-35
46	Feb 15	Lv 20-21	Mt 28	106	Apr 15	1 Sm 17-18	Lk 15:1-10
47	Feb 16	Lv 22-23	Mk 1:1-22	107	Apr 16	1 Sm 19-21	Lk 15:11-32
48	Feb 17	Lv 24-25	Mk 1:23-45	108	Apr 17	1 Sm 22-24	Lk 16:1-18
49	Feb 18	Lv 26-27	Mk 2	109	Apr 18	1 Sm 25-26	Lk 16:19-31
50	Feb 19	Nm 1-2	Mk 3:1-21	110	Apr 19	1 Sm 27-29	Lk 17:1-19
51	Feb 20	Nm 3-4	Mk 3:22-35	111	Apr 20	1 Sm 30-31	Lk 17:20-37
52	Feb 21	Nm 5-6	Mk 4:1-20	112	Apr 21	2 Sm 1-3	Lk 18:1-17
53	Feb 22	Nm 7	Mk 4:21-41	113	Apr 22	2 Sm 4-6	Lk 18:18-43
54	Feb 23	Nm 8-10	Mk 5:1-20	114	Apr 23	2 Sm 7-9	Lk 19:1-28
55	Feb 24	Nm 11-13	Mk 5:21-43	115	Apr 24	2 Sm 10-12	Lk 19:29-48
56	Feb 25	Nm 14-15	Mk 6:1-32	116	Apr 25	2 Sm 13-14	Lk 20:1-26
57	Feb 26	Nm 16-17	Mk 6:33-56	117	Apr 26	2 Sm 15-16	Lk 20:27-47
58	Feb 27	Nm 18-20	Mk 7:1-13	118	Apr 27	2 Sm 17-18	Lk 21:1-19
59	Feb 28	Nm 21-22	Mk 7:14-37	119	Apr 28	2 Sm 19-20	Lk 21:20-38
60	Feb 29	Nm 23-25	Mk 8:1-21	120	Apr 29	2 Sm 21-22	Lk 22:1-30
				121	Apr 30	2 Sm 23-24	Lk 22:31-63

DAILY BIBLE READING PLAN I

Day	Date	AM	PM	Day	Date	AM	PM
122	May 1	1 Kg 1-2	Lk 22:54-71	183	Jul 1	Jb 21-22	Ac 10:1-23
123	May 2	1 Kg 3-5	Lk 23:1-26	184	Jul 2	Jb 23-25	Ac 10:24-48
124	May 3	1 Kg 6-7	Lk 23:27-38	185	Jul 3	Jb 26-28	Ac 11
125	May 4	1 Kg S-9	Lk 23:39-56	186	Jul 4	Jb 29-30	Ac 12
126	May 5	1 Kg 10-11	Lk 24:1-35	187	Jul 5	Jb 31-32	Ac 13:1-23
127	May 6	1 Kg 12-13	Lk 24:36-53	188	Jul 6	Jb 33-34	Ac 13:24-52
128	May 7	1 Kg 14-15	Jn 1:1-28	189	Jul 7	Jb 35-37	Ac 14
129	May 8	1 Kg 16-18	Jn 1:29-51	190	Jul 8	Jb 38-39	Arts 15:1-21
130	May 9	1 Kg 19-20	Jn 2	191	Jul 9	Jb 40-42	Ac 15:22-41
131	May 10	1 Kg 21-22	Jn 3:1-21	192	Jul 10	Ps 1-3	Ac 16:1-15
132	May 11	2 Kg 1-3	Jn 3:22-36	193	Jul 11	Ps 4-6	Ac 16:16-40
133	May 12	2 Kg 4-5	Jn 4:1-30	194	Jul 12	Ps 7-9	Ac 17:1-15
134	May 13	2 Kg 6-8	Jn 4:31-54	195	Jul 13	Ps 10-12	Ac 17:16-34
135	May 14	2 Kg 9-11	Jn 5:1-24	196	Jul 14	Ps 13-16	Ac 18
136	May 15	2 Kg 12-14	Jn 5:25-47	197	Jul 15	Ps 17-18	Ac 19:1-20
137	May 16	2 Kg 15-17	Jn 6:1-21	198	Jul 16	Ps 19-21	Ac 19:21-41
138	May 17	2 Kg 18-19	Jn 6:22-44	199	Jul 17	Ps 22-24	Ac 20:1-16
139	May 18	2 Kg 20-22	Jn 6:45-71	200	Jul 18	Ps 25-27	Ac 20:17-38
140	May 19	2 Kg 23-25	Jn 7:1-31	201	Jul 19	Ps 28-30	Ac 21:1-14
141	May 20	1 Ch 1-2	Jn 7:32-53	202	Jul 20	Ps 31-33	Ac 21:15-40
142	May 21	1 Ch 3-5	Jn 8:1-20	203	Jul 21	Ps 34-35	Ac 22
143	May 22	1 Ch 6-7	Jn 8:21-36	204	Jul 22	Ps 36-37	Ac 23:1-11
144	May 23	1 Ch 8-10	Jn 8:37-59	205	Jul 23	Ps 38-40	Ac 23:12-35
145	May 24	1 Ch 11-13	Jn 9:1-23	206	Jul 24	Ps 41-43	Ac 24
146	May 25	1 Ch 14-16	Jn 9:24-41	207	Jul 25	Ps 44-46	Ac 25
147	May 26	1 Ch 17-19	Jn 10:1-21	208	Jul 26	Ps 47-49	Ac 26
148	May 27	1 Ch 20-22	Jn 10:22-42	209	Jul 27	Ps 50-52	Ac 27:1-25
149	May 28	1 Ch 23-25	Jn 11:1-17	210	Jul 28	Ps 53-55	Ac 27:26-44
150	May 29	1 Ch 26-27	Jn 11:18-46	211	Jul 29	Ps 56-58	Ac 28:1-15
151	May 30	1 Ch 28-29	Jn 11:47-57	212	Jul 30	Ps 59-61	Ac 28:16-31
152	May 31	2 Ch 1-3	Jn 12:1-19	213	Jul 31	Ps 62-64	Rm 1
153	Jun 1	2 Ch 4-6	Jn 12:20-50	214	Aug 1	Ps 65-67	Rm 2
154	Jun 2	2 Ch 7-9	Jn 13:1-17	215	Aug 2	Ps 68-69	Rm 3
155	Jun 3	2 Ch 10-12	Jn 13:18-38	216	Aug 3	Ps 70-72	Rm 4
156	Jun 4	2 Ch 13-16	Jn 14	217	Aug 4	Ps 73-74	Rm 5
157	Jun 5	2 Ch 17-19	Jn 15	218	Aug 5	Ps 75-77	Rm 6
158	Jun 6	2 Ch 20-22	Jn 16:1-15	219	Aug 6	Ps 78	Rm 7
159	Jun 7	2 Ch 23-25	Jn 16:16-23	220	Aug 7	Ps 79-81	Rm 8:1-18
160	Jun 8	2 Ch 26-28	Jn 17	221	Aug 8	Ps 82-84	Rm 8:19-29
161	Jun 9	2 Ch 29-31	Jn 18:1-23	222	Aug 9	Ps 85-87	Rm 9
162	Jun 10	2 Ch 32-33	Jn 18:24-40	223	Aug 10	Ps 88-89	Rm 10
163	Jun 11	2 Ch 34-36	Jn 19:1-22	224	Aug 11	Ps 90-92	Rm 11:1-21
164	Jun 12	Ezr 1-2	Jn 19:23-42	225	Aug 12	Ps 93-95	Rm 11:22-36
165	Jun 13	Ezr 3-5	Jn 20	226	Aug 13	Ps 96-98	Rm 12
166	Jun 14	Ezr 6-8	Jn 21	227	Aug 14	Ps 99-102	Rm 13
167	Jun 15	Ezr 9-10	Ac 1	228	Aug 15	Ps 103-104	Rm 14
168	Jun 16	Neh 1-3	Ac 2:1-13	229	Aug 16	Ps 105-106	Rm 15:1-20
169	Jun 17	Neh 4-6	Ac 2:14-47	230	Aug 17	Ps 107-108	Rm 15:21-33
170	Jun 18	Neh 7-8	Ac 3	231	Aug 18	Ps 109-111	Rm 16
171	Jun 19	Neh 9-11	Ac 4:1-22	232	Aug 19	Ps 112-115	1 Co 1
172	Jun 20	Neh 12-13	Ac 4:23-37	233	Aug 20	Ps 116-118	1 Co 2
173	Jun 21	Est 1-3	Ac 5:1-16	234	Aug 21	Ps 119:1-48	1 Co 3
174	Jun 22	Est 4-6	Ac 5:17-42	235	Aug 22	119:49-104	1 Co 4
175	Jun 23	Est 7-10	Ac 6	236	Aug 23	119:105-176	1 Co 5
176	Jun 24	Jb 1-3	Ac 7:1-19	237	Aug 24	Ps 120-123	1 Co 6
177	Jun 25	Jb 4-6	Ac 7:20-43	238	Aug 25	Ps 124-127	1 Co 7:1-24
178	Jun 26	Jb 7-9	Ac 7:44-60	239	Aug 26	Ps 128-131	1 Co 7:25-40
179	Jun 27	Jb 10-12	Ac 8:1-25	240	Aug 27	Ps 132-135	1 Co 8
180	Jun 28	Jb 13-15	Ac 8:26-40	241	Aug 28	Ps 136-138	1 Co 9
181	Jun 29	Jb 16-18	Ac 9:1-22	242	Aug 29	Ps 139-141	1 Co 10:1-13
182	Jun 30	Jb 19-20	Ac 9:23-43	243	Aug 3o	Ps 142-144	1 Co 10:14-33
				244	Aug 31	Ps 145-147	1 Co 11:1-15

DAILY BIBLE READING PLAN I

Day	Date	AM	PM	Day	Date	AM	PM
245	Sep 1	Ps 148-150	1 Co 11:16-34	306	Nov 1	Jr 31-32	Ti 2
246	Sep 2	Pr 1-2	1 Co 12	307	Nov 2	Jr 33-35	Ti 3
247	Sep 3	Pr 3-4	1 Co 13	308	Nov 3	Jr 36-37	Phm
248	Sep 4	Pr 5-6	1 Co 14:1-20	309	Nov 4	Jr 38-39	Heb 1
249	Sep 5	Pr 7-8	1 Co 14:21-40	310	Nov 5	Jr 40-42	Heb 2
250	Sep 6	Pr 9-10	1 Co 15:1-32	311	Nov 6	Jr 43-45	Heb 3
251	Sep 7	Pr 11-12	1 Co 15:33-58	312	Nov 7	Jr 46-48	Heb 4
252	Sep 8	Pr 13-14	1 Co 16	313	Nov 8	Jr 49-50	Heb 5
253	Sep 9	Pr 15-16	2 Co 1	314	Nov 9	Jr 51-52	Heb 6
254	Sep 10	Pr 17-18	2 Co 2	315	Nov 10	Lm 1-2	Heb 7
255	Sep 11	Pr 19-20	2 Co 3	316	Nov 11	Lm 3-5	Heb 8
256	Sep 12	Pr 21-22	2 Co 4	317	Nov 12	Ezk 1-3	Heb 9
257	Sep 13	Pr 23-24	2 Co 5	318	Nov 13	Ezk 4-6	Heb 10:1-23
258	Sep 14	Pr 25-27	2 Co 6	319	Nov 14	Ezk 7-9	Heb 10:24-39
259	Sep 15	Pr 28-29	2 Co 7	320	Nov 15	Ezk 10-12	Heb 11:1-19
260	Sep 16	Pr 30-31	2 Co 8	321	Nov 16	Ezk 13-15	Heb 11:20-40
261	Sep 17	Ec 1-3	2 Co 9	322	Nov 17	Ezk 16	Heb 12
262	Sep 18	Ec 4-6	2 Co 10	323	Nov 18	Ezk 17-19	Heb 13
263	Sep 19	Ec 7-9	2 Co 11:1-15	324	Nov 19	Ezk 20-21	Jms 1
264	Sep 20	Ec 10-12	2 Co 11:16-33	325	Nov 20	Ezk 22-23	Jms 2
265	Sep 21	Sg 1-3	2 Co 12	326	Nnv 21	Ezk 24-26	Jms 3
266	Sep 22	Sg 4-5	2 Co 13	327	Nov 22	Ezk 27-28	Jms 4
267	Sep 23	Sg 6-8	Gl 1	328	Nov 23	Ezk 29-31	Jms 5
268	Sep 24	Is 1-3	Gl 2	329	Nov 24	Ezk 32-33	1 Pt 1
269	Sep 25	Is 4-6	Gl 3	330	Nov 25	Ezk 34-35	1 Pt 2
270	Sep 26	Is 7-9	Gl 4	331	Nov 26	Ezk 36-37	1 Pt 3
271	Sep 27	Is 10-12	Gl 5	332	Nov27	Ezk 38-39	1 Pt 4
272	Sep 28	Is 13-15	Gl 6	333	Nov 28	Ezk 40	1 Pt 5
273	Sep 29	Is 16-18	Eph 1	334	Nov 29	Ezk 41-42	2 Pt 1
274	Sep 30	Is 19-21	Eph 2	335	Nov 30	Ezk 43-44	2 Pt 2
275	Oct 1	Is 22-23	Eph 3	336	Dec 1	Ezk 45-46	2 Pt 3
276	Oct 2	Is 24-26	Eph 4	337	Dec 2	Ezk 47-48	1 Jn 1
277	Oct 3	Is 27-28	Eph 5	338	Dec 3	Dn 1-2	1 Jn 2
278	Oct 4	Is. 29-30	Eph 6	339	Dec 4	Dn 3-4	1 Jn 3
279	Oct 5	Is 31-33	Php 1	340	Dec 5	Dn 5-6	1 Jn 4
280	Oct 6	Is 34-36	Php 2	341	Dec 6	Dn 7-8	1 Jn 5
281	Oct 7	Is 37-38	Php 3	342	Dec 7	Dn 9-10	2 Jn
282	Oct 8	Is 39-40	Php 4	343	Dec 8	Dn 11-12	3 Jn
283	Oct 9	Is 41-42	Col 1	344	Dec 9	Hs 1-4	Jd
284	Oct 10	Is 43-44	Col 2	345	Dec 10	Hs 5-8	Rv 1
285	Oct 11	Is 45-47	Col 3	346	Dec 11	Hs 9-11	Rv 2
286	Oct 12	Is 48-49	Col 4	347	Dec 12	Hs 12-14	Rv 3
287	Oct 13	Is 50-52	1 Th 1	348	Dec 13	Jl 1-3	Rv 4
288	Oct 14	Is 53-55	1 Th 2	349	Dec 14	Am 1-3	Rv 5
289	Oct 15	Is 56-58	1 Th 3	350	Dec 15	Am 4-6	Rv 6
290	Oct 16	Is 59-61	1 Th 4	351	Dec 16	Am 7-9	Rv 7
291	Oct 17	Is 62-64	1 Th 5	352	Dec 17	Ob	Rv 8
292	Oct 18	Is 65-66	2 Th 1	353	Dec 18	Jnh	Rv 9
293	Oct 19	Jr 1-2	2 Th 2	354	Dec 19	Mc 1-3	Rv 10
294	Oct 20	Jr 3-4	2 Th 3	355	Dec 20	Mc 4-5	Rv 11
295	Oct 21	Jr 5-6	1 Tm 1	356	Dec 21	Mc 6-7	Rv 12
296	Oct 22	Jr 7-8	1 Tm 2	357	Dec 22	Nah	Rv 13
297	Oct 23	Jr 9-10	1 Tm 3	358	Dec 23	Hb	Rv 14
298	Oct 24	Jr 11-13	1 Tm 4	359	Dec 24	Zph	Rv 15
299	Oct 25	Jr 14-16	1 Tm 5	360	Dec 25	Hg	Rv 16
300	Oct 26	Jr 17-19	1 Tm 6	361	Dec 26	Zch 1-3	Rv 17
301	Oct 27	Jr 20-22	2 Tm 1	362	Dec 27	Zch 4-6	Rv 18
302	Oct 28	Jr 23-24	2 Tm 2	363	Dec 28	Zch 7-9	Rv 19
303	Oct 29	Jr 25-26	2 Tm 3	364	Dec 29	Zch 10-12	Rv 20
304	Oct 30	Jr 27-28	2 Tm 4	365	Dec 30	Zch 13-14	Rv 21
305	Oct 31	Jr 29-30	Ti 1	366	Dec 31	Mal	Rv 22

DAILY BIBLE READING PLAN II

Jan 1	Gn 1-3	Feb 20	Lv 13-14	Apr 11	1 Sm 8-10
Jan 2	Gn 4:1-6:8	Feb 21	Lv 15-17	Apr 12	1 Sm 11-13
Jan 3	Gn 6:9-9:29	Feb 22	Lv 18-20	Apr 13	1 Sm 14-15
Jan 4	Gn 10-11	Feb 23	Lv 21-23	Apr 14	1 Sm 16-17
Jan 5	Gn 12-14	Feb 24	Lv 24-25	Apr 15	1 Sm 18-19; Ps 59
Jan 6	Gn 15-17	Feb 25	Lv 26-27	Apr 16	1 Sm 20-21; Pss
Jan 7	Gn 18-19	Feb 26	Nm 1-2		56; 34
Jan 8	Gn 20-22	Feb 27	Nm 3-4	Apr 17	1 Sm 22-23; 1 Ch
Jan 9	Gn 23-24	Feb 28	Nm 5-6		12:8-18; Pss 52;
Jan 10	Gn 25-26	Mar 1	Nm 7		54; 63; 144
Jan 11	Gn 27-28	Mar 2	Nm 8-10	Apr 18	1 Sm 24; Ps 57;
Jan 12	Gn 29-30	Mar 3	Nm 11-13		1 Sm 25
Jan 13	Gn 31-32	Mar 4	Nm 14-15	Apr 19	1 Sm 26-29; 1 Ch
Jan 14	Gn 33-35	Mar 5	Nm 16-18		12:1-7; 19-22
Jan 15	Gn 36-37	Mar 6	Nm 19-21	Apr 20	1 Sm 30-31; 1 Ch
Jan 16	Gn 38-40	Mar 7	Nm 22-24		10; 2 Sm 1
Jan 17	Gn 41-42	Mar 8	Nm 25-26	Apr 21	2 Sm 2-4
Jan 18	Gn 43-45	Mar 9	Nm 27-29	Apr 22	2 Sm 5:1-6:11;
Jan 19	Gn 4647	Mar 10	Nm 30-31		1 Ch 11:1-9;
Jan 20	Gn 48-50	Mar 11	Nm 32-33		12:23-14:17
Jan 21	Jb 1-3	Mar 12	Nm 34-36	Apr 23	2 Sm 22; Ps 18
Jan 22	Jb 4-7	Mar 13	Dt 1-2	Apr 24	1 Ch 15-16; 2 Sm
Jan 23	Jb 8-11	Mar 14	Dt 3-4		6:12-23; Ps 96
Jan 24	Jb 12-15	Mar 15	Dt 5-7	Apr 25	Ps 105; 2 Sm 7;
Jan 25	Jb 16-19	Mar 16	Dt 8-10		1 Ch 17
Jan 26	Jb 20-22	Mar 17	Dt 11-13	Apr 26	2 Sm 8-10; 1 Ch
Jan 27	Jb 23-28	Mar 18	Dt 14-17		18-19; Ps 60
Jan 28	Jb 29-31	Mar 19	Dt 18-21	Apr 27	2 Sm 11-12; 1 Ch
Jan 29	Jb 32-34	Mar 20	Dt 22-25		20:1-3; Ps 51
Jan 30	Jb 35-37	Mar 21	Dt 26-28	Apr 28	2 Sm 13-14
Jan 31	Jb 38-42	Mar 22	Dt 29:1-31:29	Apr 29	2 Sm 15-17
Feb 1	Ex 1-4	Mar 23	Dt 31:30-34:12	Apr 30	Ps 3; 2 Sm 18-19
Feb 2	Ex 5-8	Mar 24	Jos 1-4	May 1	2 Sm 20-21;
Feb 3	Ex 9-11	Mar 25	Jos 5-8		23:8-23; 1 Ch
Feb 4	Ex 12-13	Mar 26	Jos 9-11		20:4-8; 11:10-25
Feb 5	Ex 14-15	Mar 27	Jos 12-14	May 2	2 Sm 23:24-24:25;
Feb 6	Ex 16-18	Mar 28	Jos 15-17		1 Ch 11:26-47;
Feb 7	Ex 19-21	Mar 29	Jos 18-19		21:1-30
Feb 8	Ex 22-24	Mar 30	Jos 20-22	May 3	1 Ch 22-24
Feb 9	Ex 25-27	Mar 31	Jos 23-Jdg 1	May 4	Pss 30; 1 Ch
Feb 10	Ex 28-29	Apr 1	Jdg 2-5		25-26
Feb 11	Ex 30-31	Apr 2	Jdg 6-8	May 5	1 Ch 27-29
Feb 12	Ex 32-34	Apr 3	Jdg 9	May 6	Pss 5-7; 10; 11;
Feb 13	Ex 35-36	Apr 4	Jdg 10-12		13; 17
Feb 14	Ex 37-38	Apr 5	Jdg 13-16	May 7	Pss 23; 26; 28;
Feb 15	Ex 39-40	Apr 6	Jdg 17-19		31; 35
Feb 16	Lv 1:1-5:13	Apr 7	Jdg 20-21	May 8	Pss 41; 43; 46;
Feb 17	Lv 5:14-7:38	Apr 8	Ru		55; 61; 62; 64
Feb 18	Lv 8-10	Apr 9	1 Sm 1-3	May 9	Pss 69-71; 77
Feb 19	Lv 11-12	Apr 10	1 Sm 4-7		

DAILY BIBLE READING PLAN II

May 10 Pss 83; 86; 88; 91; 95	Jun 6 Pr 10-12	Jul 9 Mc
May 11 Pss 108; 109; 120; 121; 140; 143; 144	Jun 7 Pr 13-15	Jul 10 2 Kg 16; 2 Ch 28; Is 7-8
	Jun 8 Pr 16-18	Jul 11 Is 9-12
	Jun 9 Pr 19-21	Jul 12 Is 13-16
	Jun 10 Pr 22-24	Jul 13 Is 17-22
May 12 Pss 1; 14; 15; 36; 37; 39	Jun 11 Pr 25-27	Jul 14 Is 23-27
	Jun 12 Pr 28-29	Jul 15 Is 28-30
May 13 Pss 40; 49; 50; 73	Jun 13 Pr 30-31; Ps 127	Jul 16 Is 31-35
May 14 Pss 76; 82; 84; 90; 92; 112; 115	Jun 14 Sg	Jul 17 2 Kg 18:1-8; 2 Ch 29-31
	Jun 15 1 Ki 11:1-40; Ec 1-2	Jul 18 2 Kg 17; 18:9-37; 2 Ch 32:1-19; Is 36
May 15 Pss 8; 9; 16; 19; 21; 24; 29	Jun 16 Ec 3-7	
May 16 Pss 33; 65-68	Jun 17 Ec:8-12; 1 Kg 11:41-43; 2 Ch 9:29-31	Jul 19 2 Kg 19; 2 Ch 32:20- 23; Is 37
May 17 Pss 75; 93; 94; 97-100		Jul 20 2 Kg 20; 2 Ch 32:24- 33; Is 38-39
May 18 Pss 103; 104; 113; 114; 117	Jun 18 1 Kg 12; 2 Ch 10:1-11:17	Jul 21 2 Kg 21:1-18; 2 Ch 33:1-20; Is 40
May 19 Ps 119:1-88	Jun 19 1 Kg 13-14; 2 Ch 11:18-12:16	Jul 22 Is 41-43
May 20 Ps 119:89-176		Jul 23 Is 44-47
May 21 Pss 122; 124; 133-136	Jun 20 1 Kg 15:1-24; 2 Ch 13-16	Jul 24 Is 48-51
May 22 Pss 138; 139; 145; 148; 150	Jun 21 1 Kg 15:25-16:34; 2 Ch 17; 1 Kg 17	Jul 25 Is 52-57
		Jul 26 Is 58-62
May 23 Pss 4; 12; 20; 25; 32; 38	Jun 22 1 Kg 18-19	Jul 27 Is 63-66
	Jun 23 1 Kg 20-21	Jul 28 2 Kg 21:19-26; 2 Ch 33:21-34:7; Zph
May 24 Pss 42; 53; 58; 81; 101; 111; 130; 131; 141;146	Jun 24 1 Kg 22:1-40; 2 Ch 18	
	Jun 25 1 Kg 22:41-53; 2 Kg 1; 2 Ch 19:1-21:3	Jul 29 Jr 1-3
		Jul 30 Jr 4-6
May 25 Pss 2; 22; 27	Jun 26 2 Kg 24	Jul 31 Jr 7-9
May 26 Pss 45; 47; 48; 87; 110	Jun 27 2 Kg 5-7	Aug 1 Jr 10-13
	Jun 28 2 Kg 8-9; 2 Ch 21:4-22:9	Aug 2 Jr 14-16
May 27 1 Kg 1:1-2:12 Kg 1:1-2:12; 25a 23:1-7		Aug 3 Jr 17-20
	Jun 29 2 Kg 10-11; 2 Ch 22:10-23:21	Aug 4 2 Kg 22:1-23:28; 2 Ch 34:9-35:19
May 28 1 Kg 2:13-3:28 Kg 2:13-3:28; 2 Ch 1:1-13	Jun 30 Jl	Aug 5 Nah; 2 Kg 23:29-37; 2 Ch 35:20-36:5; Jr 22:10-17
	Jul 1 2 Kg 12-13; 2 Ch 24	
May 29 1 Kg 5-6; 2 Ch 2-3	Jul 2 2 Kg 14; 2 Ch 25; Jnh	
May 30 1 Kg 7; 2 Ch 4		Aug 6 Jr 26; Hb
May 31 1 Kg 8; 2 Ch 5:1-7:10	Jul 3 Hosea 1-7	Aug 7 Jr 46; 47; 2 Kg 24:1-4, 7; 2 Ch 36:6-7; Jr 25; 35
	Jul 4 Hosea 8-14	
Jun 1 1 Kg 9:1-10:13; 2 Ch 7:11-9:12	Jul 5 2 Kg 15:1-7; 2 Ch 26; Am 14	
	Jul 6 Am 5-9; 2 Kg 15:8-18	
Jun 2 1 Kg 4;10:14-29; 2 Ch 1:14-17; 9:13-28; Ps 72		Aug 8 Jr 36; 45; 48
	Jul 7 Is 14	Aug 9 Jr 49; 1-33; Dn 1-2
Jun 3 Pr 1-3	Jul 8 2 Kg 15:19-38; 2 Ch 27; Is 5-6	
Jun 4 Pr 4-6		
Jun 5 Pr 7-9		

DAILY BIBLE READING PLAN II

Aug 10	Jr 22:18-30; 2 Kg 24:5-20; 2 Ch 36:8-12; Jr 37:1-2; 52:1-3; 24; 29	Sep 8	2 Ch 36:22-23; Ezr 1:14:5	Oct 8	Jn 5; Mt 12:1-21; Mk 2:23-3:12; Lk 6:1-11
		Sep 9	Dn 10-12		
		Sep 10	Ezr 4:6-6:13; Hg	Oct 9	Mt 5; Mk 3:13-19; Lk 6:12-36
Aug 11	Jr 27; 28; 23	Sep 11	Zch 1-6		
Aug 12	Jr 50-51	Sep 12	Zch 7-8; Ezr 6:14-22; Ps 78	Oct 10	Mt 6-7; Lk 6:37-49
Aug 13	Jr 49:34-39; 34; Ezk 1-3	Sep 13	Pss 107; 116; 118	Oct 11	Lk 7; Mt 8:1, 5-13; 11:2-30
Aug 14	Ezk 4-7	Sep 14	Pss 125; 126; 128; 129; 132; 147; 149		
Aug 15	Ezk 8-11			Oct 12	Mt 12:22-50; Mk 3:20-35; Lk 8:1-21
Aug 16	Ezk 12-14				
Aug 17	Ezk 15-17	Sep 15	Zch 9-14		
Aug 18	Ezk 18-20	Sep 16	Est 1-4	Oct 13	Mk 4:1-34; Mt 13:1-53
Aug 19	Ezk 21-23	Sep 17	Est 5-10		
Aug 20	2 Kg 25:1; 2 Ch 36:13; Jr 39:1; 52:4; Ezk 24; Jr 21:1-22:9; 32	Sep 18	Ezr 7-8	Oct 14	Mk 4:35-5:43; Mt 8:18,23-34; 9:18-34; Lk 8:22-56
		Sep 19	Ezr 9-10		
		Sep 20	Neh 1-5		
		Sep 21	Neh 6-7		
		Sep 22	Neh 8-10	Oct 15	Mk 6:1-30; Mt 13:54-58; 9:35-11:1; 14:1-12; Lk 9:1-10
Aug 21	Jr 30; 31; 33	Sep 23	Neh 11-13		
Aug 22	Ezk 25; 29:1-16; 30; 31	Sep 24	Mal		
		Sep 25	1 Ch 1-2		
Aug 23	Ezk 26-28	Sep 26	1 Ch 3-5	Oct 16	Mt 14:13-36; Mk 6:31-56; Lk 9:11-17; Jn 6:1-21
Aug 24	Jr 37:3-39:10; 52:5-30; 2 Kg 25:2-21; 2 Ch 36:17-21	Sep 27	1 Ch 6		
		Sep 28	1 Ch 7:1-8:27		
		Sep 29	1 Ch 8:28-9:44	Oct 17	Jn 6:22-7:1; Mt 15:1-20; Mk 7:1-23
		Sep 30	Jn 1:1-18; Mk 1:1; Lk 1:1-4; 3:23-38; Mt 1:1-17		
Aug 25	2 Kg 25:22; Jr 39:11-40:6; Lm 1-3			Oct 18	Mt 15:21-16:20; Mk 7:24-8:30; Lk 9:18-21
Aug 26	Lm 4-5; Ob	Oct 1	Lk 1:5-80		
Aug 27	Jr 40:7-43:30; 2 Kg 25:23-26	Oct 2	Mt 1:18-2:23; Lk 2	Oct 19	Mt 16:21-17:27; Mk 8:31-9:32; Lk 9:22-45
Aug 28	Ezk 33:21-36:38	Oct 3	Mt 3:14:11; Mk 1:2-13; Lk 3:1-23a; 4:1-13; Jn 1:19-34		
Aug 29	Ezk 37-39			Oct 20	Mt 18; 8:19-22; Mk 9:33-50; Lk 9:46-62; Jn 7:2-10
Aug 30	Ezk 32:1-33:20; Dn 3				
Aug 31	Ezk 40-42	Oct 4	Jn 1:35-3:36		
Sep 1	Ezk 43-45	Oct 5	Jn 4; Mt 4:12-17; Mk 1:14-15; Lk 4:14-30	Oct 21	Jn 7:11-8:59
Sep 2	Ezk 46-48			Oct 22	Lk 10:1-11:36
Sep 3	Ezk 29:17-21; Dn 4; Jr 52:31-34; 2 Kg 25:27-30; Ps 44			Oct 23	Lk 11:37-13:21
		Oct 6	Mk 1:16-45; Mt 4:18-25; 8:2-4, 14-17; Lk 4:31-5:16	Oct 24	Jn 9-10
				Oct 25	Lk 13:22-15:32
				Oct 26	Lk 16:1-17:10; Jn 11:1-54
Sep 4	Pss 74; 79; 80; 89				
Sep 5	Pss 85; 102; 106; 123; 137	Oct 7	Mt 9:1-17; Mk 2:1-22; Lk 5:17-39	Oct 27	Lk 17:11-18:17; Mt 19:1-15; Mk 10:1-16
Sep 6	Dn 7-8; 5				
Sep 7	Dn 9; 6				

Daily Bible Reading Plan II

Oct 28	Mt 19:16-20:28; Mk 10:17-45; Lk 18:18-34		Lk 23:50-24:12; Jn 19:31-20:10	Dec 24	Heb 10-11
Oct 29	Mt 20:29-34; 26:6-13; Mk 10:46-52; 14:3-9; Lk 18:35-19:28; Jn 11:55-12:11	Nov 12	Mt 28:9-20; Mk 16:9-20; Lk 24:13-53; Jn 20:11-21:25	Dec 25	Heb 12-13; 2 Jn; 3 Jn
				Dec 26	1 Jn
				Dec 27	Rv 1-3
				Dec 28	Rv 4-9
		Nov 13	Ac 1-2	Dec 29	Rv 10-14
		Nov 14	Ac 3-5	Dec 30	Rv 15-18
Oct 30	Mt 21:1-22; Mk 11:1-26; Lk 19:29-48; Jn 12:12-50	Nov 15	Ac 6:1-8:1	Dec 31	Rv 19-22
		Nov 16	Ac 8:2-9:43		
		Nov 17	Ac 10-11		
		Nov 18	Ac 12-13		
Oct 31	Mt 21:23-22,14; Mk 11:27-12:12; Lk 20:1-19	Nov 19	Ac 14-15		
		Nov 20	Gl 1-3		
		Nov 21	Gl 4-6		
Nov 1	Mt 22:15-46; Mk 12:13-37; Lk 20:20-44	Nov 22	Jms		
		Nov 23	Ac 16:1-18:11		
		Nov 24	1 Th		
Nov 2	Mt 23:1-39; Mk 12:38-44; Lk 20:45-21:4	Nov 25	2 Th; Ac 18:12-19:22		
		Nov 26	1 Co 1-4		
Nov 3	Mt 24:1-31; Mk 13:1-27; Lk 21:5-27	Nov 27	1 Co 5-8		
		Nov 28	1 Co 9-11		
		Nov 29	1 Co 12-14		
Nov 4	Mt 24:32-26:5, 14-16; Mk 13:28-14:2, 10-11; Lk 21:28-22:6	Nov 30	1 Co 15-16		
		Dec 1	Ac 19:23-20:1; 2 Co 1-4		
		Dec 2	2 Co 5-9		
Nov 5	Mt 26:17-29; Mk 14:12-25; Lk 22:7-38; Jn 13	Dec 3	2 Co 10-13		
		Dec 4	Rm 1-3		
		Dec 5	Rm 4-6		
Nov 6	Jn 14-16	Dec 6	Rm 7-8		
Nov 7	Jn 17:1-18:1; Mt 26:30-46; Mk 14:26-12; Lk 22:39-46	Dec 7	Rm 9-11		
		Dec 8	Rm 12-15		
		Dec 9	Rm 16; Ac 20:2-21:16		
Nov 8	Mt 26:47-75; Mk 14:43-72; Lk 22:47-65; Jn 18:2-27	Dec 10	Ac 21:17-23:35		
		Dec 11	Ac 24-26		
		Dec 12	Ac 27-28		
		Dec 13	Eph 1-3		
Nov 9	Mt 27:1-26; Mk 15:1-15; Lk 22:66-23:25; Jn 18:28-19:16	Dec 14	Eph 4-6		
		Dec 15	Col		
		Dec 16	Php		
		Dec 17	Phm; 1 Tm 1-3		
Nov 10	Mt 27:27-56; Mk 15:16-41; Lk 23:26-49; Jn 19:17-30	Dec 18	1 Tm 4-6; Ti		
		Dec 19	2 Tm		
		Dec 20	1 Pt		
		Dec 21	Jd; 2 Pt		
Nov 11	Mt 27:57-28:8; Mk 15:42-16:8;	Dec 22	Heb 1:1-5:10		
		Dec 23	Heb 5:11-9:28		

SCRIPTURE INDEX

Scripture Index

SCRIPTURE INDEX

SCRIPTURE INDEX

Scripture Index

Scripture Index

21:1-11	105	23:33-35,39-47	341
21:12-16	106		
22:36-40	133	**John**	
22:41-46	107	1:1-5	1
26:14-25	337	1:4-5	221
26:59-68	110	1:14	173,323
28:1-10	112	1:14,16-17	173
28:18-20	177	1:29-34	103
		2:1-11	314
Mark		3:1-5,10,12-16	315
1:1-11	312	3:14-17	195
2:18-22	160	3:16	76
2:23-28	9	4:13-14	42
3:20-30	320	6:5-14	321
9:2,7	107	6:30-40	220
9:2-10	323	6:35	42
10:13-16	326	7:37-39	42
10:42-45	104	8:1-2	2,221
12:29-31	75	9:1-7	221
14:27-38	338	10:1-10	222
14:55-65	340	10:11	223,244
15:22-32,37-39	111	10:11-18	223
		11:1,4,17,21-27,43-44	224
Luke		12:1-11	334
1:46-55	68	13:34-35	75,382
2:4-14	388	14:1-9a	225
2:41-52	311	14:12-13	324
4:33-36	62	14:27	79
5:1-11	316	15:1-11	226
5:17-26	317	18:1-9	109
6:43-45	74,85	20:1-9,19-20	342
8:4-10	252	21:25	314
8:11-18	253		
9:18-22	104	**Acts**	
9:46-48	326	1:1-11	344
10:21-22	326	2:1-13	345
11:1-10	325	2:14-18,21-24,38	346
11:29-31	251	3:1-10	347
13:10-17	327	4:1-4	347
15:1-10	255	4:13-23	348
15:11-21	256	6:7-12	349
15:22-32	257	7:8-15	27
18:18-30	329	7:55-8:1a	349
19:1-10	333	8:1b-4	350
19:29-40	335	9:1-9	350
19:41-44	106	9:10-15,17-20	351
20:9-19	336	13:1-12	352
22:7-8,14-22	108	14:8-10,19-23,26-28	353
22:47-48,54-62	339		
23:3	67		

SCRIPTURE INDEX

SCRIPTURE INDEX

TOPICAL INDEX

TOPICAL INDEX

demon-possession 62, 318, 320, 324, 327
demons 47, 163, 358
destiny 212, 304
devil 253, 313, 352, 393
diet 138
discipleship 316
discipline 35, 184
disobedience 167, 168, 194, 195, 200, 209, 235, 261, 267, 270, 278, 380
divorce 156, 328
doubt 377
dreams 26
drinking/drunkenness 303, 360
dry bones 290

E

ecology 8
Eleazar 201
Eli 227-229
Elijah 104, 267-269, 307, 323
Eliphaz 35, 38
Elkanah 227, 228
Enoch 375
environment 321
Esau 24, 25, 289
Esther 304-306
eternal life 82, 84, 220, 244, 315, 329, 395
eternity 58, 61
Eve 10, 12-14, 16
evil 85, 373
exile 274, 275, 278, 279, 283, 286, 304
Exodus 52, 115-117,119, 150
eye for eye 136, 157
Ezekiel 290, 391
Ezra 302

F

faith 21, 23, 173, 179, 192, 205, 206, 238, 239, 288, 319, 324, 357, 361, 368, 375, 376, 379, 383
faithfulness 3, 54, 57, 59, 63, 67, 71, 87, 88, 122, 169, 216, 217
Fall 12
false gods 70
false teaching 358, 384, 385
false testimony 129, 340
false witnesses 349
family 142, 144, 209
fasting 160, 273
father 114, 140, 157-159, 181-184, 225, 226, 338
favoritism 39, 58

fear 4, 23, 29, 31, 45, 47, 87, 112, 114, 116, 118, 145, 151, 190, 202, 208, 237, 251, 259, 260, 282, 284, 294
fear of the LORD 4, 23, 29, 31, 45, 87, 118, 145, 151, 190, 202, 208, 251, 259, 260, 294
feasts 139
festivals 139
fidelity 185
filling of the Spirit 345, 349, 351, 352, 360
flood 17-19
food 6
foolishness 256
forgiveness 28, 76, 88, 92, 159, 170, 172, 256,257,312,317,325,333,341
found 255, 257
friendship 260
fruit of the Spirit 74, 75, 77, 79, 81, 83, 85, 87, 89, 91
fruitfulness 226, 252, 253

G

gentleness 89, 90
gift of tongues 345
giving 158, 162, 389
glory 3, 11, 56, 78, 116, 174, 178, 323, 335, 349, 366, 367, 381, 388, 391
God as Creator 60, 61, 67, 83, 121, 146, 176, 359
God as Father 114, 157-159, 181, 184, 225, 226, 338
God as King 56, 59, 61, 63, 67, 69, 118, 233, 282
God as Provider 6, 8, 128, 355
God as refuge 54, 55, 57, 59, 70, 86, 218, 281,386
God as Savior 72, 84
God as Shepherd 73, 90, 244, 260
God as the Rock 54, 69-71, 79, 354
God is one 75, 133, 179, 202
God protects 300
God relents 168, 272, 285
God remembers 51, 228, 299
God's calling 350, 351
godliness 130, 358, 372
gods 70, 121, 354
gold 389
golden calf 167, 263
Goliath 237-239
goodness 85, 86, 171, 281, 329, 355-357
goodness of God 86, 281, 329, 355-357
grace 15, 22, 72, 76, 170, 171, 173, 175, 271, 361, 374

TOPICAL INDEX

greatness   326

H

Habakkuk   288
Hagar   22
Haggai   294, 296
Ham   17
Haman   305, 306
hand of   God 354
Hannah   71, 227-229
hardness   94, 95, 97, 276
hate   26, 126, 155
healing   106, 124, 221, 317, 319, 327,
   347, 348, 351, 353
heart   4, 44, 74, 133, 236
heaven   2, 5, 40, 73, 157, 359, 366, 372
hell   126, 155, 156, 378, 393, 394
Herod   389
Hezekiah   277, 279, 280, 285
Hiram   258
Holiness   62, 67, 71, 114, 138, 174, 276,
   359
Holy Spirit   1, 40, 42, 63, 177, 179, 181,
   236, 247, 310, 312, 313, 315, 320, 326,
   344, 346, 365, 366, 379, 385, 391, 395
holy war   118, 201, 206, 207, 210, 211,
   235
homosexuality   137
honor   125, 140, 182
hope   61, 69, 72, 77, 81
Hosea   275
Hoshea   278, 279
humility   256, 367
husbands   182, 185-187
hypocrites   158-160, 162, 327

I

idolatry   150, 167, 169, 208, 209, 215,
   233, 261, 263, 267-269, 271, 277, 278,
   284, 291, 292, 391
idols   70, 121, 122
image of God   8, 126, 369, 378
immorality   169, 200
integrity   31, 36
intercession   168
intermarriage   261
interpretation   292
Isaac   22-24, 27, 28, 52, 53, 376
Isaiah   276, 280
Ishmael   22
Israel in the desert   188-191, 193-195,
   199, 200

J

Jacob   25-28, 49, 52, 53
Jael   211
James   107, 316, 323, 338
Japheth   17
jealousy   26, 27, 240, 241
Jeremiah   283-285
Jericho, battle of   205, 206
Jeroboam   262, 263
Jeshua (Joshua)   294, 296
Jesse   236
Jesus as High Priest   44, 148, 374, 387
Jesus as King   386
Jesus as Lord   58
Jesus as Savior   61, 72
Jesus as Shepherd   222, 223, 244, 308
Jesus as the King of Israel   105, 111, 308,
   335, 389
Jesus as the Lamb   5, 56, 73, 103, 114
Jesus as the Messiah   110, 322, 383, 384
Jesus as the Prophet   105, 321
Jesus as the Rock   169, 380
Jesus as the Servant of the LORD   308
Jesus as the Son of David   105-107, 310,
   387
Jesus as the Son of God   103, 111, 154,
   181, 195, 309, 311-313, 315, 318, 323,
   324, 326, 336, 340, 351, 383, 384, 386
Jesus as the Son of Man   9, 104, 110, 195,
   309, 317, 322, 333, 340, 392
Jesus as the Word   1, 67, 173
Jesus says "I am"   42, 220-226
Jethro   52
Jezebel   267, 268
Joab   245, 246
Job   29-31, 35-38, 176
Joel   273, 346
John the Baptist   103, 104, 160, 312, 325
John the apostle   107, 108, 316, 323, 338,
   347, 348, 392
Jonah   251, 270-272
Jonathan   240-242
Joseph   26-28, 49, 310, 311, 388
Joshua   191, 203-206, 208, 209, 294, 296
joy   77, 78, 302, 390
Judas   109, 334, 337, 339
judging   162
judgment   13-15, 17, 18,   93, 96, 97, 101,
   115, 117, 134, 169, 191, 193, 194, 195,
   200, 201, 211, 226, 247, 254, 259, 260,
   263, 274, 276, 277, 280-289, 292, 307,
   365, 391, 393, 394
justice   36, 38, 41, 43, 57, 63, 134-136,

TOPICAL INDEX

TOPICAL INDEX

offerings   7, 149
omnipotence   176
omnipresence   177
omniscience   178
oppression   49
orphans   134

P

parables of Jesus   252-257, 336
parents   125, 137
Passover   101, 108, 114, 139, 337
patience   81, 82, 89
Paul   349-353, 368
peace   41, 45, 79, 80, 89, 259, 301, 308,
   335, 356, 388
Pentecost   345
persecution   46, 152, 153, 157, 347-350,
   353, 373
perseverance   376, 385
Peter   104, 107, 108, 316, 321, 322, 329,
   338, 339, 342, 346-348
Pharisees   9, 140, 154, 160, 255, 315, 317,
   328, 335, 368
Philip   225, 321
Phinehas   200
plagues   96
plants   4
polygamy   147
poor   39, 83, 142, 143, 329, 334
power   3, 73, 90
praise   1, 3, 30, 54, 59, 68 71, 72, 77, 78,
   86, 118, 119, 121, 142, 145, 271, 347,
   354, 356, 357, 360, 366, 378
prayer   24, 38, 159, 162, 187, 215, 227,
   228, 280, 299-301, 325, 338, 352, 353,
   355, 374
presence of God   203, 204
priesthood   148, 149, 380
Prodigal son   256, 257
promise   22, 119, 168, 248
prophecy   11, 63, 69, 80, 90, 102,
   105-107, 180, 229, 243, 267, 269, 270,
   274, 283-285, 294, 296, 307-310, 336,
   338, 340, 346, 379, 380, 381, 386, 387,
   389, 392
prostitution   147
proverbs   250
punishment   76, 122, 123, 137, 176, 246,
   269
purity   44

Q

Queen of Sheba   251

R

Rabab   205, 206
Rebekah   24
rebellion   192, 193
redemption   55
Rehoboarn   262, 263
renewal   247
repentance   246, 247, 272, 273, 346
respect   187
rest   9, 124
restitution   135, 306
restoration   273-275, 282, 290, 293, 295
resurrection   69, 102, 104, 112, 113, 224,
   319, 338, 342, 343, 347, 365, 367, 369,
   370, 376, 393, 394
retaliation   136
retribution   35, 57
revenge   157
reward   35, 38, 85, 128, 153, 158, 159,
   217, 329, 365, 368, 393, 395
rich   39
riches   128, 329, 372
righteousness   15, 17, 21, 36, 42, 46, 57,
   63, 79, 154, 161, 173, 180, 307, 368
Ruth   216-219

S

Sabbath   9, 124, 137, 286, 327, 343
salvation   58, 59, 68, 71, 72, 84, 101, 102,
   113, 114, 116, 173, 175, 195, 209, 239,
   247, 252, 253, 255, 271, 280, 282, 284,
   287, 288, 289, 308, 315, 329, 333, 343,
   346, 353, 357, 358, 361, 366, 369, 379,
   385
Samson   212-215
Samuel   228, 229, 233-236
Sarah   20, 22, 376
Satan   29, 31, 313, 320, 327, 393
Saul   234-243, 349-352
Saul (Paul)   349-352
Scripture   373, 381
sea   4, 6
Second Coming of Jesus   72, 81, 82, 309,
   370, 395
security   47, 57, 59, 70, 123
self-control   91
Sermacherib   280
Sermon on the Mount   152-163
serpent   12, 13, 195
Servant of the LORD   102, 104, 308
service   334
shame   282
Shem   17

TOPICAL INDEX

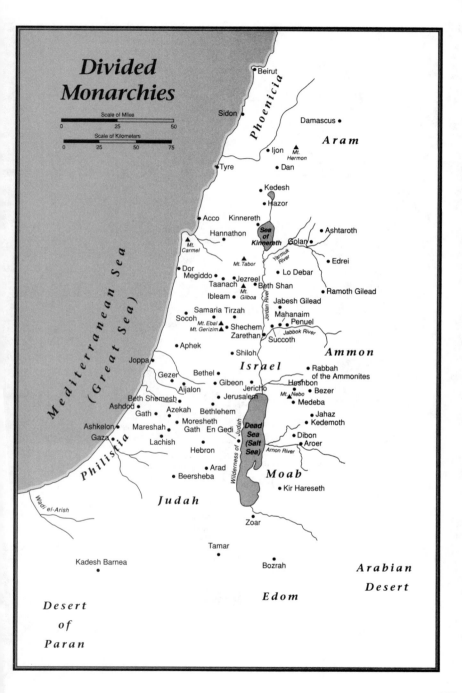

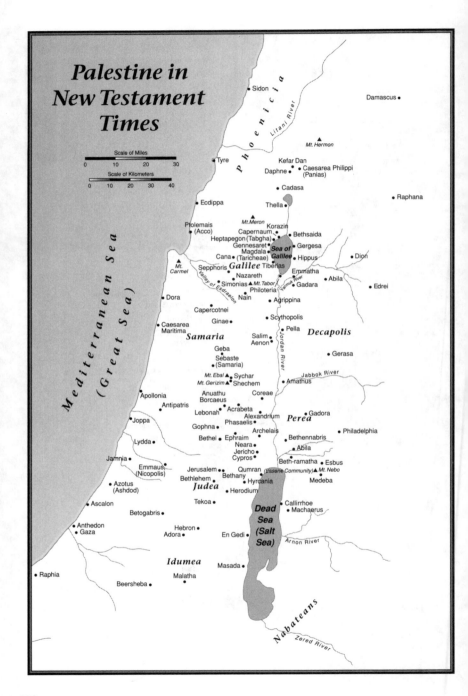

Palestine in New Testament Times

Scale of Miles

0   10   20   30

Scale of Kilometers

0   10   20   30   40

Mediterranean Sea (Great Sea)

Phoenicia

Litani River

Sidon

Damascus

Mt. Hermon

Tyre

Kefar Dan

Daphne

Caesarea Philippi (Panias)

Cadasa

Raphana

Ecdippa

Thella

Ptolemais (Acco)

Mt. Meron

Korazin

Capernaum

Bethsaida

Heptapegon (Tabgha)

Gennesaret

Gergesa

Magdala

Sea of Galilee

Cana (Taricheae)

Hippus

Dion

Mt. Carmel

Sepphoris

Galilee

Tiberias

Emmatha

Nazareth

Gadara

Abila

Edrei

Dora

Simonias

Mt. Tabor

Philoteria

Yarmuk River

Valley of Esdraelon

Nain

Agrippina

Capercotnei

Ginae

Scythopolis

Caesarea Maritima

Samaria

Pella

Decapolis

Salim

Aenon

Jordan River

Geba

Gerasa

Sebaste (Samaria)

Mt. Ebal

Sychar

Jabbok River

Mt. Gerizim

Shechem

Amathus

Anuathu Borcaeus

Coreae

Apollonia

Antipatris

Acrabeta

Alexandrium

Gadora

Perea

Lebonah

Phasaelis

Philadelphia

Joppa

Gophna

Archelais

Bethennabris

Lydda

Bethel

Ephraim

Abila

Neara

Jamnia

Jericho

Beth-ramatha

Esbus

Emmaus (Nicopolis)

Cypros

Jerusalem

Qumran (Essene Community)

Mt. Nebo

Bethlehem

Bethany

Medeba

Azotus (Ashdod)

Hyrcania

Judea

Herodium

Ascalon

Tekoa

Callirrhoe

Betogabris

Dead Sea (Salt Sea)

Machaerus

Anthedon

Gaza

Hebron

Adora

En Gedi

Arnon River

Idumea

Masada

Raphia

Malatha

Beersheba

Nabateans

Zered River

418

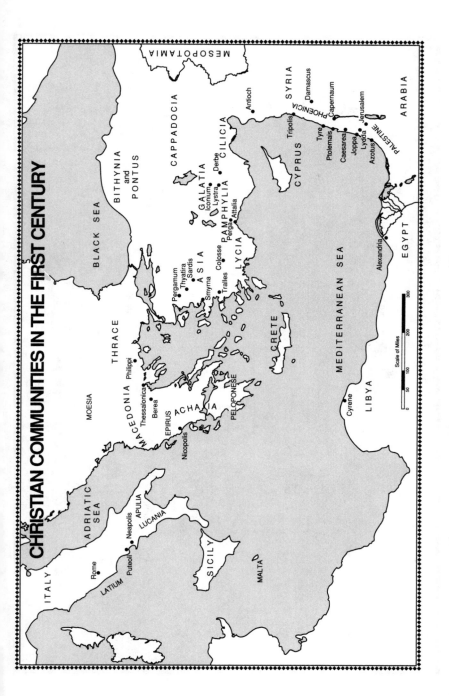

CHRISTIAN COMMUNITIES IN THE FIRST CENTURY

MESOPOTAMIA

SYRIA
Damascus
Antioch
PHOENICIA
Capernaum
Tripolis
Tyre
Ptolemais
Caesarea
Joppa
Lydda
Jerusalem
Azotus
PALESTINE
ARABIA

CAPPADOCIA

BITHYNIA
and
PONTUS

CILICIA

GALATIA
Derbe
Iconium
Lystra
PAMPHYLIA
Perga
Attalia

CYPRUS

BLACK SEA

Pergamum
Thyatira
Sardis
ASIA
Smyrna
Colosse
Tralles
LYCIA

LYCIA

EGYPT

Alexandria

THRACE

MACEDONIA
Philippi
Thessalonica
Berea
EPIRUS
ACHAIA
PELOPONESE
Nicopolis

CRETE

MEDITERRANEAN SEA

MOESIA

LIBYA
Cyrene

ITALY
Rome
LATIUM
Puteoli
Neapolis
APULIA
LUCANIA

ADRIATIC
SEA

SICILY

MALTA

Scale of Miles
0   50   100   200   300

419

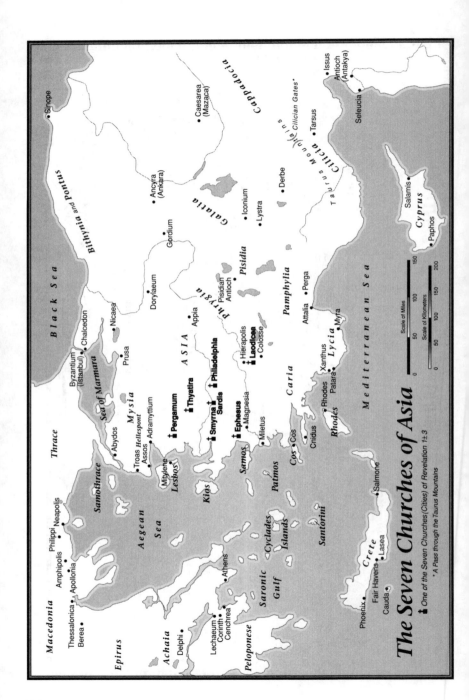

The Seven Churches of Asia

⛪ One of the Seven Churches (Cities) of Revelation 1:3

* A Pass through the Taurus Mountains